157
1049

The County Books Series

GENERAL EDITOR : BRIAN VESEY-FITZGERALD

HEREFORDSHIRE

THE COUNTY BOOKS SERIES

FOLLOWING ARE THE FIRST TWENTY
VOLUMES IN ORDER OF PUBLICATION

PLEASE WRITE TO THE PUBLISHERS
FOR FULL DESCRIPTIVE PROSPECTUS

HEREFORDSHIRE

by

H. L. V. FLETCHER

Illustrated and with a Map

London
Robert Hale Limited
18 Bedford Square W.C.1

First published 1948

THIS BOOK IS PRODUCED IN
COMPLETE CONFORMITY WITH THE
AUTHORIZED ECONOMY STANDARDS
PRINTED IN THE UNITED STATES AT
THE COUNTRY LIFE PRESS, GARDEN CITY, N. Y.

TO MY MOTHER AND FATHER

ACKNOWLEDGMENTS

I HAVE received so much kindness in the writing of this book that to thank everyone here would mean making a very long list. My special thanks for help or the loan of material are due to Mr F. C. Morgan, the librarian of Hereford; Mr Harry F. Davies, Secretary of the Hereford Herd Book Society; Messrs Bulmer, Ltd.; The Ven. A. J. Winnington-Ingram, Archdeacon of Hereford; Mr Robert Gibbings; and Mr David Smith.

CONTENTS

CONTENTS

ILLUSTRATIONS

ILLUSTRATIONS

ACKNOWLEDGMENTS

*The illustrations above, numbered 4, 9, 12, 13, 16, 17, 18, 19,
25, 26, 28, 30, 33, 34, 37, 38 and 39 are reproduced from photographs by Mr Reece Winstone, A.R.P.S., of Bristol; 14, 15
and 32 by Mr E. W. Tattersall of St Albans. The remaining
29 are from photographs supplied by Miss M. Wight of Hereford.*

INTRODUCTION

HEREFORD 26 MILES

AT THE back of my house a tiny stream, what is known locally as a "prill," comes hurrying down from the hills. This stream runs through my bit of ground. A few years ago I dug out a piece of it to make a pool where I could grow water lilies and raise goldfish and become childish again by playing with water and getting myself muddy and wet. I put a bridge over the stream where it entered the pool, and this was as good a place to be lazy in as one could ever wish to find, watching the fish and the lilies, shaking my head over the things I should never have planted, and making myself acquainted with all the uninvited creatures that appeared to share my view that my pool was rather a nice sort of place.

One day while I stood on the bridge I looked for a long time at the water as it ran into the pool and presently ran out again. It would, I reflected, presently run into the brook Dulas, and with the Dulas would join the Ithon, and after that, the Wye.

It was not a wise thought, or a profound one; it was not even of the slightest significance. It was only the sort of lazy thought a man would get on a warm sunny day as he looked at his own stream and his own pool. It gave me a lot of pleasure.

My little stream was on its way "down-country." It would turn its back on Wales at Hay, pass Clifford and Monnington and Bridge Solers and then run through Hereford, almost under the shade of the Cathedral. Then on to Dinedor, past Holm Lacy and Balstone, Ballingham, Kings Caple, and Sellack, and so to Ross with its tall elms and taller spire. It would go under Wilton Bridge, down to Goodrich, pass through Symond's Yat and onwards. . . .

But I wasn't so concerned with it after that. I was thinking that if a river could choose its course it could hardly ask a

I

kinder fate than to be allowed to meander unhurriedly through Herefordshire.

The first time I ever went to Hereford was on a lovely day in late spring. We had just bought a motorcycle and sidecar, an acquisition over which I had some doubts, though, once it gave up its unpleasant habit of throwing me violently into the near-side ditch, I wasn't afraid of it any more. It certainly was useful for getting us to places and there was something to be said for that. On this particular day we had been wandering about on Radnor Forest and then suddenly there was the signpost: *Hereford 26 Miles*. Reading it was like an invitation and we looked at each other. "Looked at each other with a wild surmise." Twenty-six miles wasn't much— provided the strange new beast between my knees would behave reasonably. Twenty-six miles? Why, you could do that in an hour. Saving the presence of the two babies sharing the sidecar with their mother, you could even do it in half an hour. Twenty-six miles—pooh, what was twenty-six miles! Long live the internal combustion engine! I steered cautiously in the direction indicated by the signpost and recklessly opened the throttle, increasing speed from fifteen miles an hour to at least twenty.

In Hereford they had the flags out. I don't know what the occasion was, but as we entered the city flags were hung from every window and festooned across the streets.

"What are all the flags for?" demanded the babes.

"Why, to welcome us, of course," I said confidently.

And for all we learned to the contrary, that might have been the truth.

The funny thing was that for quite a long time afterwards we hardly ever went to Hereford without the flags being out. I don't know if the people just liked flags, or if we always happened to pick a day when there was a flower show or an agricultural show or a music festival; but the flags were always out and we accepted it as a personal compliment. If Hereford was glad to see us, well and good: we were glad to see Hereford.

The fact was we'd fallen in love with the place from the start. Not only the city, though it did seem to be the nicest, quietest, wisest city we'd ever been to, but the whole district.

2

We liked the jolly winding roads along the Wye; we liked the long straight bits that had been long straight bits since the Romans laid them out and strode out of Kenchester to march along them; we liked the spreading uninterrupted views of wide countryside; the little, friendly hills (though years later they weren't so little, I found, when I came to do schemes up their slopes with my platoon of Home Guards). We liked the rich vegetation, so much earlier than our own back in the hills behind the Forest; the early flowers, the roses; the good red soil; the hops on poles; the grand oak trees and even grander beech trees. We liked the little black-and-white cottages and the kind, drawling, slow people who lived in them, who boiled water for us and spared milk for our tea, or something essential we had forgotten. We liked the birds we saw, even down to the silly pheasants that dawdled in front of our machine and invited us to run over them—not that we ever did—we liked the white-faced red Hereford cattle feeding in rich meadows. We liked—why, we liked everything.

The place grew into a habit. Going to Herefordshire became almost second nature to us. Four people, two of them babies, of course—though they didn't stay babies long—in search of somewhere to go. We weren't very original. We did try other places: Shrewsbury, Aberystwyth, Brecon. They were well enough, but always in the end we came back to our first love. *Hereford 26 Miles,* we'd read when we were nearly halfway there, and smile that we'd ever wondered if it was too far. We had no money, but I believe we had nearly everything else—everything that mattered, and I don't think the money did.

"Let's go to Hereford," we always said when we wanted to go somewhere. "What about Such-a-place, for a change? Or Somewhere-else?" But no, it would be Hereford—or Leominster—or Ledbury—or we'd threaten to go to Gloucester, and stop when we got to Ross. And there were all the little places in between that we got to know like old friends.

The rainfall in the hills averages sixty to eighty inches a year. In Herefordshire it ranges from twenty to thirty inches. The winds crossing the hinterland of Wales dump

3

all their moisture in rain and, when they can do no more, in fleecy mists on the hill-tops. By the time they reach Herefordshire they are practically dried out. Perhaps that is why the sun always seemed to shine for our visits. No, not "seemed to shine." It really did shine.

A journey into Herefordshire was a reward or a consolation as occasion provided. If I sold a story we celebrated: "Let's go to Hereford." And we each fingered the cheque in turn. If all my stories came thumping back on the mat my family patted my shoulders and said: "Never mind, we'll go to Hereford and you can forget all about it."

The motorcycle and sidecar grew up and became a three-wheeler, and the babies grew up a little more slowly—and had two little back seats to themselves where they could argue or fraternize as the mood took them; the three-wheeler matured into a car, and the back seat was wider and served for free fights or romps. But whatever the conveyance, it soon got so that it could find its way through down-country lanes without almost any help from the driver.

We were never guide-book tourists. Not that I want to belittle guide books. For those who find their pleasure in sucking dry the facts about a place before going on to the next a guide book is invaluable. But it did not happen to be our way. We went to a place because we had a fancy for it. If the fancy were strong we went a dozen times. We would go to the same grove of sweet chestnuts time after time to have our tea and roll on the grass; call at the same cottage to beg water or buy a jug of milk; spend half an hour watching a ploughman at work, or a reaper and binder clattering rhythmically round and round a field, or gossiping to a leisurely roadman; and all the time, close at hand, might be a Norman church we had never entered, or an ancient earthwork we had never stood on. Yet I don't think we were the losers in the end. We gained an intimacy with an unequalled part of England; an intimacy that could never have come through reading memorials in churches. If looking at churches gives one satisfaction, then, naturally, one should go after churches for all one is worth. We didn't happen to be feeling that way at the time. And, anyhow, sooner or later, I expect we went into most of them.

4

When William the Conqueror had his foot firmly planted in England he looked round for a way to keep his liveliest spirits occupied. Any schoolmaster knows that the best way to handle the naughty boys is to give them plenty to do, and William, in this, at any rate, showed all the instincts of an excellent schoolmaster. He packed them off to the Marches, the broad belt of the old Kingdom of Mercia that lay close against the mountains of Wales. What they could subdue and keep in order they could claim for their own, he told them, or words to that effect. So blithely came the Lords Marchers to the borders of Wales and a lively time they had. In the hills were the Welshmen, the descendants of the Silures, men to whom warfare, and wily warfare at that, was not second but first nature.

> Taffy was a Welshman,
> Taffy was a thief
> Taffy came to my house
> And stole a leg of beef;
> I went to Taffy's house
> Taffy wasn't home . . .

Of course he wasn't home. He had too much sense.

And the people in the Marches themselves? They, too, were descendants of the Silures, where they were not descendants of the warlike Mercians. They, too, were warriors. Living next door to their Welsh cousins, what else could they be?

The Lords Marchers did their job in the end. Or perhaps it would be more accurate to say that Time did it for them. And when the job was finished they faded away. Their castles remained; their noble names: Mortimer, de Lacy, Fitzborn; the churches they built and endowed—but the Lords Marchers themselves became a memory, a memory of cruelty, of greed, rapacity, tyranny, very occasionally of wisdom and stern justice.

A few of the great Marcher names may still be found, but for the most part their greatness has gone. I have heard of Mortimers, descendants of men whose names were the terror of the Border, who were roadmen and labourers. Parry in his *History of Kington* gave a well-authenticated

5

example of the decay of a noble family. He found in the churchyard there a tombstone: *Susan Scull, died in October 1814.* The Sculls had been important people. The pedigree of the family was adopted in the reign of Edward II and "extends to a remote era." They had a mansion, or manor, Ty-mawr, in Breconshire, and Sir William Scull was High Sheriff for the county in 1422. They held important offices under the Tudors and settled at Much Cowarne (in Herefordshire) but by Stuart times were little more than small gentry: one of them, John Scull, being a captain in Charles I's service, another being Rector of Presteign in Radnor in 1658. At the time Parry wrote his book, 1847, there was one Scull left. "Miles Scull is the present collector of the toll [market tolls] and resides in Duke Street." How are the mighty fallen! From the days of the Reformation a new aristocracy had arisen and the old names were no longer potent.

From prehistoric times until the end of the Civil War, Herefordshire was too often a battlefield. Here was the cockpit for all the struggles between east and west. The rich red soil of the Marches was often stained a deeper red with blood. But after the Civil War—and enough of that struggle was fought out in the county—peace came at last. We've been peaceful for three hundred years. But the fighting spirit still lives even if the occasions are, on our own ground, happily no longer with us. I've seen a man, after a few quarts of good Herefordshire cider, feel the instincts of his forefathers liven him up quite a lot.

From living in the hills and at the same time being often in the comfortable plains I conceived in my mind a sort of allegorical picture of the country. On the slope of a steep rocky hillside stands a spare man, lean, a little wizened, sharp-featured, quick, gimlet-eyed. He looks down on the plain and there, sleeping in the sun, is a woman, full-proportioned, full-bosomed, warm, long-haired, luxurious. Once she could not sleep in the sun, but now the wars are over and the corn grows richly round her, and she has time to be kind. In my picture, dream—call it what you will—the figures are gigantic, spread over half a countryside. The woman is Herefordshire and the imagined man personifies the hills.

It isn't so silly a picture as it sounds. In the hills living is still hard, often a struggle, and the hill-men think of the easy crops of the Old Red Sandstone with some envy. But they laugh last. The saying goes that Hereford farmers live rich but Radnor farmers die rich.

An old hill-farmer put it to me in a slightly different way. "They d'get too neish [tender] down Hereford way. Living like gentry, with stables for the hunters and all sorts of fal-lals. Then the money's gone and a hill-farmer steps in and buys cheap."

There is, indeed, a good deal of changing all along the Border. There are nearly as many Welshmen on the wrong side of Offa's Dyke as there are on the right side. But for that matter there always were. Half the village names of Herefordshire are Welsh names; their churches commemorate Welsh saints. You are as likely to come across a sing-song Welsh intonation as the slow, comfortable Herefordshire drawl. Indeed, when the Saxons drove the Welsh back from the plains into the hills there was one part of the county of which the Welshmen never were dispossessed. This was *Ergyng* or *Ereinwg,* meaning a pear orchard; that is, a fruitful country, known still as Archenfield, a district extending from the western end of the Forest of Dean to Madley and Moccas. The inhabitants here came to terms with the invader, kept their own language and customs— even the peculiarly Welsh system of inheritance known as *gavelkind* in which property is shared among a man's descendants at his death instead of going to the eldest son. The men of Archenfield sent six representatives to the Shire Mote at Hereford, fought with the Mercians against their wild kinsmen, and enjoyed the privilege, which could be given to none but brave and trusted allies, of marching in the vanguard of the army whenever it advanced against the Welsh, and in the rear-guard as it retired.

Viri de Archenfield, cum exercitus in hostem pergit, per consuetudinem faciunt Avantward, et in reversione Rereward.

They were a state within a state, kept their Welsh customs, were governed by their Welsh laws, for at least two centuries after the Norman Conquest.

Most of the churches in the present Deanery of Archenfield are dedicated to Welsh saints: St David, St Dubricius, St Deinol, St Beuno. St Beuno—one of whose miracles was to restore to life St Winifred—famed for St Winifred's Well in Flintshire—originated an unusual way of telling a Welshman from an Englishman. He planted an oak tree by his father's grave and, as the tree grew, one branch bent over to the ground. Any Englishman passing between this branch and the trunk died instantly, but Welshmen could do so without coming to harm.

Another of these old Welsh saints, St Dubricius has a good deal of legend attached to his name. He was a Bishop of Hereford, before the coming of St Augustine, when it belonged to the ancient Celtic church. He was born at Madley in a fire made by his grandfather, a local king, to destroy his mother, after he had failed to drown her in the Wye. When he grew up he gained a reputation for sanctity and established a sort of college at Hentland near Ross. Later he moved to Moccas—or *Moch-rhos,* the pigs' damp meadow (a *rhos* in Wales is a damp marshy moor), being led to the spot by a white sow with a litter of pigs. (A similar story is told of Æneas by Virgil.) According to legend, it was Dubricius who crowned King Arthur at Cirencester in A.D. 506. He ended his life in a monastery on Bardsey Island off the Caernarvonshire coast, and later his remains were taken to Llandaff, an occasion marked by rainfall which ended a seven weeks' drought.

Whatever one thinks of the legends that have grown up around the names of these ancient British saints, there is no doubt that the men themselves were men of saintly character, who genuinely strove to teach and spread the Gospel. They left behind them a strong impression of holiness and service.

One of the privileges, though not one of the oldest, of landowners in Archenfield lasted until the present century. This was the possession of rights of free-fishing in the Wye between Holm Lacy and Stansford. There was, however, a condition attached to this. In order that poor people should be able to buy small amounts of the fish caught it had to be exposed for sale for two hours on the turnpike road between Llanfrother and Hoarwithy (a name meaning the boundary willows) before it was taken to a market town. The right was granted or renewed in the time of Charles I (1639) at a court leet of the manor of Wormelow. This free-fishing lasted until 1911. Two fishermen had a case brought against them in 1907 challenging their privilege and the court decided against them. The decision was reversed by the Court of Appeal in 1908, but in 1911 the House of Lords decided (by a majority of one) against the fishermen and in favour of the plaintiffs, the Earl of Chester, and Mrs Madeleine Foster.

Welsh was so essential to the life of Hereford that as late as 1855 the Clerk to the Hereford magistrate got his appointment because he was able to speak Welsh.

The Welsh influence on place names is seen nowadays by the prefixes and suffixes. In the eastern half of the county, though no doubt in very early times many of the names must have been Welsh, one comes across the Saxon -ton (Ashton, Yatton), -ham (Brockhampton), -wick (Ullingswick), -hope (Woolhope), -ley (Putley), -low (Wolferlow), -bury (Bosbury). West of the Wye the Welsh names become more common: Tre- (Tretire), Llan- (Llanveyno), Pen- (Pencoyd).

PART I

TOWN

CHAPTER I

HEREFORD

HEREFORDSHIRE is above all a county of villages. It contains five places that can claim to be called towns: the city of Hereford, the county town; Kington on the Welsh border; Leominster, Ross, and Ledbury in the south. But don't be taken in by them. Towns and a city they may pass for, but villages they are, even Hereford itself, villages that have grown up. That is to say, they still have the desirable characteristics of villages. They are not too large, they are friendly, they are in touch with the countryside. There's mud on their boots. They may (if they are what is wrongly known as progressive) hate to be told so, but people who dislike real towns and generally avoid them bless them for it.

Somebody must, presumably, live in large towns, and quite a lot of people like living in them and do live in them; but others prefer what has come to be associated with the country life of England, and like towns in small doses. They want fields and rivers and woods and orchards; hedges where there are plenty of wild flowers and bird-life, clean air, hills and valleys. To suit such tastes we shall be hard driven to find a county that has more to give than this one. Here are some eight hundred and forty square miles containing about one hundred and twenty thousand people; less than one hundred and fifty to the square mile, which, when you take into account the five towns and a number of the good-sized villages, is not too bad. There are, or were before the outbreak of war, about seventy square miles of woodland. I daresay a good deal of this has been cut down, though a surprising amount of fine timber is still standing. In a lot of places it hardly seems to have suffered at all. I don't know what accounts for this: lack of patriotism, or love of trees, or the price wasn't good enough, or the timber wasn't? I suppose there *is* a reason. Whatever it is, one can't help being grateful for it. Any fool can cut timber, but there are too few wise enough to plant it.

The soil of Herefordshire is Old Red Sandstone and it is very fertile. It is exactly the same soil as the Old Red Sandstone of Devonshire (which may account for the fact that both counties grow cider apples to perfection) with one striking difference: the Old Red Sandstone of Devonshire was once below the sea and that of Hereford never was. Here and there older rocks strike through, Silurian in the extreme north-west, a strip in the east and in the Woolhope valley, and a few acres in the south-east belonging to the Cambrian. The Old Red Sandstone gives fertility; the older rocks add a touch of grandeur or the picturesque here and there, but there is nowhere anything more picturesque than the red soil itself. The mud on our boots is red, and, as I said, it is seen in the big villages (that pass for towns) as well as in the small ones.

It is seen in Hereford. Never was a city less offensively cityish. It possesses a cathedral, noted for having embodied in it all the principal styles of architecture, not omitting some unfortunate Victorian neo-Gothic; it has noble churches, wide streets (some of them), handsome houses, good shops, a first-rate library and museum. At times there is the unmistakable odour of sanctity—"the sly shade of a rural dean"—that attaches itself peculiarly to cathedral cities— and then suddenly it is gone. Through the traffic comes a farmer whacking the rumps of the hardiest of a fine bunch of white-faced Herefords—and you smell the country again. Should the cattle not materialize, and, it must be admitted, the stock-lorry is doing its best to keep livestock off the roads, it is only necessary to go to the market. Here there are some stalls that have the full townish flavour. But they hardly count. Right down the middle of the Market Hall, sit or stand the country people with their poultry (live and dead), their vegetables and fruit gathered that morning from a cottage garden, and most appealing of all to me, the little posies. Whatever time of the year you go into Hereford Market the stall-holders seem to have a few flowers to sell. Violets and anemones in the winter, daffodils and wallflowers in the spring, then the tulips, later some roses, a mixed bunch of hybrid teas perhaps, but as likely as not moss or cabbage roses or a bunch of Zephyrine Drouhin picked from the big bush by the kitchen window. The roses will give way to early chrysanthemums and then a few of the later kinds from a small greenhouse, and for Christmas you may buy a bunch or even a pot of Blanche Poitevene, or a little plant of winter cherry. There is no self-conscious air about any of these flowers, no suggestion of the florist; as likely as not the flowers will be in a mixed bunch; no skill in setting-out, no compelling display that insists on a purchase. You wonder can it be worth-while selling them—there aren't many, the price is modest—and then you get the spirit behind it all. Cottagers must grow a few flowers—and they must pick them and bring them to town, if only because it is town.

The traffic can be as thick as it likes in High Town. Go into the market and get a smell of wallflowers and you know it is all pretence. This is country all the time.

"For which the Lord be thankit."

Nobody seems to be positive about the meaning of the name, Hereford. There has certainly been a ford over the Wye here since earliest times so the Welsh name of *Hen-Fordd* (Old Ford) may be as near a guess as any, though the Welsh see of which it was the centre was known as Caeffawdd.

The Romans were here—they had a camp of some importance at Kenchester—and the Saxons, and, of course, the ubiquitous Welshmen, but the first person of historical importance to make much impression was Offa, King of Mercia. He drove the Welshmen back into the hills, and then, optimistically, built his famous Dyke—Offa's Dyke—running from Dee to Severn. To the west of this famous boundary (parts of it may be seen in Herefordshire, as well as in the neighbouring counties, to-day) the Welshmen were to keep themselves. Perhaps they did; perhaps they did not.

> Taffy came to our house
> And stole a leg of beef.

It takes more than a dyke and a fence to keep a Welshman from where he wants to go—and there was good fat mutton and sweet beef grazing on the Hereford fields. But the shades of his druids aid him if the Mercians caught him on the wrong side of the dyke!

Offa seems to have established Hereford as the head of an English see, though he had his own palace at Sutton Walls nearby. To Sutton Walls, in 793, came Ethelbert, "a noble impe," King of East Anglia, suitor for the hand of Offa's daughter, Elfrida. Offa's queen, Quendreda, had some of the qualities of a Lady Macbeth. She suggested to her husband that, with Ethelbert out of the way, East Anglia might easily be added to Mercia. Offa agreed to the proposal, and between the betrothal and the wedding, Queen Quendreda having drugged the young man's wine, he was murdered by a mercenary soldier named Gunbertus, though his East Anglian followers managed to escape.

Even in those wild days neither murders nor murderers were popular, and then, as now, it was afterwards that the trouble started. Offa took East Anglia as planned, but his daughter vowed herself to virginity and entered a nunnery, and two months later Quendreda died.

Eadwulf, Bishop of Lichfield, reproved Offa in these words: "Because thou has repented of thy evil deed thy sin will be forgiven, nevertheless the sword shall not depart from thine house. It was in thy heart that Mercia should be the greatest of English kingdoms and so it might have been. But now the glory shall depart from thee and another king, even the King of Wessex, shall be greater in power and shall become the first king of the whole of England."

It was Eadwulf who ordered proper burial to be made, the resting place of Ethelbert, at Marden, being disclosed by divine revelation.

The body was brought to Hereford and a shrine erected over it, and the church which had until now been dedicated to the Blessed Virgin was now dedicated to St Mary and St Ethelbert. Miracles were performed at his tomb, and at Marden, where the body had been left before burial at Hereford, a holy well sprang up that was never polluted even when the neighbouring Lugg overflowed its banks.

Offa, to make up for his crime, built a wonderful shrine for his victim and gave gifts to the Cathedral. It was prob-

16

ably, at this date, of wood, but later Milfrith, a Mercian nobleman, in honour of the cures being wrought at Ethelbert's tomb (paralysis was one of the diseases cured there), built one of stone, which was rebuilt by Bishop Athelstane early in the eleventh century. This building did not last long. In 1056 Elfgar, the outlawed son of Leofric, Earl of Mercia, and Gruffydd, Prince of Wales, swept across Herefordshire and destroyed and burned the city and Cathedral, putting the defenders to the sword. So savagely did they behave that thirty years later the Domesday surveyors were reporting that Archenfield had not recovered from the invasion. The relics and tomb of St Ethelbert were destroyed in the fire.

It was 1079 before Robert of Lorraine, the first bishop to be appointed after the Conquest (he was astrologer, mathematician, and architect as well as priest), began the rebuilding of the Cathedral, taking as his pattern the church built by Charlemagne at Aix-la-Chapelle, but not for centuries to come could the work in any way be regarded as completed.

Quite recently I have come across a very different version of Offa's crime. The story, as related above, is more or less as the old monkish chroniclers told it. My new version alleges that what they were mainly concerned with was to whitewash Ethelbert and extract as much as possible for the church from Offa. According to this story, the young prince of East Anglia spent his time between his betrothal and marriage in trying to seduce his future mother-in-law. Quendreda complained to Offa and he did the only possible thing.

One does get different versions of the same stories, especially stories as old as this. But even the worst club bore never relates two or three variations of his favourite story, so with such yarns as I pick up I make a point of believing either the story I like best, or the one told to me by the person I like best. It is the only thing to do. Either one says the yarn about Alfred and the cakes is all rubbish, or one sticks to it like grim death and to blazes with all debunkers. But I thought I would be fair to the shade of Offa —and who knows but what I might meet his wrathful spirit any evening glowering from the Dyke—and tell both sides.

Though, on the evidence, unless Ethelbert was a confirmed profligate, I don't think the second version will hold water.

The see of Hereford has not been one of the greatest or the richest in England, but it has had a long and interesting history and it was to produce one more saint, and he the last Englishman to be canonized.

Thomas de Cantilupe was born in the year 1220, and was related to some of the noblest families in England. When his uncle, the Bishop of Worcester, asked him as a child what he wanted to be, he said he would be a soldier.

"Sweetheart," said his uncle, "thou shalt be a soldier and serve the King of kings and fight under the banner of the glorious martyr, St Thomas."

He studied and took degrees at Oxford and at Paris, became Chancellor of Oxford and later Chancellor of England, was Archdeacon of Stafford, a prebend of Lichfield Cathedral, a canon of York and of St Paul's, and a prebend of Hereford. In 1275 he was consecrated Bishop of Hereford.

He was intensely devout, but no fool. His devoutness he showed in various ways. He would never allow his sister to kiss him and he wore an iron girdle and a hair shirt, which, following the example of St Thomas à Becket, he allowed to become infested with lice (*pediculi*) to make it more uncomfortable. His shrewdness forbade any trifling with the rights of the see, and he kept a champion, Thomas de Bruges (who was paid six shillings and eightpence a year for his services), to defend his causes where more peaceable methods failed. At one time he concerned himself in a dispute with the Earl of Gloucester about the ownership of the chase of Eastnor and Colwall. Thomas de Bruges's services were not needed. The Bishop excommunicated the Earl and then appealed for a trial by a jury, and won his case giving him the right, which dated from Domesday, to capture "buck, doe, fawn, *wild cat,* hare, and all birds pertaining thereto."

The wild cat, at any rate, is extinct to-day in Herefordshire, though evidently it was once not only common, as common as buck and hare, but also served as an article of food.

He was successful also in a dispute with Llewellyn, Prince of Wales, and after a quarrel with Lord Clifford, who had ill-treated some of his tenants and stolen his cattle, he compelled the offending nobleman to do penance in the Cathedral, the Bishop himself beating him with a rod as he walked.

Following a quarrel with Peckham, the Archbishop of Canterbury, Bishop Cantilupe made a journey to Rome and received a decision in his favour from the Pope. On his way home from this journey he was taken ill and died at Monte Fiascone near Orvieto. He was buried in the church of St Severus, near Florence, the Bishop of Palestrina, afterwards Pope Nicholas IV, preaching the funeral sermon. Later the flesh was removed from his bones by boiling, and the bones were brought home and buried in Hereford Cathedral, the heart being deposited in a shrine in a monastery at Ashbridge, Buckinghamshire, which held as a holy relic some of our Lord's blood.

It is related that when the bones were deposited at Hereford three hundred sick people were cured of their ailments and so many candles were given that the Cathedral officials found it worth-while to quarrel about who should have the wax.

Five years later the bones were transferred, in the presence of Edward I—on Maundy Thursday, April 6th, 1287—to another part of the Cathedral.

Richard Swinfield, Bishop Cantilupe's chaplain and disciple, succeeded his master and gave much time to trying to persuade Pope Nicholas IV that his predecessor deserved canonization. But Bishop Swinfield had been dead four years, when the canonization took place in 1320. Before that (1307) the Bishops of London and San Miniato had come to Hereford to enquire into the miracles that were being performed at the dead Bishop's shrine. These miracles were some four hundred and twenty in number and varied from the curing of sick animals (King Edward I on two occasions sent favourite falcons to be cured) to restoring the dead to life (in sixty-six cases). The two bishops arrived at Hereford on August 30th and stayed until November 16th, in which time they investigated and passed a satisfactory verdict on seventeen miracles and heard, less fully, the particulars of two hundred and four others.

The shrine by this time was especially rich in gifts. Among

them were images in silver and in wax of men, ships, animals, birds, and vehicles; crutches, nightgowns, gold and silver rings and brooches, garments of gold thread and of silk.

The treasure has departed. And the bones . . . ?

Well, the bones seem to have been dispersed at various times, for as early as 1380 Edmund Mortimer, Earl of March, left one of St Thomas's bones to the Abbey of Wigmore. They would not in any case have been likely to survive the Reformation, but what probably happened was that some, at least, were removed before His Majesty's Ecclesiastical Commissioners reached Hereford. At any rate, some of St Thomas's bones were carried through the city in 1610 when there was an outbreak of the Plague, "giving total succour to the same." These bones were dispersed during Lord Stansford's occupation of the city in 1642. None were left in the tomb.

In 1846 Dean Merewether opened it, but it was empty.

I believe there are still St Thomas relics in existence. One bone, at least, was said to be at Stonyhurst in 1888.

As a special compliment to the memory of St Thomas de Cantilupe the see of Hereford was allowed to change its armorial bearings for those of the family of Cantilupe, and these have been borne by Bishops of Hereford ever since.

On the road into Hereford from the west, a short distance outside the city, stands a tall and lovely cross on the left-hand side of the road. On this spot, legend tells us, Bishop Thomas stayed to rest one day as he came towards the Cathedral from his palace at Sugwas. And as he rested there the bells of the Cathedral rang out of their own accord to welcome him, and the cross was erected in honour of the miraculous event.[1] In Queen Elizabeth's time it was "pulled down by one Gernoras afterwards called Kill-Christ." It was re-erected later.

Was he really a saint? There is no need for those who object to miracles to believe in them—though enough happen around us every day—but I think he was more saintly than anyone most of us have the good fortune to meet.

"Blind zeal may close her stomach and make up her mouth with the sweetmeats of his memory."

[1]There are other stories of the origin of the White Cross.

20

Most visitors to Hereford, if they stay in the city for any length of time, or, more particularly, if they visit the Cathedral, go to have a look at the Mappa Mundi. This map of the world was made in Bishop Swinfield's time by Richard of Hallingdon, a native of Battle, in Sussex, Treasurer of Lincoln, later a prebendary of Hereford and Archdeacon of Berkshire, and a friend of the Bishop.

The Mappa Mundi is a treasure artistically (apart from its quaintness) and, like other early maps, pretty weak cartography. If it were a more useful map it would be much less highly thought of. As a rule it does not get the attention it deserves—it is worthy of more than a quick glance before hurrying on to look at something else. Richard of Hallingdon, as he looked at his work, no doubt thought he had done something mighty clever, not to say useful. His shade must feel pretty indignant to see it passed by as a tourists' peepshow. That great traveller, Sir John Mandeville, showed much more respect for it. It was on the strength of the accuracy of the Mappa Mundi that he received the Pope's guarantee of the truth of his book *Voyage and Travayle*.

In Bishop Swinfield's time, too, the order was made expelling the Jews from England. It is hardly likely that the Bishop was anything but pleased by this as he had already excommunicated some of his flock who had been guests at a Jewish marriage. The familiarity between some of the Christian citizens and the Jews had already given him deep offence. It was 1290 before the sentence of expulsion was carried out, and then the houses and land of the numerous Jews in Hereford were given to citizens (those who had not fraternized with the accursed race nor attended their wedding feasts?) and some of it went to the Knights Templars. But their tenure was to be short, for in 1308 their order was suppressed and the preceptors of Garway and Upleadon as well as other Herefordshire knights went to the Tower.

Happy the man who has no history, and presumably the same may be said of a town. Hereford's pace through the ages has been pedestrian, its part in history-making (excepting the time of the Civil War, and even then its share can hardly be said to have affected the conflict decisively one way

21

The Woolhope Hills

or the other) a mere touching on the fringes of national events. Interests were often local, even parochial, and very often ecclesiastical, yet, at the same time, what went on in the world did not entirely pass by unnoticed.

After all, Hereford was a city. It had a cathedral and it had, most of the time (not during all of the Protectorate), a bishop. And bishops, with all due respect to them, have a habit of getting their fingers into pies.

The bishop who succeeded Bishop Swinfield, for instance, was Adam of Orleton, a Herefordshire man, Orleton being in the north-east of the county. He took a lively part in the intrigues that were to pull Edward II from his throne, siding with the Queen against Edward, and being the one to take the Great Seal from him when he was eventually captured at Neath Abbey. The King was taken to Kenilworth and his death. But two of his companions were brought to Hereford, one of them, Hugh Despenser, crowned with nettles, and on his garments being written the first six verses of Psalm 52: *Why boasteth thou thyself in thy mischief O mighty man* . . . was hanged there on a gallows fifty feet high while the people cried "hue" at him in mockery of his name.

By 1340 the Black Death had reached Herefordshire and the mortality was great, one hundred and fifty-one people dying in four parishes alone. But the course of the disease in the city was checked by carrying the shrine of St Thomas of Cantilupe in procession.

"The devil was sick; the devil a monk would be." It may have been fear of the Plague which caused Bishop Trilleck in 1348 to forbid the acting of "theatrical plays and interludes" in churches. There was, however, a Corpus Christi pageant performed in the city and this was not affected by the Bishop's ban, for it was performed until the middle of the sixteenth century. Another survival of the ancient mysteries went on until 1706 and was unique in being the only example in England. This was the Hereford Riding in which, during Passion Week, a labourer rode into the city on an ass.

Bishop Trilleck, like both his predecessors and successors, fell out at times with the citizens, each side being jealous of its privileges. A man named William Corbet showed his contempt of the Bishop by entering the palace by violence, carrying off the palace keys and the porter, and locking up the latter in the city gaol. But Corbet had gone too far and ended up by making complete public submission in the Cathedral. Hardly an event of national importance, but how the people must have enjoyed it.

The bishops and the monks of the various monasteries (especially Leominster) had their quarrels, too, the brethren being often in need of reproof. Sometimes the monks complained to, not of, a bishop, as when the Prior of Leominster reported angrily about some "sons of iniquity" who had, among other things, killed his peacocks and stolen two swans.

In 1361 the Black Death was stalking the country again and Hereford Market was moved out to the White Cross, the spot from which St Thomas had heard the Cathedral bells welcome him.

The bishop of this time, Lewis Charleton, bequeathed books to the Cathedral, expressing a wish that they might be chained to their places in the library. Hereford has two of the finest chained libraries in the country, one at the Cathedral and one in All Saints Church, though the latter narrowly escaped being sold to America not many years ago.

A later bishop, Bishop Gilbert, was, for a time, Treasurer of England but was driven out of office by Richard II. It was he who founded the Cathedral Grammar School.

Owen Glyndwr was ravaging Wales and the Marches impartially at this time. He led his army as far as Leominster, plundered the priory, and destroyed or damaged other churches in the district. He did not come as far as Hereford, though the plump citizens must have wondered what was going to happen, the town being Henry IV's base for his campaigns against Wales.

The fifteenth century was most notable for the quarrels with the Lollards, and there were some famous (or infamous, according to how one looks at it) Lollards in the diocese. "Ye poure lege man of ye kinges and your poor prst, William of Swynderby" was one of the best known and prcved too clever for the Bishop of the time. Another,

Nicholas de Hereford, did a large, if not the principal, part of the translating of Wycliffe's Bible, and Sir John Oldcastle, whose home was at Almeley, is well known as a Lollard martyr.

A bishop of a later date, Thomas Mylling had been a monk, and later Abbot of Westminster, and was a friend of the first English printer, William Caxton.

Thirty years or so later the Bishop of Hereford was one of those sent to Spain by Henry VII to bring home the Infanta Katherine of Aragon who was to marry the heir to the throne, Prince Arthur. His successor was summoned by the King, Henry VIII by now, to accompany him to Calais, on which expedition he was to be attached to the following of "his dearest wife, the queen." It was still the same Katherine of Aragon though her sun was near setting. The Bishop was to be accompanied by "thirty tall personages," of whom six were to be "gentlemen, well and conveniently apparelled."

The Reformation was at hand and again the Bishop of Hereford had a part to play. This was Bishop Foxe and he showed no unwillingness to play his part. On the whole Hereford and Herefordshire clung to the old religion, but Foxe was not one of them.

With the exception of the Cathedral there were in the county only two monasteries, Leominster and Wigmore, large enough to escape the Act of 1535–36 granting to the King all religious houses with an income of less than two hundred pounds a year; there being one more in the diocese, at Wenlock. There were fifteen others and one by one they were disposed of, some being given away, others bought, and the King's treasury benefiting to no small extent. The larger houses followed, and, in 1545, came the "third meal of Church property," the chantry chapels, which had escaped so far, largely because of the interest taken in them by great families. There were seventy-seven of these in Herefordshire, and the Act transferring their revenue to the Crown pleaded, not doctrine, but mismanagement and, ingenuously, the expense incurred by the King in his wars. Again the purchasers of good property going cheap did not miss their opportunity.

After the accession of Edward VI the pageant given every

year on the Feast of Corpus Christi was discontinued, and
the money spent on it was ordered to be used on the city's
roads, ditches, and the like. So ended a notable link with the
past, but the people refused to give up their custom of decorating their churches at Christmas and Easter.

Hereford did not like the Reformation. Hereford, like
Wales, so near at hand, and so nearly akin, was "popishly inclined." And it mistook a breathing space for a complete
change of policy, greeting Mary's accession with bonfires in
the streets, the ringing of bells, and a throwing up of caps
and hats. Small wonder that the one small rising in the county
on behalf of Lady Jane Grey, which took place near Leominster, was put down without bloodshed. But after Mary
came Elizabeth and the Reformation went on to its appointed end. By 1563 Bishop Scory of Hereford was helping
the Welsh bishops to supervise the translation of the Bible
into Welsh (which sounds as if the Bishop of Hereford did
not disdain to speak and read Welsh himself) and he helped
in the drawing up of the Forty-two Articles which were
presently to be reduced to thirty-nine.

When Spain threatened England with her Armada the
Queen called on the bishops for "knight service." Each
bishop had to provide one demi-lance and one light horseman armed in a corselet and other light horseman's stuff
and carrying a pistol. The dean and the archdeacons had
to provide a demi-lance each, the members of the chapter two
demi-lances between them, and the deaneries a certain number of corselets, muskets, calivers, and bills (that is, men
armed with these weapons).

The leanings towards the old religion died hard. In spite
of prohibitions and penalties the "popish sympathizers"
would not be put down. And it was not all underground work,
either. On Whit Tuesday in 1605 a woman, Alice Wellington, was buried at Allensmore, not far from the city, according to the rites of the Roman Catholic church, "tapers burning and other trumperies." Some fifty or sixty people were
present and those who were not taking part in the ceremony
were armed to prevent interference. Some of these were later
arrested and sent to London, but the majority escaped. In
1610 a priest named Cadwallader (a Welsh name) was ar-

rested. This was the year of the Plague in Hereford, so he was tried at Leominster where he was sentenced to death. After execution the body was quartered and the portions hung up in different parts of the town, the head being put in the market-place.

So the pursuit of recusants went on, the Privy Council writing to Bishop Godwin in 1626 asking him to arrest "the Popish priests, of whom many lurk about the country."

"I have laid all the gynnes I can think of," the Bishop wrote to Mr Scudamore. He would need to; Hereford folk were springing them before they could hurt anybody. The services were still "a fountain of superstition throughout the whole country . . . strange gesticulations, crouching, ducking, shifting from place to place, one blowing, another piping and fiddling, others bellowing, some praying, the congregation in confusion, few understanding what is said or sung, with a world of other ceremonial trinkets and forgeries devised to make gaze upon the outside of empty ceremonies and superstitious pompe."

But a new struggle was on the way. Herefordshire was soon to see its last battles, hear its last martial music. The "Great Rebellion" was boiling up and once more the sympathies of Hereford people were to be on the losing side. And, the rights of the case apart, they were none the worse for that. It is often the nicest people who espouse lost causes. To sympathize, and to be prepared to back one's sympathies, however, are two different things. On September 30th, 1642, little more than a month after the King raised his standard at Nottingham (and had it blown down—a bad omen, people said), Lord Stamford and Sir Robert Harley, under the command of Essex, marched into Hereford unopposed. It was only a few days later that the Parliamentary soldiers showed their contempt by dancing in the Cathedral to the music of the organ during Divine service. Lord Stamford left the city in December, and the city suffered hardly at all during his stay, but a good deal of plundering went on outside it. Goodrich was one of the places that suffered in this way, but seeing that Thomas Swift, grandfather of the famous Dean Swift, was the parson of Goodrich, and made no secret of his Royalist sympathies, that is hardly surprising.

It was Thomas Swift who later in the war put caltrops in the Wye at a place where Roundheads were to cross and caused the death of many of them. Caltrops were spiked iron balls thrown on the ground to maim cavalry horses. He also, at the end of the struggle, visited the King at Raglan to present him with his waistcoat, a useful gift, seeing there were three hundred guineas sewn into the lining. "No gift the king received," wrote Lord Clarendon, "was more seasonable or acceptable." Swift kept his place until 1646 (he was to be restored later) but he, his wife (who was the aunt of the poet Dryden), and his children were repeatedly molested and his house plundered, largely by Colonel Kyrle, Governor of Goodrich Castle, as long as he stayed.

April, 1643, saw Hereford once more in the hands of Parliamentary forces, this time under Waller, but he did not stay long. In Royalist hands again it became almost a sanctuary for Roman Catholics, and had the reputation, from the Puritan point of view, of being "a very malignant town."

Four days after Naseby, King Charles reached the city and stayed a couple of days. This was on June 19th. The Scottish army, under Lord Leven, besieged Hereford after the King had gone, but had to retire on September 1st, and on the 4th the King visited the city again. He was to come for the last time, on September 18th, when he passed through on his way to Presteign. Still Hereford had not suffered greatly—with one exception. An exception that seemed to be a rule in those days. One is forced to wonder how the war could have gone on without the lead from the roofs of churches and cathedrals. Both sides seem to have taken it indiscriminately.

The same year, 1645, was to see one more siege, and by a trick the city was taken on December 18th by Colonel Birch and Colonel Morgan, Governor of Gloucester. Both of them wrote to Lenthall, Speaker of the House of Commons, to announce their victory, and Morgan announced that they had taken "one hundred and twenty Lordes, Knights and Officers in Commission. Eleven pieces of Ordnance and Great Store of Ammunition." Birch, giving the same information, adds, of the prisoners, "most of them being Papists." He told how "it being so deep a snow that they could not possibly imagine we could march; which indeavour the Lord was pleased to bless."

Again Hereford may be said to have had better fortune than it might have expected. One of Birch's principal officers was Captain Silas Taylor, who was something of an antiquarian. Soldiers over-ran the city after it was taken, and they did damage to windows, ornaments, and monuments in the Cathedral as well as to the library. But Captain Taylor exerted himself to prevent excesses, and though a lot of harm was done it was less than might have been feared, and it certainly was less than happened to cathedrals in many other cities.

Outside Hereford the Scots went in for plunder on a grand scale, sometimes adding murder for good measure. They were not invariably successful. There is, or was, a portrait in Treago at St Weonards showing a lady with her hand on a dagger. She was a mistress of the house who chased the plunderers away. The county could have done with an army of such women.

A man named Miles Hill, who had been employed by Parliament to get in provisions for the Scots, published in 1650 an account of their thefts. It is called *A True and Impartial Account of the Plunderings, Losses and Sufferings of the County of Hereford by the Scottish Army during their siege before the city of Hereford, Anno. Dom. 1645. Since brought in by the Country in writing.*

It contained "an abstract taken of the losses, damages and plunderings of one hundred and six small parishes within the County of Hereford by the Scottish Army commanded by General Leven . . . in the prosecution of which were divers boxes riffled, doors, chests and trunks broken open, severall familes undone, most of all their cattle, horses and goods taken from them, much mony, plate, jewels and all kind of rich household-stuffe, rings and other rich commodities as wearing apparrel, linnen, books; the plate and linnen of divers churches, neere all the horses, mares & colts that ever they set their eyes upon as wel from friends as others as the reader may see if he please in an inventory . . ."

The values of the losses sustained by various places are then listed. They vary from:

	£	s	d
Taken and plundered from the Brough and Forren of Rose to the valew of	1189	15	0

down through—

	£	s	d
Taken and plundered from Mr Monnington of the parish of Sarnfield to the valew of	1000	00	00

to—

Taken and plundered from the Inhabitants of Kentchurch.	0006	14	06

Kentchurch, perhaps having least, suffered least.

The

Summe totall of all the aforesaid particulars is	31743	05	02

No wonder Dr Johnson said that the best view to a Scotsman was the highroad to England.

The Scots went at last, and it was almost three hundred years before an army from another country was quartered in Herefordshire. But this time the visitors did not come to plunder. Indeed it was rather the other way round—the demanding voices being those of Herefordshire children, and the booty chewing gum.

Naseby was the beginning of the end; and the end, if not in sight, was ordained, and once again began the confiscations and sequestrations that had been seen only a century earlier.

Hereford seems to have made the best of the Protectorate, for on Cromwell's death the well-to-do people of both city and county presented an address to Richard Cromwell offering their sympathy and loyalty and hoping he would be "as Solomon was to Israel after David." But the feelings that prompted this address could not have been very deep. By February 17th, 1660, they were making bonfires and calling for a king and free Parliament.

The Restoration was followed by a certain amount of Nonconformist-baiting, but, strangely, it was the hunting out of Roman Catholics that continued the chief sport. In-justice was done on more than one occasion, the most notorious case being that of John Kemble, a Franciscan Friar, who came from St Weonards and belonged to the family that later was to produce the great actors.

John Kemble was a priest in Herefordshire for fifty-four years, a quiet, gentle man, nearly eighty years old when he was arrested in 1679, accused of being implicated in the Popish Plot. He was taken to London and returned from there, *on foot,* to Hereford. There he was tried and sen-tenced to be hanged and beheaded on Widemarsh Common.

The appointed day came and Mr Digby, the under-sheriff, arrived to take Kemble to the place of execution. The old man asked a favour: could he have time to say his prayers and smoke a last pipe of tobacco? Digby agreed, and joined him in his pipe. Kemble finished his smoke first and declared himself ready to go, but Digby had not finished his and asked his prisoner to be good enough to wait until he had. From this happening arose an old Hereford saying: a last smoke became "a Kemble pipe." John Kemble was buried in Welsh Newton churchyard and a stone bearing his initials and the date when he died was placed over his grave.

It is often claimed that the last trial for witchcraft to take place in England was held in Hereford. Actually this happened in Hertford and was in 1712 when Jane Wenham, the witch of Walkerne, was found guilty and condemned to death. She was later reprieved. But in 1662 a witch, Mary Hodges, did stand her trial in Hereford, though there seems to be no record of what happened to her.

In 1717 the first meeting of the choirs of Hereford, Gloucester, and Worcester cathedrals took place, a meet-ing that was the birth of the famous Three Choirs Festival.

History was passing Hereford by quietly, and Hereford was now little more than a quiet spectator. All the same things did happen. In 1802 a butcher exercised a husband's undisputed (if illegal) right to get rid of a wife he had no more use for. This butcher sold his by public auction in Hereford Market for one pound four shillings, and a bowl of punch. There was another case recorded in the city and this time the woman went even cheaper, going for as little as a shilling. Hardy, of course, made use of this custom as part of the plot of *The Mayor of Casterbridge,* but it is not likely that such sales took place many times later than those recorded at Hereford. From a woman's point of view it seems a barbarous business and yet, if a man were prepared to sell his wife, perhaps the wife would come off better in the end by being sold. That may be why none of them appear to have protested against their transfer. It is not a method of separation anyone would recommend should be revived, yet there have been divorces quite as thoughtless, and much more cruel.

To-day, Hereford smiles placidly after its thousand years of history and on the margins of history. It is a quiet friendly city—no, village, I stick to that. A big village, if you like, a village that sometimes looks like a city and speaks like a city and acts like a city, but that still preserves about it in its happiest moments some of the unspoiled freshness of the village.

CHAPTER II

KINGTON

KINGTON is the smallest town—or the smallest large village, according to how one looks at it—in Herefordshire. It stands so close to the Welsh border as to be more like a small Welsh market-town than are many small Welsh market-towns. In fact, it seems to be different from any of its Welsh neighbours in only one respect: opening its public houses on a Sunday, a thing strictly forbidden in Wales. This gave it—in the petrol age—a sort of notoriety among visitors to Welsh places within motoring distance. It used to be a habit of the thirstier ones to go for a run to Kington on a Sunday evening; and they would return with their thirst quenched. Not that they really need have bothered. I never knew a thirsty Welshman wander far afield—even on a Sunday. But I did notice that weary Home Guards, returning from a Sunday's exercise in Herefordshire, always found on the way home that the 'bus needed a short rest when it reached Kington.

Before Kington, to the east, stretches England, with its woods and meadows and winding streams; at its back, to the west, stand the mountains, Radnor Forest looming dark and purple against the sky. The town could be (Sundays excepted) of Wales or of England. It is little more than chance that it happened to be England. Not far away is as good a section of Offa's Dyke as can be found on the Border, and through the town runs the River Arrow. This is the stream crossed only a few miles away, between Pembridge and Eardisland, by Henry Tudor on his way to Bosworth (by way of Leominster), and he reminded his followers of an ancient saying that "who would win a national strife must shoot the arrow first." They took it to be a good omen—and so it was, as events were to prove.

Kington has a lovely old church in the Early English and

32

Decorated style. There are fine monuments to some of the Vaughans, a notable Welsh family who had their seat at Hergest Court nearby. It was in Hergest Court that Lady Charlotte Guest found the Red Book of Hergest from which she compiled the book of Welsh mythology known as The Mabinogion.

The best known of the Vaughans was Ellen Vaughan, Ellen Gethin (Ellen the Terrible), who belonged to the Hergest Court branch of the family in the fifteenth century. She was young (at the time of this story) and she was beautiful, but from all accounts she fully earned her nickname, *Gethin* (the Terrible). Her most notable exploit was an act of revenge. Between the Tretower (Breconshire) Vaughans and their Hergest kinsmen there were constant feuds, and in Ellen's day they broke out afresh when John Vaughan of Tretower killed her favourite brother. Ellen dressed herself in man's clothes and went down to Breconshire, ostensibly to compete in an archery tournament. She knew Shon hir (Long John), the man who had killed her brother, was certain to be there, as indeed he was. When it came to her turn to compete she fitted an arrow to her bow and then suddenly turned and shot and killed Shon hir. In the confusion she escaped— and many consider her lucky to have done so, for she would have had short shrift had she been caught. Even to-day feelings can run pretty high between neighbouring Welsh villages, without a killing to rouse their feelings.

But, in spite of what happened, Ellen Gethin later married a Vaughan of Tretower. He was a man of spirit himself and may have recognized a kindred soul. He was killed in the Wars of the Roses and fine effigies of them both can be seen to-day on their tomb in Kington Church.

Ellen's husband was Black Vaughan and a fit mate for her. His death was not the end of him. Lesser men and gentler men become memories, but such as Black Vaughan cannot cease from troubling, nor be at rest. He returned as a ghost, and became so obnoxious a ghost that it was determined to lay him. No less than twelve parsons tackled the job; twelve parsons with twelve candles to read Black Vaughan down into a silver snuff-box. And they had with them a newborn babe to provide that element of innocence so necessary in

33

exorcism. But one by one they gave in and retired from the contest, until there was only the last of them left (together with the baby, presumably), and he was so stubborn only because he was drunk and did not realize the size of the task. In the end it was good Herefordshire beer (or it may have been cider) that prevailed. Black Vaughan's spirit was in the snuff-box at last and safely fastened down. Asked where he would lie, he answered that they could put him anywhere they liked, only not in the Red Sea. For some reason I cannot trace in all the cases of exorcism the spirit always begged not to be laid in the Red Sea. So they put him in Hergest Pool for a thousand years. He still has quite a while to go, but I'd hate to be on hand when he starts his tricks again.

This is not the only case of exorcism in Herefordshire. The ghost of a Mr Hoskyns (one of the Hoskyns of Harewood, perhaps), which came from Ireland, was laid in Hereford Cathedral in 1786. This one, too, expressed an intense dislike of the Red Sea and was put (I don't know in what) under Byster's Gate in the city. There is another spirit laid under a bridge in Eardisland; and another, that of a lady who, as a ghost on a gray horse, is imprisoned in a goose-quill in Haugh Pool near Yarpole.

This business of exorcizing spirits is not so far away in history. Stephen Hawker, a vicar of Morwenstow in Cornwall, wrote in one of his books a fairly full account of such a ceremony; and quite recently I was told the full story of a "laying" that occurred near Llanidloes in Montgomeryshire —and the father of the man who told me was present. Only in this case it was the devil who was "laid." He turned up as a stranger at the house of some people who played cards on Sunday, and a number of spectators actually saw the cloven hoofs under the table when they peeped through a keyhole into the room where the card-playing was going on. He was coerced into a goose-quill this time and put away—but not for long; not for nearly long enough. He's been about again of late years.

There are no Vaughans at Hergest Court now (though the family is still going strong elsewhere), so the Black Dog of the Vaughans of Hergest hardly troubles the place any more. It used to appear when one of the family was to die.

Margaret Vaughan of Tudor times (she was one of the ladies of Queen Elizabeth's bedchamber) became the wife of Sir John Hawkins, sea-dog, pirate, hero, and—the one black mark on his name—slave trader. Lady Margaret Hawkins left money to found the Grammar School and it bears her name—Lady Margaret Hawkins Grammar School—to-day. Perhaps some of Sir John's sins have been blotted out by this good use of money badly gained; perhaps that was what she wanted.

In 1845 a book, *The History of Kington by a Member of the Mechanic's Institute,* was published at Kington. Mr F. C. Morgan, Librarian of Hereford Library and Curator of the Museum, writes in a recent copy of the *Transactions of the Woolhope Club* that he marvels how, with the material then available, they did the job, for it was both well printed and well bound. Only a hundred copies were printed and it is difficult to get a copy today. The "Member of the Mechanic's Institute" was Richard Parry, and since the only Richard Parry in the list of "principal persons in the town" was a coal and slate merchant (an unpleasant-sounding combination) and he was hardly likely to have carried anonymity so far as to leave his own name out of the "principal persons in the town," I take it that it was the coal and slate merchant who was the author.

Parry's *History of Kington* has no claims to great literary quality, but it does give a lot of information about Kington and is, besides, a most entertaining book to anyone familiar with the life of small towns and prepared to read between the lines. He starts off by quoting somebody else whom he calls "an eminent author."

"In former days this town was awake only once a week and that was on a market day. If you had passed through it at any other time you may have seen the shops open and the houses open, and a few persons walking about the streets with their eyes open; but the shops and the houses and the people therein were all asleep; the few persons who walked about looked as if they did not know whither they were going or what they were doing. The shops were cold for want of glass in the windows, and the articles exposed for sale appeared as if they had been in that state ever since Noah's

flood, and old-fashioned enough to have come out of his
Ark; the shop-keeper was often standing at his door, not
looking for customers, for that would have been vain employment, but merely gaping for something to fill his eyes;
and if a neighbour happened to be sauntering by he had a bit
of a chat with him . . . propping their backs against a wall,
and thrusting their hands into their breeches pockets, talked
for a time about things in general, and when tired they
parted; the one lounger wandered down the street to seek
for somebody else to gossip with, and the shop-keeper retired
into the shop to keep himself awake by killing flies and
wasps. Whenever a coach came into the town, and changed
horses at an Inn, all the indolent, gaping, staring and yawn-
ing population of the town came out to look at the said
horses, and the coach, and the coachman, and watch the
interesting process of taking off one set of horses and putting
on another: the very horses themselves appeared to wonder
what the people could be staring at, and when the coach left,
the town became so quiet again that the quack of a duck or
the squeaking of a pump-handle could be heard from one end
of the town to the other."

Now observe the way Mr Parry presents this to you. "An
eminent author says . . ." as much as to say, "This is the
way people talk about us." But who was the eminent author?
Nobody I have asked can tell me. And was he so eminent?
It would not be wise nor becoming to poke fun; we all trip
up at times. But the tenses certainly appear to get into a
muddle as early as the second sentence. I wonder was the
eminent author Richard Parry himself. Was he in a thoroughly bad temper with the town or with some part of it and
did he use this method of giving it a hearty punch on the
nose? Whether he wrote it or not, I am sure something had
annoyed him; and, if it was not his own work, it appealed
to him very much indeed in the mood he was in.

Having knocked the town flat, with the aid of an eminent
author, Mr. Parry, by his own exertions, proceeded to pick
it up and brush the dust off its jacket.

"The town, however [his own words now], is since much
improved and at the present time the inhabitants in business
are as active and lively as in any town of the same size in the
kingdom."

36

Farmhouse at Madley
Thatcher at work, Bartestree

He couldn't say fairer to-day.

He went on to give fuller praise where such praise was due:

"On the first of January, 1841, a very ingenious young man, Henry Sharratt, an inhabitant of the town, placed an illuminated dial in the front of his shop, which is considered an exquisite piece of workmanship and shows the time equally as well by night as in the day-time when required."

My own feeling about Parry's book is that he started it in a very crotchety frame of mind. Something had made him cross and he was going to take it out of somebody. That may have been when he decided on the anonymity of "A Member of the Mechanic's Institute." But he liked his native place and, having worked off his spleen in the early stages, found himself enjoying his self-appointed task, and made the best job he could of it.

One of the high-lights of the Kington of his day was the Kington Railway or Tram Road, which came from the Hay Railway at Eardisley (there is still a Tram Inn at Eardisley) round through Almeley and Lyonshall to Kington, and, from there, continued to the lime works at Burlingjobb near Old Radnor. Royal assent to the project was given May 23rd, 1818, and the section from Eardisley to Radnor cost twenty-three thousand pounds. The railway—trucks drawn by horses—was opened on May 1st, 1820. "A band of music preceded the tram carriages of coal and on arrival at Kington a considerable quantity of coal was given to the poor on the Upper Cross."

But there was better to come. Mechanically minded man must for ever be trying to improve on what he has.

"On Monday the 5th May, 1841, a new machine made its appearance on the Tramroad. Two men started from the town of Kington in an ingenious vehicle which they contrived to propel by means of cog-wheels set in motion by a winch, the handles of which were turned by the men who were seated in the machine. They proceeded at the rate of about six miles an hour; they reached Brecon the same day and returned to Hay about five o'clock on Tuesday with a ton of coal, but leaving the machine near the gas-house whilst they refreshed themselves, some boys began to meddle with the novel affair, and contrived to break one of the wheels to the great dis-

37

appointment of the men, who, instead of coming to Kington which was their intention that night, only reached Eardisley by pushing the machine before them. A scientific gentleman has stated his conviction that a machine might be made to suit the purpose of carrying passengers and goods of every description."

I can imagine very vividly the exaltation and pride in the hearts of those two men as they propelled their "ingenious vehicle" along the tramway. What glorious vistas opened before their eyes! They were inventors, creators. They were on the threshold of a new era of travel—"at six miles an hour"—and it would all be due to them. George Stephenson was no prouder of his Rocket than they of "the novel affair." And then those accursed boys! It was enough to break the inventors' hearts. To have started so promisingly only to come to this! Two tired men pushing their invention to Eardisley—very likely to the very great joy of, and with unpleasant comments from, the men who had always said there's nothing to equal a good horse. I wonder what happened to the boys; it is to be hoped they were good runners.

One day in the Red Lion at Weobley I was talking to an old man who remembered the Eardisley–Kington Railway.

"They used to take their time," he said, "specially when mushrooms was about. If they saw mushrooms in any field near they'd stop to pick 'em."

Very sensible, too, I thought. After all, you can travel on a railroad any day in the year, but mushrooms, like opportunity, must be plucked at the appointed time.

Even in these hustling days Herefordshire people don't always allow Time to prod them on. One November day I was at a small railway station in the south of the county, waiting for a train that would take me back to Hereford. A local train (two coaches, I believe) was there, but I was not taking particular notice of it. Ever since I read about Sherlock Holmes counting flights of steps—or was it the man Doyle used for his model of Holmes?—I have had the counting habit, though, fortunately, I immediately forget the number I get to; and I was occupied in counting the long string of trucks loaded with sugar beet. I did notice that the "local" was in charge of a woman guard. Gradually my attention was drawn from sugar beet to passenger train. The guard was growing restless. I looked at my watch and found the train should have puffed off two minutes ago. A middle-aged lady came leisurely on to the platform. This seemed to be the guard's cue.

"Oh, Mrs Pobjoy, are you coming on the train?"

(Obviously, Mrs Pobjoy was not the name she used. I don't want to get Mrs Pobjoy or anybody else into trouble.)

"Yes," said Mrs Pobjoy briefly.

"Well, do 'urry up, love. We're nearly three minutes late."

But Mrs Pobjoy wasn't going to be hurried. "I got to go in the office," she said briefly, and disappeared, neither hurrying nor promising to hurry.

The guard grew a little fidgetty. "Mrs Pobjoy," she called. " 'Urry up, Mrs Pobjoy. We're five minutes late."

Heads began to appear at carriage windows.

"Come *on,* Mrs Pobjoy," called the guard.

"Come on, Mrs Pobjoy," shouted the heads.

" 'Urry *up,* Mrs Pobjoy," cried the guard.

"Hurry up, Mrs Pobjoy," yelled the heads.

Eventually Mrs Pobjoy came, and a woman less in a hurry I never saw.

"We're late," complained the guard, as she bustled Mrs Pobjoy into a compartment, but even she wasn't particularly unhappy about it. She signalled the driver to get on with his business and the train moved off into the Herefordshire dusk.

Didn't Mussolini make the trains run to time in Italy? Perhaps that's what was wrong with him.

One can't be certain whether Parry approved or disapproved of the theatre. He is certainly very respectful to Mrs Siddons. He writes: "In a barn still standing on the Talbot premises, but now converted into stables &c., the celebrated Mrs Siddons whom the first painter of his day immortalized as the 'Tragic Muse' made her first public appearance on the stage."

But, apart from Mrs Siddons, he is much less approving, though again, characteristically, he shifts the blame on to somebody else.

"A judicious writer remarks, that the stage has flourished most in the most corrupt and depraved state of society; and in the exact proportion that the drama has thriven or declined in any place, so as [*sic.*] it been the faithful barometer of the depraved or ameliorated state of morals in that community."

He goes on to quote Dr Johnson and Sir Matthew Hale against the theatre. He may have been getting at somebody, or he may have been trying to please two sections of public opinion. The worst of writing for a small, local circle of readers is that one has to do it with an eye on their likes and dislikes.

Parry made a complete list of the tombstones in the churchyard in his time, giving the full inscriptions on most of them. For the greater part they are no more interesting than one would expect to find them in a country churchyard. A tombstone is interesting if you knew the person buried under it or—if it *is* interesting. There were one or two in the latter class.

"Christopher Blaxland, died October 18th, 1812, aged 42 years. He lived an affectionate husband, a tender parent, and sincere friend."

Then comes the story (not on the tombstone) of Christopher Blaxland. "This man came to Kington from Gladestry on the day of his death and purchased a brace of pistols, and on his road home called upon a gentleman with the intention, it is supposed, of inviting him to fight a duel. The gentleman could not be prevailed upon to leave his residence, and therefore most probably saved his life. Mr Blaxland soon after his arrival at home put an end to his own existence by shooting himself through the head." He was determined to kill somebody, and, poor devil, may have had good reason to do so. But was he really a good husband, parent, or friend?

Another on the same page is in direct contrast. "Philip Turner, late of the Royal Oak, gentleman. After entertaining a society of his friends in his usual cheerful manner, he retired peacefully to repose, and in that interval gently passed from this world into immortality on the 26th day of September, aged 69 years."

Parry records: "The churchyard formerly contained a stone with an inscription which recorded the death of four children who were born at one birth in the town."

He has more to say about the churchyard than to make a record of the tombstones, and for once I am heartily with him. The virtues of the countryman seldom include a great regard or feeling for anything of antiquarian interest—unless it happens to suit his particular purpose to show regard or feeling. I'm not thinking in particular of the present day, and, of course, Parry was writing of his own times. How many beautiful buildings, monastery buildings mostly, have been pulled to pieces in the past because a neighbouring farmer wanted to build a new cowshed? How many dolmens have been pulled down to provide a few useful big stones? How many tumuli have been opened in the hills because somebody thought they might find inside something that could be sold? Personally I'm no more sympathetic towards people who open them in order to put bones in a museum: to me the grave of a Neolithic man is still a grave and his bones may stay where they were put. Other people, other tastes. "Us d'open her up," said an old hill-farmer to me, talking about a mound on his farm, "but there warn't nothing there but some ol' bones. Us d'put they in a bottle and on the kitchen window they d'stand for years and then mother d'get the fidgets an' us had to take 'em back where they come from." Some abbeys have been despoiled to a state where they have become picturesque, ivied ruins, and if you happen to care for picturesque, ivied ruins that is not so bad. But I happen to live near where one of the largest Cistercian abbeys in Wales once stood. *Once* stood! With the exception of a very small portion of crumbling wall there is nothing left. *Nothing at all!* But there are some very fine stone buildings in the neighbourhood! I don't think (and I say this of people whom I like, people who are my friends) that anyone in the district would feel much compunction about using that remaining fragment of wall if it could be made into something useful.

In the Kington of Parry's day it was the gravestones that suffered. Anything, in fact, about a grave that could be made to serve other purposes was shown scant respect. Parry himself, in the year 1835, saw the sexton and his assistants at work during the night. They were demolishing a brick grave in order to sell the materials to the relatives of somebody who had just died. I don't know if the historian made a fuss about it, but he does record that the people in question refused to buy and the stuff was carted away (not replaced!), probably to be sold to someone less squeamish. Parsons, not only in Kington, but in most of the country parishes, had a habit of taking old gravestones to serve as flag-stones and such-like. In this connection I might mention that I found a piece of a tombstone, inscribed in lettering that obviously was very old. I found it in the bed of a mountain stream, though there is a church not far away. But this was not in Herefordshire.

"They be quite se'af, the owd gravestones," said a Herefordshire sexton to Parry. "Mr So-and-So had they to lay flurs wi', they be quite se'af wi' their faces down'wrts." What a lot of priceless material—to say nothing of much that was worthy of more respect—must have gone in the past to serve some passing need that could have been served equally well by stuff of less intrinsic value.

In the *History of Kington* there is a list—mentioned earlier—of "principal persons in the town." Some of their occupations are interesting: currier, butcher, solicitor, tanner, tallow chandler, widow lady, cooper, spinster, fellmonger and malster, miller, gentleman, surgeon, barber, coal and slate merchant (probably the author), wheelwright, model-maker (it does not state models of what), cornfactor, gunmaker, schoolmaster, schoolmistress.

A number of these could be found in the Kington of to-day—and a number certainly could not. This was still the hey-day of the self-contained community and the town or village craftsman.

There is no mention of poet. Yet there had been one of those, too, though, since his principal effort was sixty years old, he may have been dead by the time the *History* was written. Parry included this poem in his book. "The town of Kington and places in the neighbourhood poetically described by Thomas Parker, Joiner, an inhabitant in the year 1785." Now some of this poetry is not bad rhyming at all.

And parts of it are shocking. But all poets turn out poor stuff at times. It starts:

> By fancy led through pleasing rural scenes,
> To range where art with nature intervenes
> For pure amusement some fair themes I choose,
> And court improvement from the tuneful muse.
> And though unskill'd in versifying rules,
> Nor blessed with wealth, or time to spend in schools
> Yet I'll attempt to show my country's worth,
> And praise the little town that gave me birth.
> This town is by the name of Kington known;
> Its situation in the temperate zone,
> Its northern latitude near fifty-three,
> Its western longitude the third degree.

After a flying start I'm afraid Mr Parker descended into bathos. But is it so much worse than Wordsworth at his worst? The first thing that struck me as I read it was how lucky Mr Parker was that Kington *was* in the temperate zone. But frigid or torrid would have scanned equally well. I'll not say it's not too bad for a joiner who had probably never been to school—it is not necessary to go to school to be a poet, and a poet may follow any calling—but poets with better opportunities have done worse.

He was conscious of his poor education, though not lamenting it overmuch, as when he writes of the Lady Margaret Hawkins Grammar School.

> One gen'rous Lady gave a whole estate
> Had I received my education there
> More merit in my verses would appear;
> Tho' now insipid, yet I own I find
> 'Tis an amusement that unbends the mind.

Mr Parker was intensely patriotic, both locally and more widely.

> Of all the counties England can record,
> Few are so blessed as this of Hereford
> For wheat and wool, and wood and water famed,
> And for good cider very much esteemed.
> Few counties can afford a better place

For fishing, fowling, or the healthy chase:
England has not more rich or fertile fields,
None that a better annual produce yields.
Far from America's destructive war,
Where Mars in dreadful glory drives his car—
Where carnage, death and desolation reign
With hostile ruin o'er the bloody plain!
But while that side the globe fierce discord frowns,
Here peace with plenty all our labour crowns,
And tho' the meagre sons of vicious France,
Perfidious slaves of falsehood and romance,
With native pride and intolerance do boast,
And threaten to invade Britannia's coast—
Dare they attempt it?—No, they never dare!
For Britain's thunder fills their mind with fear.
Nay, they should think on't, sure they have no chance,
Have we not fought the Colonies and France.

Those last eight lines—except that they were written
defiantly at France when a French invasion was expected—
somehow struck a sympathetic note at a time when once
again invasion seemed not merely possible but probable.

There are one hundred and fifty-four lines of his poem.
Parry gives it all. I give a taste of its quality as well as its
weakness. Perhaps some of it raises an involuntary smile. I
still say there have been worse poems.

Mr Parker was no teetotaller—unless he was forced by
sheer lack of invention to include that rather bad rhyme
about cider. One can imagine the poem being read or recited
in the poet's favourite inn to the tune of much applause. I
wonder did our joiner ever go home drunk with success and
fuddled with "cider very much esteemed" thrust on him by
his admirers.

"You did ought to ha' bin a parson, Parker," they would
have said to him. "Thee bist a queer quist, boy. Enough learning in thy head to be usher up at the Grammar School."

Alas, poor poet! His success went to his head. Poetry is
like drink, "it gits a holt on you." Not content to rest on his
achievements, he must attempt another poem (also given in
full in the *History*). But it was watery stuff, typical of the

churchyard-tombstone school of poets. It was entitled *A Search for Happiness* and the last verse is enough to show how the mighty had fallen.

> Thus happily I'd pass the time,
> Till Heaven decreed my death;
> Then, conscious of no evil crime,
> In peace resign my breath.

Parry's quotation of the Communtation Survey of 1845 is interesting for the amount of common land it shows still existed. Out of a total area of 8,313 acres, 6,391 acres were enclosed lands and woods and 1,830 acres were commons. The remainder was roads, 75 acres, and rivers and brooks, 17 acres.

I cannot get hold of reliable figures for the present day, but in 1910 there were in the county 11,245 acres of moorlands which, roughly speaking, is the same thing, and I am very sure that not a sixth, nor anywhere near it, is in Kington Parish. Of course, lying so close to the hills, Kington would contain a lot of what is, up here, vaguely referred to as "hill" (rough grazing for sheep) and that is very often common land. But there is nothing like a quarter of the parish as there was in Parry's day.

"Hops are not cultivated in the parish," reads a following sentence. They would not be. The most northerly line to which hops are grown runs roughly halfway through the county.

Quite a number of pages of the *History* is devoted to local customs. Burning the bush was still going on. A new bush was made each New Year's Day and labourers went round singing "Old Cider." It was an old bush that was burned, the new one being kept for the ceremony to take place a year hence. "It is a common case to see numbers of labouring men early on New Year's morning in a beastly state of drunkenness arising from this foolish custom."

The plain fact was that the "foolish custom" was kept up largely by men thrown out of employment by work coming to a standstill on the farms during the quietest part of the winter, and it gave them a chance to beg and not be ashamed, to eat, drink, and be merry at small expense.

There were so many fires on a New Year's morning that on one occasion a doctor going to a confinement (perhaps Mr Parry's surgeon among the "principal persons") was lit all the way without having to use a lantern.

Burning the bush was soon to die out. Like wassailing the cider trees, it was probably a custom of great antiquity, being part of the annual votive offering to Ceres, and one of those pagan customs that Pope Gregory instructed St Augustine not to try to destroy but to utilize in new and Christian channels.

Bell-ringing also went on on New Year's Day, and it is on record that Kington people in the fifteenth century gave each other gifts of pins, much more highly considered than the wooden skewers in general use.

On Shrove Tuesday there was another local custom, a less ancient one, that would hardly have met with Pope Gregory's approval and which Parry disliked even more than he disliked labourers getting drunk as they went round burning the bush. The boys used to take out the fire engine on this day and parade round the town collecting contributions. Their habit was to turn the hose through open windows or doorways belonging to those who refused to give them anything, or even on the people themselves. A playful trick that Parry denounced sternly.

"Cock-fighting was still one of the chief amusements." That is quite understandable, for it went on in the hills only a few miles away long after it was stamped out elsewhere. Even in the twentieth century now and then—but never mind about that. Cock-fighting had declined in popularity for a while, but when Parry wrote it was on the increase again. He noted the fact with regret.

Bull-baiting was, however, thirty years away, the last event having taken place in 1815. However pleased the humanitarians may have been at the end of this robust amusement, which used to take place near the Market Hall, a great roar of protest must have gone up from the poor people of the town. It wasn't their sport they missed so much, as food. The amiable custom had been that—after the battle —they should be allowed to buy the meat of the bull for next to nothing. I never hear of some unpleasantness that should be continued because of the employment it provides without thinking of the good case the hungry paupers had for the continuing of bull-baiting.

Parry knew that hot cross buns never go mouldy. It is a belief that has lasted until the present day.

A jolly, talkative Herefordshire baker waved his pint pot at me. "Now here's something that will interest you." Knowing I could be depended on not to interrupt him, nor laugh at him, he came and sat down by me. "D'you know this? A bun baked on a Good Friday will never go stale."

"Spice?" I suggested.

"It's not spice. You can bake 'em without spice. You can bake 'em exactly like you do any other day. And the other days only keep 'em a bit and they'll go green as a toad's belly. But not if it's baked on Good Friday."

"Well, what does happen to them then?"

"Nothing. Nothing at all. Just dries up. But they *don't* go mouldy. They don't go bad."

More things in heaven and earth, Horatio! I'm anybody's fool when it's an old story, I admit that.

"Look," said my friend, "you drop in. We always keep one for a year. I'll show you. [This was about November, I think.] I got one. If I'm not there ask the Missus. You'll see."

I did call and I did see. It sounds ridiculous, but there it is. There's no catch. Of all crafts, that of baking bread has suffered most horribly under the juggernaut of speed and efficiency we miscall Progress. But my baker had something left. His Good Friday buns wouldn't go mouldy.

"We'm important men, us bakers," he told me. "The birth of our Lord and His death. We'm at both. We makes mince pies for His birthday and hot cross buns for His deathday."

Which, of course, is quite true.

A hundred years ago Parry was telling how bakers always kept some of their Good Friday buns for luck—and the buns, he said, never went bad.

It was not until some time later that I came across the legend that explains this favour shown to bakers. It is related that as Jesus was on His way to be crucified He passed a woman by the wayside washing clothes. The woman, taking the side of His persecutors, mocked at Him, and to show her contempt threw her dirty washing water over Him. There was a woman standing near with new-baked bread in her arms. She chided the washerwoman sternly for her want of charity, and, after wiping the water off Jesus, gave Him one of her loaves.

He ate the bread and said: "From henceforth blessed be the baker and cursed be the washer."

April 1st was All Fools' Day. Too frivolous. Mr Parry frowned on it. May 1st was quite a festival; he had little to say of that, but he does tell us that on May 29th, Oak Apple Day, the boys all wore oak leaves and oak apples in their caps and were inclined to disapprove—and show their disapproval roughly—of those less loyally inclined. Royalist sympathies were still alive.

November 5th he disliked very much. It was not the special Form of Prayer in the Prayer Book he objected to. But the bonfires! The guys! The fireworks! "This fiery zeal has decreased with the last fifty years, the sober and the thinking classes of the community take no pleasure in the destruction of fuel and expenditure of money, which if given to the poor would tend to make them comfortable and happy." A good thing the poor are always with us; what else would serve so well for reproving extravagance?

Christmas was an occasion for decorating church and houses—so also were Easter and Whitsun—and the old legend of the oxen kneeling on Christmas Eve is mentioned. Many of the old people believed implicitly that this happened.

Easter was a festival celebrated by ball-playing. This may have been the old form of football, played at many places along the Marches, when whole parishes, sometimes more than one, took part. Parry did not have much to say about it, but the game often used to take the better part of a day, the goals being miles apart. Broken bones were not uncommon by the end of the match, nor, often, were broken heads.

Curfew was still being rung in Kington when the *History* was written, a custom that had gone on since Norman times. It was rung in Leominster until 1855, and at All Saints,

Hereford, until 1860. The curfew (*couvre-feu*) was originally not a bell, but the covering put over the fire to extinguish it, the object of curfew being to prevent the fires that so easily broke out in the wooden houses of Saxon England by making people put out their fires and go to bed early.[1] It was only after many years that the word curfew came to be used for curfew-bell, the bell that gave warning.

"The curfew was made of copper, rivetted together, as solder would have been likely to melt with the heat. It was ten inches high, sixteen inches wide and nine inches deep."

A bell was also rung in Kington at five o'clock in the morning until about 1820.

Parry also mentioned sin-eating, which he says was discontinued about the time of Charles II, but whether he had any certain knowledge of it is doubtful. He also writes of fairies, corpse candles, and will-o'-the-wisps, all firmly believed in by the country people in his day—and not altogether forgotten by them in this.

He gives one or two peculiarly local words. One of them, *frum,* meaning early, has survived in the Kington district up to the present time. There are still people who speak of their potatoes being *frum.* The word is said to be of Norse origin and an isolated survival from one of the rare incursions of the Norsemen into Mercia. It is peculiarly local to Kington.

Cider is said to *fret* if it ferments, and tufts of dead grass are called *fegs,* a word that is still in common use in the neighbouring county of Radnor. "Them old fegs," said a roadman, "they d'spoil the edge" (of his sickle).

A *ruck* of stones meant a heap of stones, but the word is seldom used now.

"There's nothing like a good murder," is a saying many a smart newspaper proprietor might use as motto for his coat-of-arms. Parry relates one murder that was committed at Kington and another case where a man was hanged for wounding someone, a reminder of the times when other crimes than murder were punishable by death.

I fancy, from the description he gives, that he may have seen the latter execution. He could have done so unless he

[1]Or it may have been to prevent the fire from burning out.

was a very young man, and I don't think he was. It took place at Hereford on Saturday, April 12th, 1817. Thomas Langslow, the son of a currier, had got into bad company, and during a quarrel wounded James Green, a solicitor's clerk, aged twenty-seven. The whole town seems to have been horrified at Langslow's fate, but I daresay a good many walked the twenty miles to see the spectacle. It was a double execution, the other being a man called Hardy, who was hanged for robbing his master's house at Kilgwyn, near Llandovery.

The murder related was unintelligent and brutal. Francis Smyth killed his uncle, Walter Smyth, a tanner, by shooting him and he buried the body in the tan-house after taking five shillings and sixpence from his pockets. The crime may have been caused by the fact that the tanner was going to be married and the younger man feared to lose an inheritance. The body was soon found and the murderer hanged at Hereford. Sordid, unhappy tale that can hardly move one to-day, but it is said to have provided the theme for "Lillio's once admired tragedy, *George Barnwell*."

One omission in the *History of Kington* is surprising. Three years before the book was written the scandal of the increasing tolls on every road had driven the Welshmen in neighbouring counties and all over South Wales to take the law into their own hands in a very determined fashion. In 1842 the Rebecca Riots broke out, and they spread like a flame. Men dressed themselves in women's clothes, made rough wigs of horses' hair, blacked their faces, and, their leader always nicknamed Rebecca, turned out in the dead of night in their hundreds to smash and burn the hated gates. This was no petty revolt of a few disgruntled farmers, but a concerted movement, carried on with an almost religious fervour, by a whole peasantry. A few miles from Kington the gates were going down like elm-branches in a gale. Twenty-five miles away, in Rhayader, a Radnor hill-town, Rebecca smashed and burned gates, waited for them to be put back, and then smashed them down again. The country was in an uproar; poor people were delighted, and those who found the Turnpike Trust profitable, angry and frightened.

Parry does not say one word about the Riots. They are

bound to have been in his mind when he gave an account of the local meetings of the Turnpike Trust, and wrote down a full and exact list of the tolls charged at the town gates. Why, I wonder. Local politics? Fear of giving offence to some of his wealthier customers? Something of the sort, no doubt. A pity, for he could have spoken surely with authority on a movement that, because of its peculiar nature, has all too many gaps in its history. He could have given us local gossip, and local gossip has more than once hauled truth out of her well. And that may be the reason he kept his mouth shut; for Richard Parry was Richard ap Harry, and he may have reflected that the best way of getting none of his kinsmen into trouble was to say nothing.

The Rebecca Riots achieved their purposes, but, though some results were immediate where the Rioters had been most active, not all at once or in a spectacular manner. They sowed a seed and the fruit came later. At Kington there were still substantial tolls in 1845.

> For every horse or other beast (except as hereinafter is excepted) drawing any hearse, coach, chariot, landau, chaise, chaise-marine, car, calash, berlin, barouche, chair, or other such light carriage or any cart drawn by only one horse, six pence.
>
> For every horse or other beast (except as aforesaid) drawing any waggon, train, cart, car, or any other such carriage with wheels of less breadth than four and a half inches, the sum of sevenpence.

There were eleven separate classes, each set down as carefully as the ones quoted.

One-horse carts with wheels between four and a half and six inches in breadth paid sixpence. Those with wider wheels —six inches to nine inches—saved a further penny and paid fivepence.

One-horse carts "with the felloes of the wheels of less breadth or gauge than four and a half inches" paid one halfpenny only, as long as it was carrying "any stones, bricks, timber, wood, gravel, or any materials for making and repairing the said roads or any bridges thereon, or bones or salt to be really and truly used solely for manure."

51

The next class is interesting in mentioning an animal we certainly don't use to pull carts in these days.

"For every ox, meat cattle, ass or dog drawing any waggon, train, cart, car, or other such carriage, the sum of threepence."

A horse or mule laden but not drawing a vehicle paid "one penny-half-penny."

A laden ass paid a penny. Cows or oxen paid three-farthings a head. Smaller animals, calves, swine, hogs, sheep, or lambs were charged fivepence a score.

The few toll-gates left in the country now (there is one near Hay) are amusing anachronisms. But a hundred years ago these gates were found every few miles. The toll-farmers were supposed to repair the roads. When the expense of doing so affected their pockets they (with the connivance of the Turnpike Trusts) put up fresh gates. Rebecca acted none too soon.

What were the tolls worth? In 1790 the Town Gates were let for £391. And we can be sure there was a good profit; very good if one is to judge by the way their value rose.

"The meetings [of the Trustees of the Turnpike Trust] are now held at the King's Head Inn, kept by John Roberts. The tolls received at the gates are let to the highest bidder, in the month of November, for one or three years from January following. The last letting amounted to the sum of £1,530 for the gates in the district, and for those leading into Kington the sum of £800."

That is, £2,330 for one small district, and the takings made such an investment worth-while!

Well, you can go into Kington for not one penny nowadays. Not a penny. Free as air. That is, if you've paid the horse-power tax on your car, and five shillings for a driving licence, and, willy-nilly, some quite unreasonable number of pennies per gallon of petrol, and, I daresay, taxes on various other parts of the car. Don't laugh and say you haven't a car. You pay your tolls some way. I wonder if we really *are* so much wiser and so much better off than our forefathers were!

Mark Stone and Cross, Pembridge
The Old House, Hereford

Chapter III

LEOMINSTER

LEOMINSTER is the second largest town in Hereford-shire and, but for a rather shabby trick played by the cities of Hereford and Worcester, it might easily have become the largest.

From the earliest times Leominster was famous for its wool. So precious was it that it was commonly referred to as "Lemster ore." That was what Drayton called it:

Where lives the man so dull on Britain's shore
To whom did never sound the name of Lemster ore
That with the silkworm's web for smallness doth compare?

The county is now so noted for Hereford cattle that it is often forgotten how important the wool trade was. Up to Stuart times Leominster had the best wool-market in England. Wool was the first of the six Ws of Hereford: Wool, Water, Wood, Wheat, Wine, and Women. The Wine was apple wine, cider—and Women came last. (To be fair, they came second in Camden's list and he left out Wool altogether: Wine, Women, Wye, Wells, and Woods.)

There was something special about the wool of these parts. "Certain fields near Leominster," wrote Izaak Walton, "a town in Herefordshire, are observed to make the sheep that graze upon them more fat than the next and also to bear finer wool."

The noted local breed was the Ryeland, and it was nearly cross-bred out of existence, but some enthusiasts remedied this and there are now a few pure-bred flocks. Nowadays the Black-faced Shropshire Down is perhaps the most common in the locality, but cattle-grazing has long since taken precedence over "Lemster ore."

And the shabby trick of Hereford and Worcester? Well, it concerns market days. Those jealous cities, seeing Leom-

53

inster catching them up and likely to forge ahead in the race for prosperity, had the market days fixed so that it was impossible for the London merchants to attend both their markets and that of Leominster. So Leominster had to fall back (in the county) into second place.

An annual wool fair held in the town lasted from Saturday to Friday. Quite likely it was held on the Sunday as well. They certainly were just across the Border, for in the seventeenth century Gualter Stephens, a licenced preacher, incumbent of Bishop's Castle for fifty-three years, gained much credit for obtaining the suppression of fairs in Wales on the Lord's Day. The Welsh Sunday is no innovation.

So important was the wool trade that (perhaps as it showed signs of declining) a law was passed which eventually gave country people the idea that it was not quite proper to be buried in a shroud of any other material than wool. This law, passed in 1678, in the time of Charles II, enacted that no corpse should be buried "in any shirt, sheet, shift, or shroud or anything whatsoever, made or mingled with flax; or in silk, hair, gold, silver or in any other stuff or thing, other than what is made of sheep's wool only on pains of penalties."

Two witnesses were supposed to testify within eight days of a funeral that the law had been carried out, but there were those who preferred to choose the material for their shroud and pay the fine incurred.

The Parish Registers give some interesting accounts of this. An entry in 1713–14, for instance: "Wife of Mr Thomas Harris was bur'd, September 19th."

And in the next column: "Bur'd in linen and information made before Mr Powell and ye money paid to the Overseers of the poor."

Pope mentioned it, too:

> "Odious! in woollen: 'twould a saint provoke!"
> Were the last words the fair Narcissa spoke.
> "No, let a charming chintz and Brussels lace
> Wrap my cold hands and shade my lifeless face."

The prohibition was so unpopular among people of means (no doubt the shepherds were consoled at receiving no less than their due consideration) that the Act fell into disuse and finally was repealed in 1814, in George IV's reign.

Leominster has had a stormy history. It was too near the Border for comfort and was big enough to be worth the trouble of sacking.

Its original name was Welsh, Llanlieni—the Church of Nuns—so called because there was a nunnery there. This was probably the original minster built in the seventh century by Merewald, King of Mercia. A holy man in the town dreamt that in a certain spot a lion came and fed out of his hand. And on the same night Merewald had a dream about an anchorite who had important news for him. The next day they met. It was evident to the King that he had met his anchorite; and the anchorite knew that the lion feeding out of his hand must be Merewald, whose nickname was the Lion, and as a result of their meeting the King built the church in the spot indicated by the dream.

Things were never peaceful at Leominster for long. In 760 the Welsh ravaged the town on their way to Hereford. Two centuries later the Danes came as far and Leominster suffered a horrible massacre. A town has to be tough to rise from destruction every hundred years or so.

Merewald's minster was probably completely destroyed in the savage Danish attack, for presently Leofric, Earl of Mercia, was building a minster in the town, from which time it became Leofric-minster, or Leofminstre, the name by which it was called in Domesday.

Leofric was the husband of the famous Lady Godiva. She had a sister, Wulviva, much less known, because she never did anything so interesting as to ride naked through a city out of pure goodness of heart (nor for any other reason). But perhaps she never had the chance. Some people say the story of Lady Godiva's ride through Coventry is not true. True? Of course it is true! I've been believing that story ever since I was a very small boy, and a lovely story I thought it, and I'm not going to stop believing it now to please anyone. Godiva and Wulviva gave the parish of Preston-on-Wye and the Manor of Woolhope as gifts to Hereford Cathedral, and very highly they were esteemed by the good churchmen, naked ride or no.

Whatever damage was done by Sweyn, or Swegen, eldest son of Earl Godwin, on his way to and from Wales, he seems to have been content with less than the whole town.

"This year [1046] went Earl Sweyn into Wales and Griffyd, king of the northern men with him, and hostages were delivered to him. As he returned homeward he ordered the Abbess of Leominster to be fetched to him and he kept her as long as he list, after which he let her go home."

The nunnery seems to have come to an end about this time, which may or may not have been due to Sweyn's carrying off Edgiva, the Abbess, and when the nuns had gone the minster became a monastery.

Harold, another son of Godwin, soon to be defeated at Hastings, was one of the most successful adversaries of the Welsh. He avenged the sack of Hereford in 1056, driving the Welsh back into the hills, so that Leominster was cleared of them for a while.

The town was to suffer three times more, twice badly, and the third time, when its history of warfare, like Hereford's, was coming to an end, not quite so severely.

On the first of the three occasions William de Braose, instigated by his wife, Maud de Haie, or, as she was more commonly known in the Marches, Moll Walbee of Hay, took the town and burned half of it to the ground. Later he had to fly to the continent, and his wife and son, taken prisoner by King John, were imprisoned in Windsor Castle until they died. She had earned John's hatred by taunting him with the murder of Prince Arthur.

The next time Leominster suffered was when Glyndwr came ravaging out of the west. He, whatever his merits as a Welsh patriot, destroyed towns, churches, and monasteries impartially—even Welsh ones—and he did not spare Leominster.

The last time the town became a battlefield was when it was taken by Colonel Birch during the Civil War, but cruelty had lost some of its venom by the year 1645.

In the reign of Henry I, Leominster Abbey was transferred to the Monastery of Reading, of which it became a cell, a sort of younger brother. All its considerable rights went with it:

"With their appendages, with woods, and fields and pastures, with meadows and water, with mills and fisheries, with churches also and chapels, and churchyards and oblations, and tythes, with money and one monier, at Reading. The monks of Reading, their family and effects shall be free from all gelt and toll, and every other custom, by land or by water, in passing over bridges and seaports throughout England. And the Abbot and his Monks shall have all hundreds and places, with soc, and sac, and tol and theam, and infangenthef, and utfangenthef, and hamsoken within-borough and without-borough, in ways and paths, and in all places and all causes which are or may be from their men, and all their possessions, and from aliens forfeiting therein; and the Abbot and Monks of Reading shall, within all their possessions, have the whole cognisance of assault and thefts, murders, shedding of blood, and breach of the peace, as much as belongs to the royal power, and of all forfeitures. . . . He [the Abbot] must not sell the demesnes nor make knights unless in the holy vest of Christ, in which he must take care, modestly, of entertaining children, but prudently to entertain adult and discreet persons, as well clergy as laity."

The old Anglo-Saxon words have a healthy ring to them.

Gelt was a fine; *toll* (this word has remained unchanged though the meaning has altered slightly) was the charge made on goods taken into a town. *Soc* (the old English for jurisdiction) was the authority to minister justice and execute laws; *tol* was the liberty to buy and sell anywhere (the city of Worcester, for instance, gave charters to the monks of Leominster exempting them from toll on their way to Worcester and Droitwich and allowing them to trade in Worcester without paying any tolls). *Theam* was a privilege granted to the Lords Marchers allowing them to judge bondmen, bondwomen, and villeins in their courts; *infangenthef* was the right to judge thieves in one's jurisdiction and *utfangenthef* was a similar right over thieves from one's own manor who committed their crimes elsewhere. *Hamsoken* was the privilege of freedom which every man enjoys in his own house.

Reading was a monastery of some importance. Henry I

57

gave them "the hand of St James the Apostle which his daughter, Matilda, wife of the Emperor of Germany, had brought from that country with much care and ceremony."

King John visited Leominster in 1216, after de Braose had sacked most of it. Since John and de Braose were enemies, he was, not unnaturally, sympathetic to the town's sufferings. He confirmed the charter of the monks and at the same time gave them a singular concession:

Nullus Dominicos canes abbatis et Monachorum expaltare cogat. Verum canes hominum quorum intra fforestam manentium abbas et Monachi expaltari faciant.

"Let none compel the great dogs of the abbot and monks to be expeditated, but the abbot may compel the dogs of the men living in the forest to be expeditated."

Expeditation (*expaltare*), sometimes known as "lawing," was a cruel business. In order to make sure that dogs did not hunt the King's game, the ball of the forefoot was cut out to make them useless for hunting. Only the larger ones were so treated, but pet-dogs and lap-dogs would have been rare enough then. The penalty imposed on a man whose dog had not been expeditated was three shillings, a considerable sum for those days.[1]

The expeditation was altered a little in the reign of Henry III, though it cannot have been a much less painful operation, by making it obligatory for only the claws of the forefeet to be removed instead of the ball of the foot.

Both Reading and Leominster were particularly rich in relics. Bishop Swinfield of Hereford made out a list of sacred relics at Leominster round about 1170.

Reading's possessions, as might be expected of the parent monastery, make the most imposing list. Dr. London, Visitor of the Monastery, catalogued them, "Inventory of Relyques of the House of Redyng." It begins:

Imprimis.   Two peces off the Holye crosse.
Item.   Saynt James hand.
Item.   Saynt Phelype scolle.
Item.   A bone off Marye Magdolene with other more.

---

[1] In 1333 the Rector of Harewood was excommunicated for cheating the tithes payable to the King of the sum of 4s. 4d.!

and ending with:

There be a multitude of small bonys &c, wyche wolde occupie iiii schets of papyr to make particularly an inventorye of eny part thereof.

Dr. London (quoting Swinfield's list) wrote to Cromwell that "at Leominster there were sepulchral remains of 2 Saxon Kings and martyrs, also a portion of the linen that was wrapped the body of our Lord, of the sponge used at His crucifixion, of the rod of Moses, one of the stones with which Stephen was stoned, some of the frankincense and myrrh offered by the Magi, some of the soil of Bethlehem and Gethsemane."

Those credulous days! What men would believe in! The illnesses that were cured by these holy "relyques." We're much wiser to-day.

"I never came across such humbug in my life," a friend said to me when I showed him the list. "What *good* did it do them?"

I tapped the bottle of the widely advertised, but almost worthless, preparation he had been taking after the meal we had just shared.

"Exactly the same good as that does you."

"You needn't make fun of that. I've great faith——"

"So had they," I interrupted. "It moves mountains and if there aren't mountains, and perhaps not even molehills, the results are even more wonderful."

Oh dear no! Considering the success of the patent-medicine vendors in the twentieth century, I think it is very unbecoming of us to scoff at people who put their faith in relics.

Leominster Priory was dissolved in 1539, and its last Prior, John Glover, was one of the sensible ones who obliged His Majesty's Commissioner, and safeguarded his own future, by giving him all the information he could. There had, in the past, at one time and another, been complaints that the monks of the Priory were not all they might have been, but at its end it was sober and well-behaved. And its worldly state was as satisfactory as its spiritual.

"I assure you," ran a letter to Cromwell, "that I suppose there is not such another turf within the King's realm lying so nigh together within itself, and within so small a compass, and of such value and commodity as that is, for it is worth a 1,000 of marks of rent of assize and casualties and all lying within the compass of five or six miles at the uttermost, so that one bayly may gather all the rents of the lordship."

The letter went on to recommend it as a right goodly thing for himself or his son.

But the King kept it and in time it was broken up. Some was sold here, some there; and the priory church—the church was one large building, part the parish church and part for the use of the monks—the priory church fell into ruin, and once again there was good building material at hand for anyone smart enough to get his hands on it.

I feel like paraphrasing Count Smorltork:

"The word smart comprises (by himself) a variety of sins."

Leominster was as Royalist as the rest of the county during the Civil War, but it was captured for Parliament in 1645, by the same commander, Colonel Birch, who took Hereford the year before.

Colonel Birch was, locally, one of the most colourful figures of his time. He was originally a pack-horse dealer—that is, a trader in charge of his own goods—and early in the war he was attacked by some Parliamentary soldiers, most of whom, at that time, were the scum and sweepings of taverns and much more interested in loot than in the cause they were supposed to serve. Their attempt to collect from Birch was one of those mistakes we all make. There was a lion in this ass's skin. The action attracted the attention of Oliver Cromwell, who was so struck by the pack-horse dealer's potential qualities that he offered him a command in his troop. It was a good move for the Parliamentary side, and also for Birch. His campaigns in the west were uniformly successful, and he took in turn Hereford, Leominster, and Goodrich.

He may have been a good Roundhead; he certainly did not lose sight of the interests of Colonel Birch. Proscribed estates were going cheap and he was, after all, a good businessman.

He appears to have had some of the qualities that made the Vicar of Bray immortal, for he took part in the negotiations for the return of Charles II and, many years later, was prominent in support of William of Orange.

He was M.P. first for Leominster and later for Weobley, a Herefordshire village that then returned two members. He settled at Weobley, where he bought the mansion of Garnstone and beautified it. He died in 1691, his line dying with him, both his son and daughter pre-deceasing him, and was buried in Weobley Church, where a life-sized monument to him stands in the chancel.

Charles I visited Leominster, as told in the *Iter Carolinum,* an account of his travellings. He was in the town in 1645.

"September 1645, Friday, 5th. To Lemster. Dinner at the Unicorn. To Weobley—supper. The Unicorn."

The Unicorn at Weobley was renamed the Crown in honour of the visit. Two good places to visit in the same day, for Camden wrote in his *Britannia,* "Renowned also it is for wheat and bread of the first floure, that Lemster Bread and Weobley Ale are grown into a common Proverbe."

Weobley ale I have no quarrel with, but Lemster bread is now no better than it is anywhere else. Bread, like beer, is not what it used to be.

Leominster, in spite of being Royalist, accepted the Commonwealth with a good face, as the following items in the Chamberlain's accounts prove.

		£. s. d.
1652–53.	Paid for pulling down the King's arms and for making up the wall, and for making the glass window.	7.0.
1656.	Paid for wine and beere on that day when the Protector was proclaimed to the Trumpetrs.	1.1.6.

But it is not difficult to see where their sympathies were. £1.1.6. for beer for Oliver Cromwell. In 1661—

	£. s. d.
Paid to the Ryngers on the Coronation Day.	10.0.
At the Crowne on the Coronation Day.	2.12.0.

	£. s. d.
Hogshead of Bere.	1.10.0.
Widow Wanklin.[2]	5.0.
More to do.	1.0.

They liked something to celebrate at Leominster, as later entries prove—in 1689:

	£. s. d.
Pd. Samuel Seaward for a hogshead of Syder.	1.10.0.
Pd. Mr Spender, 1 of Ale, 1 of Syder.	3. 0.0.

That the Civil War, no less than later and bigger wars, was followed by distress is shown by entries in the same accounts of doles paid to "distressed souldiers."

Two interesting pamphlets have come down to us from the seventeenth century, both originating at Leominster, though both were printed in London. They have something of the flavour of the wonderful found in those forerunners of the newspapers, the *Fugger News-Letters,* letters sent from their correspondents to the merchant-prince family of Fugger in Augsburg.

The first of these pamphlets was printed in the year 1649 and is entitled *Vox Populi or the Prophetical Child.* Its preamble gives a good idea of the matter it contains.

"Being a true relation of an infant that was found in a field near Lemster in Herefordshire, July 16th, 1649, that did declare and foretell of many strange things that shall ensue in England and Ireland, within the space of three years, concerning the crowning of Charles the Second, King of England, Scotland and Ireland, his great victories, with the destruction of this present parliament and army, and many other passages touching the death of our late King.

"This relation is attested to bee true, as appears by the hands of severall witnesses annexed to the booke."

No doubt the *Vox Populi* caused much excitement among zealous and hopeful Royalists, but the prophecies seem to have been no more successful than such prophecies usually are.

"The present parliament and army" had a longer run for

[2]Landlady of an inn.

their money than they were promised (if we take them to mean the regime that was just starting), but after prophesying to the best of his ability the Infant was discreet enough to vanish.

The other came thirty years later.

"Licensed, May the third. Printed for B. Harris, 1679."

This time it was no miraculous infant. It was more in the style of the Fat Boy: "I wants to make your flesh creep."

It is called *Strange News from Lemster in Herefordshire,* and begins:

"Being a true narrative, given under several persons hands there, of a most strange and prodigious opening of the earth, in divers places thereabouts, also, a true relation of several wonderful sights, viz., a hand, an arm and a shoulder of the bigness of a man's; and of blood colour which were seen to arise out of the earth and ascend up to the skyes. Likewise a strange and terrible noise of fighting, which was heard during this miraculous accident.

"All attested by several persons of worth and reputation and exhibited for public information."

No doubt the local jeremiahs shook their heads as this was read out in the ale-houses, but no cataclysm in history seems to have followed. How nice it would be to mock at the credulity of our forefathers—but one remembers the extraordinary popularity of half a dozen or more astrologers in 1939—and later—and mockery hardly seems discreet.

The truth is, you can fool most of the people most of the time, and the fact was as well known by clever people in Lemster in Herefordshire in 1649 as it is by clever people to-day.

Most people who visit Leominster go to see the Ducking Stool, which is in excellent repair and is kept in the church. I don't know if there is a better example in England, but I should think not. The Ducking Stool was really a chair mounted at the end of a long beam fixed see-saw fashion so that it could be raised or lowered at will by someone operating it from the other end. The whole contraption was mounted on a carriage with wheels, so that it could be drawn round the town and, naturally, to a convenient piece of water. It was chiefly for the punishment of over-talkative women—though it also served for the punishment of sellers of adulterated food. Fastened in the chair and paraded through the streets, they could then be ducked, a treatment that was supposed to cure a too-free tongue. It must have been great fun for everyone except the poor woman concerned.

Leominster Ducking Stool was last used over a century ago. In 1809, Jenny Piper, "a notorious scold," was paraded round the town and actually ducked near Kenwater Bridge. The next victim (or culprit, according to one's point of view), and the last, was more fortunate. In 1817, Sarah Lecke was taken through the town on the stool but not ducked, as the water was too low. These are the last instances of the use of a ducking stool, not merely in Leominster, but in the whole country. One can imagine many a Leominster man shaking his head sadly at the folly of allowing the custom to fall into disuse.

Other methods of chiding refractory females lasted a great deal longer. Riding the Stang was done in Leominster, and in Weobley as well, as late as the end of the nineteenth century. This, too, has fallen into disuse, but I believe it is of very much older origin than the Ducking Stool or its allied punishments, like the Brank (Scold's Bridle), the Stocks, and the Pillory.

Riding the Stang was not so much a punishment as an expression of disapproval by ridicule, and men as well as women were the victims. An effigy was made of the person in question (it seems most often to have been a protest against adultery) and carried on a pole round the parish, village, or town, after which it was burned in some public place with suitable accompaniments in the way of rude remarks and missiles. I was particularly interested to learn of its happening in Herefordshire because I thought I knew of the last time it had happened anywhere—in a small Pembrokeshire village about forty or more years ago. I was too young to remember its happening or it may have been a year or two before I was born, but I knew intimately up to the time of her death the old lady whose effigy was burned (not, in this case, for adultery) and I knew intimately the people who made her "ride the Stang." I was not, to my sorrow, for I was intensely interested, ever allowed to discuss the matter with the victim, but I could, and did, get all the details from the other side and it stirred my childish imagination very much. It all happened at night and I always enjoyed a bonfire.

Riding the Stang was almost certainly a survival from an age when not an effigy, but the culprit in person, took the ride; and indeed, riding a rail, after an extra preliminary in the way of being rolled, first in tar and then feathers, is a boisterous pleasantry familiar to most readers of American fiction.

Village justice was, and sometimes still is, rough justice; its chief weakness was (and is) that sometimes it was (and is) not justice at all.

An idea of some of the trades carried on in Leominster in olden days may be gathered from the Chamberlain's Accounts. The guilds met in the council room of the Corporation and paid a fine (rent?) for using it.

Thus in the accounts for 1580, twenty-seven years after the town received its first charter from Queen Mary:

Item—recceaved of the warders

of thoccupacion of Mercers	xxd.
of thoccupacion of Taylors.	xxd.
of thoccupacion of Walkers³ & Dyers.	xxd.
of thoccupacion of Glovers.	xvd.
of thoccupacion of Shoemakers.	xxd.
of thoccupacion of Tanners.	xxd.
of thoccupacion of Bochers.	xxd.
of thoccupacion of Bakers.	xxd.

But why did the glovers come off 5d. easier than everybody else? A special piece of favour, or were they less able to pay?

The Chamberlain's Accounts have many other interesting items.

"Monday, September 30th 1754. That Ward the Player have leave to make use of the Schoolhouse to act in."

"Ward the Player" was the grandfather of Mrs Siddons and of John and Charles Kemble. He died on October 30th,

³Fullers.

1773, at the age of sixty-nine, and was buried at Leominster, and so was his wife, who lived to be seventy-five, dying in 1786.

There is a rather curious entry for January 19th, 1766:

"That Mr Williams, Master of the Grammar School have the use of the Charity School for washing his boys in the future."

In winter! Perhaps he had been accustomed to washing them out of doors. But why should he have to wash them at all?

Bull-baiting, as at Kington, was still a popular sport at the end of the nineteenth century.

"November 6th, 1794. By cash to a labourer for cleansing the Corn Market after Bull-baiting.   1/6d."

So there were poor people here, also, to lose good cheap meat by the thoughtless abolition of a harmless amusement (if we except the bull and the dogs)! To say nothing of an honest labourer trying to make a living.

Leominster, like Kington, also had a murderer. William Cadwallader murdered his wife one cold night. He carried the body out and placed it under a neighbour's hedge. But the ground was covered with frost and when the body was found and moved it was noticed that there was frost under the body, proving that it had just been put there. Cadwallader was hanged at Hereford on April 1st, 1816. Curiously, his grandfather who had lived at Ludlow was executed for a similar crime, shooting his wife and hiding the body in a cellar.

How the past can come echoing down the years from a few dry written words. In 1740 the Churchwarden's Accounts record:

"Gave 12 poor people (being slaves that came from Algier) by a pass signed by a justice.   3.0."

In the words of the old song, "It don't seem much." Very little compared with the money paid for hogsheads of "bere" and hogsheads of "syder." But even threepence would buy a pint of beer and a fair amount of "Lemster bread" in 1740, and if you'd been a slave in Algiers. . . .

Some of the entries in the church accounts give an interesting sidelight on salaries.

1554. Itm. to Mr Powell for techynge the Schole.   xvl.
Itm. to Edward Davis for his techynge.   iijl.
1555. Itm. paid to the Scholemaster for one yere. xvij vis viij.
Itm. pd. to the Husher for one yere.   iiijl.

From which it will be seen that the masters had a rise in the salary and the poor "Husher" had none.

And now for some news of Leominster from a neighbouring county. Wright's *History of Ludlow* tells how "in 1594 a great barne in Lemster was fired by a comett and burned 15 dayes."

To which one is tempted to add: What a comet! And what a barn!

Chapter IV

LEDBURY

LEDBURY is one of the pleasantest little towns in England. It was given a chance to be the wealthiest as well. St Catherine of Ledbury, a holy, pious woman, promised the town that if the door of the chapel dedicated to her in the church were not opened until it opened of its own accord Ledbury should become the richest town in the country. For very many years the townspeople kept the door shut, no doubt watching it all the time and hoping for the best. But one night some drunken men broke into the church and opened the door and put an end to their hopes for ever. So the town has had to put up with being only charming, and perhaps it was all for the best. It is not so poor as all that, either.

This is the centre of the hop and sugar-beet country, a market-town, lively enough on market days, quiet on many of the others. It stands above the River Leadon, from which it takes its name (though some people suggest a Welsh origin for it), and is rich in Ancient British and Roman memories and remains. Before it took to hops the district possessed one of the old English vineyards, for Blount writes of Walls Hill that there were "almost thirty or forty acres encompassed with high mounds which has three entrances to it, one of which is called the King's Gate, and on the south was heretofore a vineyard."

So often does one come across references to vineyards in old writers (there really was an English wine industry) that one is driven to wonder if there was a hardier species of *Vitis* than we know that has gone out of cultivation.

St Catherine of Ledbury was Catherine Audley. She had been told in a vision that the place she should settle and make her home was the place where she would be welcomed by

68

The Ducking Stool in Leominster Church

bells that rang of themselves. She and her maid, Mabel, wandered from place to place seeking her home, but not until they approached Ledbury was the prophecy fulfilled.

Wordsworth made the end of her journey the subject of one of his lesser sonnets, *St Catherine of Ledbury*.

> When human touch (as monkish books attest)
> Nor was applied, nor could be, Ledbury bells
> Broke forth in concert flung adown the dells
> And upward high as Malvern's cloudy crest;
> Sweet tones, and caught by a noble Lady blest
> Is rapture! Mabel listened at the side
> Of her loved mistress: soon the music died,
> And Catherine said, Here I set up my rest.
> Warned in a dream the Wanderer long had sought
> A home that by such miracle of sound
> Must be revealed:—she heard it now, or felt
> The deep, deep joy of a confiding thought;
> And there a saintly Anchoress, she dwelt,
> Till she exchanged for heaven that happy ground.

In recognition of her piety Edward II, to whom she was related, granted her a pension of thirty pounds a year. Did he think of that when in 1327 he was lodged in the Bishop's Palace at Ledbury on his way to Kenilworth after his capture by the Queen's party?

Twice Ledbury has had a market charter. The first of them Robert de Bethune, Bishop of Hereford, obtained from King Stephen. This market was to be held on a Sunday, a common day for markets and fairs in medieval England. This fell into disuse and a new charter was granted by Queen Elizabeth. Ledbury was a borough in the early days and sent two Members to Parliament. Generally it is Members who have a difficulty in supporting the constituency, but in Ledbury's case they surrendered their right on the plea of not being able to support the Members. That is what comes of not keeping doors closed.

Ledbury Church is one of the finest in Herefordshire. There are many beautiful houses here, St Katherine's Hospital, the Biddulph Mansion, the old Market House, old

Grange Court, Leominster

inns, Church Lane, with its timbered houses that make you think you are still in Tudor England. And over them all the spire of the detached tower points benignantly to better things.

Ledbury Church used to consist of two prebends, known as Overhall and Netherhall, and a Vicarage. It probably became portionary about 1180 when the church was built. Domesday Survey mentions one priest who held two and a half hides of land from the lord of the manor. Right through its history until 1828 the church was portionary, having two lay Rectors who had the right to appoint a Vicar. Two Rectors are mentioned in 1232 when Bishop Hugh Foliot founded St Katherine's Hospital and they granted a licence to the masters and brethren to celebrate divine service in their chapel.

A Commission of 1348 found that:

"We say that the churches of Ledbury and Bromyard are Parish Churches and not Collegiate but Portionary, that is to say, in the church of Ledbury there are two free portions commonly called Over Hall and Netherhall and a vicarage in the same with a cure, nor have they Common Seals, Common Chests, Common Bells, nor Common Chapter Houses for Transacting Common business in the same, nor have they a Dean, Provost, Master or Warden or any other as Chief head in the same. . . ."

Some doubt has arisen in the past as to whether Ledbury Church did or did not become Collegiate. There is no evidence that it ever did. What happened was that in 1401 John Trefnant, Bishop of Hereford, obtained a licence from the Crown to enlarge a chantry he had hoped to found in the church into a college of nine perpetual chaplains having the prebends of Overhall and Netherhall and the advowson of the Vicarage.

The nine stalls in the church have caused people to believe that it became Collegiate, but whereas there is no mention anywhere in the Episcopal Registers of Masters or Chaplains of the College, there is an unbroken list of Portionists and Vicars.

There are no longer lay Rectors in Ledbury now, the Rector holding both Portions and the Vicarage.

The Parish Registers contain many interesting entries. The late sixteenth and early seventeenth centuries seem to have seen many violent deaths in the town.

"A.D. 1583. Jane Bordland (being murdered at Donnington by one Wm. Farr of Eastnor) was buried the XXV day of February, 1583, which said Farr was hanged on the gallows hill the XVI day of March, next following the same fact."

"A.D. 1590. Ann Wells a poore wanderinge woman being frozen to death at peese bridge in the grete snow and cruell cold was buried XXVI day of December."

Most of these violent deaths were of people "slayne," but in A.D. 1600 "Evan Priest . . . fell out of a withie tree at Priors Court and died and was buried the XXVII day of April."

And three years later, "John Williams coreister drank himself deade."

A later entry is puzzling:

"A.D. 1605. Nell Biggor an aged pson was cast into a pit in the brooke the VIIth day of May."

Apparently to be buried was a term only to be used with reference to consecrated ground. Reference to a person being "not buried" is curious.

"A.D. 1593 Thos. Barker being an excommunicat pson was put into a grave out of Christian burial and was not buried the VIIth day of April."

In 1609 the Plague broke out.

"At this time the plague began at Wall Hills, about ten persons died and Michaell the son of Francis Hall of Bromiard died of the plague and was buried the XXIst day of October, 1610."

Ledbury probably saw the most exciting times of its history during the Civil War. Between it and the badly behaved Welshmen lay the whole width of Herefordshire. In the most turbulent days, when, for example, the county dreaded the approach of Owen Glyndwr, Leominster and Hereford stood to take the first blows, but the Great Rebellion, the usual local title of the War, swayed backwards and forwards, like the struggles of a pack of schoolboys scrambling for a handful of nuts.

Ledbury, like the rest of the county, was loyal. Hopton came here recruiting. He had promised the Earl of Stamford that he could raise a thousand dragoons in four days' time. He "came to Ledbury and brought with him his colours and his drum and there in a commanding manner called all the countrymen in order to bring in their dragonnes.

"The first man answered him that he had received His Majesty's book to the contrary and that he durst not lest he should be held a traitor. The others did answer alike so that he went out of Ledbury and his colours and drum were taken from him."

There was really nothing noteworthy in a Herefordshire town proving solidly loyal. Even Herefordshire birds were that, as is proved by a story related by Aubrey.

"At Stretton in Herefordshire in Anno. 1648 when King Charles I was Prisoner, the Tenant of the Manor-house there, sold excellent Cider to Gentlemen of the Neighbourhood; where they met privately, and could Discourse freely, and be merry, in those Days so troublesome to the Loyal Party. Among others that met, there was old Mr Hill B. D. Parson of the Parish, Quondam Fellow of Brason-nose College in Oxford. This Venerable good old Man, one Day (after his accustomed fashion) standing up, with his Head uncover'd to Drink his Majestie's Health, saying, *God bless our gracious Sovereign,* as he was going to put the Cup to his Lips, a Swallow flew in at the Window and pitched on the brim of the little Earthern-cup (not half a Pint) and sipt and so flew out again. This was in the presence of the aforesaid Parson Hill, Major Gwillim, and two or three more, that I knew very well then, my Neighbours, and whose joint testimony of it I have had more than once in that very Room. . . . The Cup is preserved there still as a Rarity."

Fortunately for Ledbury it was not suitable for permanent fortifications or it might have had a siege instead of a battle.

In April 1645, Colonel Massey had his forces stationed in the town. There was, apparently, some carelessness in the matter of placing outposts, for on the 22nd Prince Rupert, with six thousand men, made a surprise attack, advancing through orchards and gardens unobserved in the dawn. The suddenness of this approach took the Roundheads completely off their balance. There was a running fight right through the streets and out into the open country, four miles along the Gloucester Road. As usual Rupert was too impetuous. He did not lack courage; in the Battle of Ledbury he tried to engage Massey in personal encounter, and shot his horse from under him. The battle, like all Rupert's battles, degenerated into a chase. The prisoners numbered only two hundred. A more cautious general might, with that advantage, have taken the lot.

Bullets fired in this encounter were, long after, taken out of the church door, and are carefully preserved. Sir Robert Harley was not as fortunate as the door. The bullet he got he carried as long as he lived.

Naturally the Cavaliers were jubilant.

" 'Twere endlesse to reckon whats printed at London for then should we repeat all Master Massey's flying victories who on Tuesday last was sent broken and bruised to Gloucester by his Highnesse Prince Rupert."[1]

Massey (whose father was a Royalist) later became a fugitive from the side he had fought on. He was presented to Charles II at The Hague and became his supporter.

The Parliamentarians had their revenge some seven months later when sixty of Sundamore's Horse were chased through Ledbury streets and out of the town by a quarter their number under Major Hopton. Hopton, remembering his humiliation and his lost colours and drum, had an old score to settle in Ledbury.

But in eighty years a town can change its mind. In 1715 Ledbury bells were ringing cheerfully at "the news of Rowting the Rebels."

In 1735 there were Turnpike Riots in the Ledbury district. Just over a hundred years later the Welshmen forty or fifty miles away were to stir themselves in the same enterprise—and with better success. It was a miller, Francis Rolland, who

---

[1] This account says a hundred and twenty of Massey's forces were killed, and four hundred taken prisoner.

tried to rouse the Herefordshire men to do something about the gates that were breaking the farmers' hearts and keeping their pockets empty. Some gates around Ledbury were broken down, but the Herefordshire rioters had not the unanimity of the Welshmen nor a Rebecca to lead them and at their first attempt on September 25th two of their number were taken prisoner. They were held in the house of a magistrate, Mr Skip of Upper Hall, and the next day there was an attempt at a rescue. Mr Skip held on to his prisoners, a fight took place, and three people were killed and many wounded. This must have resulted in more arrests, for, of four ringleaders, two were hanged at Worcester and two, one of whom, James Bayliss, was later reprieved, were sent to London.

The other was Thomas Reynolds, aged twenty-eight, a local farmer's son, and he was indicted before "Lord Hardwicke, Lord Chief Justice of the King's Bench and the Honourable Justices of His Majesty's Kings' Bench of Westminster." He was charged, not with destroying a Turnpike Gate, but under what was known as the Black Act for "going in disguise, armed with offensive arms, contrary to the said Act of Parliament."

A special jury was called for the trial and sentence delivered at Westminster Hall on July 10th, 1736, nearly a year after he had been captured. He was condemned to death by hanging at Tyburn.

A strange execution it was to be.

The day before he was hanged he made arrangements with James Bayliss's wife to take charge of his body when he was dead, provide a coffin and see to his burial. He was hanged, and when he was thought to be dead his body was cut down and handed over to Mrs Bayliss. The coffin was carried to a grave that had been prepared and then, just before it was put into the grave, a woman expressed a wish to look at him. The coffin was opened and Reynolds was alive!

They carried him away in haste along the Oxford Road, fearing he would be taken from them if the law-officers found what had happened. He was not, of course, conscious, but he was breathing. A surgeon was found who bled him and after the bleeding he vomited. His friends next carried him to Paddington. If they could get him to bed and find a doctor to attend him he might survive. But alas for their hopes! Nobody would take him in. They were all afraid of the consequences if they were found out. He was given sack and brandy in an effort to revive him, but either they were the wrong remedies or they were given too late, for he collapsed finally and died. A fresh grave was dug for him in the Oxford Road and there he was buried at last.

Ledbury has records of licences being given to people to eat flesh during Lent. The Vicar was allowed to make a charge for giving this licence, for in Queen Elizabeth's reign a law had been passed limiting the fee to fourpence. Another fee chargeable was a maximum of twopence "for writing a testimonial of any servant changing from one place to another."

Cock-fighting was, as in the neighbouring towns, a favourite pastime; but bull-baiting in Ledbury had its fame spread abroad through a description in a local book, *Malvern Chase*, by the Reverend W. S. Symonds. In this particular case the bull escaped and endangered the life of—one would never guess—the heroine.

Another local piece of literature was a drama entitled *Catherine Audley*, but its fame stayed local and the author's name is not known, though it was highly praised in the town at the time of its production. The family of Philips, the author of the long poem *Cyder* (and other and better poems), lived at Ledbury for a time.

But these are trifles, small-town gossip in a place that cannot boast a Shakespeare, or a Dr Johnson. In Jacob Tonson, Ledbury had firmer and wider connections with the world of literature. Tonson, son of a barber-surgeon, and born in 1656, was the publisher of the greatest writers of his day. Dryden was the first author he published, and he had to borrow the money to pay him. He published for Congreve, Otway, Vanbrugh, and Pope, for Addison, Steele, and Swift, and he printed the *Spectator*. He was responsible for a renewed interest in Shakespeare, bringing out new editions of his plays. But he is chiefly remembered for printing *Paradise Lost*, buying the rights of it when the possession of those rights was a poor proposition, Milton, as a Parliamentarian being very much out of favour. When Tonson did decide to publish, the poem leaped into instant favour, and the publisher enjoyed the reward. He has been criticized sometimes for making so much more out of *Paradise Lost* than Milton did, but he deserved what he earned. He bought an unpopular commodity and it became popular. That was his luck, not his fault.

He left London and his Kit-Kat Club, of which he was secretary, in 1720, to come and settle in Ledbury. He is said to have sent his literary friends in London presents of casks of cider made from his apples, and when he died in 1736 he was worth forty thousand pounds.

In one direction at least Ledbury can claim a lead where others follow. The question of providing dinners for school-children is well to the fore nowadays. Ledbury was providing them over sixty years ago.

One of the town's many charities was Miss Elizabeth Hall's Charity School. Miss Hall left money to pay "an honest and able schollmistress to teach twenty-four children to read and work." For this simple task the mistress was to receive seven pounds ten shillings a year, but there was further provision for a schoolmaster who was to teach eight of the twenty-four to write. Not being handicapped by having to make them work as well, he received only four pounds ten shillings a year for his trouble.

The number of pupils must have been increased as time went on. This charity was later diverted to purposes with a wider educational scope.

On January 8th, 1884, "a series of cheap dinners were commenced at the school. . . . The cost of provisions for these dinners for 3 weeks was £1-17-4½ and for this sum 450 dinners were provided. On an average 32 children remain to dinner daily (out of 40). In addition to this a person is paid to cook the dinners; firing is found and all utensils.

"The bill of fare for each week is: Monday, pea-soup; Tuesday, rice-pudding; Wednesday, Irish stew; Thursday, boiled beef and suet pudding; Friday, pea-soup. The children bring ½d each and a piece of bread. Mr M. Biddulph finds the remainder."

It is not a wildly exciting menu, but for a cost of a half penny a head they seem to have got the maximum filling power. The information is added that the children could eat as much as they liked and thoroughly enjoyed the dinners.

I'd like to know what they paid the cook, though.

CHAPTER V

ROSS

W H E N E V E R I go to Ross I feel I am really getting into England, which is a silly idea because Ross stands on the south-eastern edge of that Welsh territory that elected to stay under the invading Saxons. Yes, there lies Archenfield to the north of Ross and one has only to strike towards the Black Mountains to realize it. Llandinabo, Llanwarne, Pontrilas, and south of these, Llangarren, Llanrothal, Welsh Newton, Ganarew; who would say at a guess that these were English villages? Yet they are every one in Herefordshire. And there are as many Joneses and Morgans as Smiths and Browns.

Ross is sometimes called "The Gateway of the Wye," meaning the gateway to its lower, better-known reaches, rather than the wilder Wye winding up through Hereford to Hay and so back to its source in the loneliness of Plynlimmon. If you go to Ross, you naturally go the few miles down-river to see Symond's Yat. Everybody goes. That's the one place nobody must miss seeing. It is lovely; it is magnificent; it is the most beautiful stretch of the river. There's only one person who never went to Symond's Yat. The only reason I didn't go was obstinacy. I was told I certainly must see it, so I stayed away. I, who had been a friend of the river when it was no more than what we call a prill, who had encouraged my wicked children to tickle its trout where you only needed to roll your trousers up to the knee, who had found the grey wagtail's nest on the first little bridge that crosses it, who . . . no, I just didn't want to see Symond's Yat. There was a sort of disloyalty in the thought.

But, like everybody else, I daresay I'll go to see it someday.

Ross was, by tradition, called Rose-town, and a pun explains that it rose gradually up the hill from the river.

It certainly does give that sort of impression as you approach from Hereford. The Wye is crossed by Wilton Bridge, and then the road winds up the side of the hill to the town itself, dominated by its lovely church with the tapering spire. Ross is the sort of town I like. Its streets are much too narrow, as is Wilton Bridge, but there's no sign of their widening them so that the char-à-bancs can go snorting carelessly through, and I hope they never will. Outside the town, especially on the Gloucester side, the roads are good and wide and modern. Only in the centre of the town itself they are as they were (some of them)—lanes with houses on each side.

It must be quite a work of art manoeuvring, say, a car and good-sized caravan past the old Market Hall that stands in the centre of the town. The Market Hall is a pleasant red sandstone building that was built in the seventeenth century, still bearing a rather weather-worn bust of Charles II on one end, and on the side an anagram made up of a C and L and a heart, meaning "Love Charles to the heart," both put there by the Man of Ross to show his loyalty to the Stuarts. He died a bachelor, so later he may have had doubts about his wisdom as he looked at the bust from the windows of his house. If he had, he kept them to himself.

Ross Church is lovely, both inside and out. Its spire seems to dominate the countryside. I don't know how far away it can be seen, but from certain directions it must be a considerable distance. The present spire has not been up very long, the old one being struck by lightning in the summer of 1852. Sixty feet of it had to be rebuilt.

The trouble with Ross is you can't get away from the Man of Ross. The Man of Ross was a good man and there's a saying that you can have too much of a good thing. I'm not at all sure that you can. You can have too much of something you imagine is good. People are inclined to laugh at the Man of Ross. "Of course you know all about the Man of Ross?" And they nod and laugh. But the fact is they don't. They've heard that Pope praised him in verse; that he did this and that for the town, was a philanthropist. But not *all* about him.

I'll admit it becomes something of a relief to read something other than fulsome praise. A. G. Bradley was light-hearted about the old gentleman, though he couldn't but admit his virtues. An earlier writer, Robinson, in his *Manors and Mansions of Herefordshire,* was quite reproving.

"In dealing with the past associations of Ross it is impossible to omit all mention of John Kyrle, although our notice must be curtailed by our belief that he has too often been made the subject of extraordinary laudation. A country squire who does his duty to his God and to his neighbour, displays some public spirit and a zealous attachment to the church of his choice is, we hope, not a very rare character even in these degenerate days, and it is certainly one for which a parallel might be found in the annals of almost every neighbourhood. The good deeds of the Man of Ross had the great merit of having been done with some expenditure of trouble and substance on the part of the doer; they had also the good fortune to attract the notice of a poet whose Court and City life had made him almost a stranger to the virtues of outspoken honesty and unostentatious benevolence."

To parody a well-known advertisement:

A bit of debunking now and then
Is relished by the best of men.

It quite does one good to think that perhaps things aren't as good as they are painted.

But: "a parallel might be found in the annals of almost every neighbourhood." Oh no, I'm afraid not! There was one Man of Ross. Only one. If there were only one country squire in every hundred as unselfish, country squires, as a class, would be so valuable there would be a special Act of Parliament to protect and preserve them.

John Kyrle was probably descended from the ancient family of Crul. He was born on May 22nd, 1637, at Dymock in Gloucestershire. His great-grandmother was John Hampden's sister, and his grandmother a sister of the poet, Waller.

He went to Oxford and studied law at the Middle Temple. Then, with his income of five hundred pounds a year, he came to settle at Ross and his early life seems to have been entirely uneventful. I say *seems,* because anything that happened in those early years may have been accountable for the extraordinary benevolence of his disposition later on.

"Only God and I know what is in my heart," says the proverb.

By the time he reached maturity even his dress was worth noting.

"His usual dress was a suit of brown Dittoes and a King William's wig, all in the costume of his day. He declined much company except in the present custom of dinnering his friends upon the Market and Fair-days. This is to be understood—of *set* company or *formal visiting;* for in another view he may be said to have kept a constant public table there being scarcely a day but someone or other called and dined with him. He was, indeed, particularly pleased with his neighbours dropping in,—loved a long evening,—enjoyed a merry tale,—and appeared always discomposed when 'twas time to part."

So he was a man who loved pleasure and company. Goodness is often coupled with austerity, but not in the case of John Kyrle. In fact, desire for companionship appears to have been almost a weakness in him, and it is reflecting on that, and those last eight words in the passage quoted (I found it in a book on Ross published in 1821), "appeared always discomposed when 'twas time to part," that brought the proverb to my mind.

"He was a genuine Herefordshire man," we are told, "with a spade on his shoulder and a glass bottle of liquor in his hand." The liquor was always beer or cider.

His hobbies were horticulture and planting. And what he loved best to plant were trees. This tree-planting did much to beautify Ross. Many of his elms are still alive and as flourishing as his memory, and some he planted in the churchyard sent up suckers that for a while grew in the church itself—according to the story, in Kyrle's pew.

He made an additional hobby of the gentle art of giving.

He had the spire of Ross Church raised by forty-seven feet. He gave one of the peal of bells, going to see it cast, and into the molten metal, after drinking a loyal toast, throwing his silver tankard from which he had always drunk his favourite beer or cider.

Nobody ever knew all he gave. Then, as always, there must have been spongers. To them he must have been a godsend. He helped children with their education, and started them on their careers. He gave to the poor daily (and the poor were always with us even more constantly then than now), sending bread where it was most needed. Food from his table was sent daily to Rudhall's almshouses. He and his housekeeper were quite good amateur physicians and they concocted medicine for simple ailments and distributed them free to any who needed them.

But more indicative of the way his neighbours thought of him was the fact that he was on different occasions called in to arbitrate in quarrels and disputes. If any people disliked him it must have been the lawyers, for he kept money out of their pockets more than once.

And even more eloquent, at the time of his death on November 20th, 1724, at the age of eighty-nine, he owed nothing and he had no money in the house.

After he had been dead some time a man went to one of Kyrle's relations who was settling his estate and gave him a sum of money, which, he said, Mr Kyrle had lent him.

"I can't find any record of it," said the relation.

"No, sir. There was nothing put in writing. You see, Mr Kyrle didn't think I'd be able to repay it during his lifetime and he said he didn't want anybody worrying me to pay it until I was able to."

That hardly requires comment.

John Kyrle never refused help. He managed to enjoy life and at the same time he gave all he had. The only fortune he made was the affection of his fellow-townsmen, and they all mourned him when he died. "A parallel in almost every neighbourhood"? No such luck!

Ross is proud of the Man of Ross. So she should be.

"In Rosse are seven hides geldable. In demesn is one carucate and there might be another. There are eighteen villains and six bordars and a Priest with twenty-three carucates. There are three serfs and a mill of six shillings and eightpence, and sixteen acres of meadow. There is a wood in the King's fence. The villains pay eighteen shilling rent."

That is how Ross is described in the Domesday Survey. At that time there were about seventeen hundred acres subject to the tax called Danegelt.

Ross was in quite good condition when the survey was made, largely due to the hundreds of years of occupation by the Romans, for Ross was said to have risen out of the ruins of Ariconium. Roman remains have been found at Ariconium (Bolitree now), though it was not as important a station as Magna Castra (Kenchester). Here, as at Kenchester, the coins that were found were known as "Fairies' money."

Ross became a market-town in the days of Stephen and its privileges were renewed when it was made a borough in the reign of Henry III. The people of Ross apparently did not give these matters the consideration due to them, for which fault they were referred to rather slightingly by one writer as "A colony of Blacksmiths, the general profession of the town from the fall of Ariconium to the days of Camden."

Bishop Trilleck of Hereford had a lot of trouble with Walter Morton of Ross. First of all it was fishing. Morton, who seems to have loved worrying the Bishop, had an action brought against him about fishing rights. The jury found the Bishop entitled to the exclusive fishing rights in the mill-dam and awarded him four shillings damages.

The next quarrel was over game. The Bishop brought a fresh action for trespass. He alleged that William Morton had entered his chase and taken fifty stags, fifty deer, and three hundred goats.

Again the Bishop won the action. Morton was found guilty and fined. I am a bit uncertain about that fine. I have read two separate accounts of this action. One says the fine was four shillings. The other gives it as four pounds.

But if it were four pounds, *and* taking into consideration the difference in the value of money, I can't help thinking that if Morton had fifty stags, fifty deer, and three hundred goats he was not paying an extortionate price for them.

During the Civil War, Ross was an important place because of the nearness of Wilton Bridge. Wilton Castle itself had been made into a dwelling-house some century or more earlier, and while its owner, Sir John Bridges, was trying to decide which side he was on, Barnabas Scudamore came and burned it for him as a way of helping him to make up his mind, which, of course, it did, Bridges becoming a Parliament man at once.

William Rudhall, a member of a local family—his tomb is in the church, with himself shown as a Roman soldier, a most unroyalist-like garb—destroyed part of Wilton Bridge to check the advance of Massey. The Scots repaired it on their way back from the siege of Hereford and repaid themselves for their trouble by taking more plunder from Ross than they had taken from any other place in the county— which is saying a lot.

A few miles down the Wye is Goodrich. Goodrich Castle was the last in Herefordshire to hold out for the King, but in the end it was taken by Colonel Birch. From the castle he helped himself to as much of that fascinating metal, lead, as he could find. You'd think soldiers were alchemists and needed only the base metal. They certainly turned it into gold. I wonder what Birch did about the floors, for when Goodrich Castle was built by the Clares soil was brought over from Ireland for its floors so that no toad could live in it. The timber, also, was Irish, this being a certain way to keep out spiders and cobwebs.

Below Goodrich Castle was the ford known as Walesford, or Walford. Henry IV, while he was still Earl of Derby, was crossing the ferry at Walford when he heard that his son, who was to become Henry V, had been born at Monmouth. He was so delighted at the news that he gave the boatman rowing him the monopoly of the ford for life.

Goodrich has another, and a much later, claim to fame, for it was here that Wordsworth, on one of his visits to Herefordshire, met the obstinate youngster of *We Are Seven*. I've been told that some years ago quite a number of old ladies in the district made capital out of being the heroine of *We Are Seven*.

Ross celebrated the Restoration with a spontaneous piece of merriment that is reminiscent of "riding the Stang." It was "not enough to celebrate the day with praise and prayer as well as a sermon." They made an effigy of the late Pro-

tector, fixing a wooden face on it, and on the breast they made an order of the "Solemn League and Covenant." There was an inscription on it, as well:

> Who set three kingdoms on a flame
> 'Tis just should perish by the same.

After parading this effigy through the town it was burned with much rejoicing.

A hundred years ago the customs we have nearly forgotten were flourishing around Ross.

On New Christmas Day and the First Monday in the Year a woman must not come first into the house or it would have no luck for the year.

The superstition is widespread. In fact, it is in many parts practised almost as much to-day as ever.

But "New Christmas Day"! How the country people everywhere resented those days they lost in 1752. It is only a few years since many old people who were my friends counted only Old Christmas Day and Old New Year's Day as worth celebrating.

"Buying fire" was common in Ross as it was all over Herefordshire. This was for Old Christmas Day and on that day no person must borrow fire, but buy it from a neighbour with something, no matter how slight a trifle, a pin being considered quite satisfactory currency.[1]

Burning the witch seems to be similar to burning the bush.

"On 12th day also they make 12 fires of straw one large one to burn the old witch. They sing and dance around it. Without this festival they think that they should have no crop."

Toasting the oxen appears to be, in Herefordshire, peculiar to the Ross district. On New Year's Day the finest ox was toasted in beer by the workpeople on the farm.

> Here is to you, Champion, with your white horn.
> God send our master a good crop of corn.
> Both Wheat, Rye and Barley and all sorts of grain,
> If we meet this time twelvemonth will drink to him again.

---

[1] To borrow fire from a neighbour was the usual way of relighting a fire that had gone out in those days.

Ross, from the Wye

Thee eat thy pousse, and I'll drink my beer.
And the Lord send us a Happy New Year.

Corn-showing, which took place at Easter, combined a
holiday and utility. Corn-showing was really weeding, pull-
ing the corn-cockle (the *Lolium* of Virgil) from the field,
and the one who did best was allowed to claim a kiss from
the prettiest maid, and the largest piece of cake from the
feast provided. Married men, I suppose, if their wives were
present, took the cake and let the kiss go. The seed of corn-
cockle, if it were among the wheat to be ground, therefore
getting into the bread, was supposed to be poisonous, caus-
ing giddiness and vertigo.

There were Harvest Homes, Maypole and Acorn dances.
Ross people knew how to enjoy themselves.

"The young peasantry have been known to adopt the idle
classical superstition of Love-Philtres and Powders" and
there was a case recorded when a young chemist in the town,
on being asked for these, indulged his sense of humour by
giving an emetic instead.

Cock-fighting was "in high vogue." Indeed, Ross would
have been unique in the times if it had not been.

A custom at funerals was to sing psalms before the corpse
on the way from the house to the grave.

In earlier days an effigy of the dead person had been carried in front of the coffin, and not far away, at Much
Marcle, they had a wooden figure which was carried into the
church before every funeral, a custom that lasted until 1878.
The figure is still there and is said to be the effigy of a Sir
Hugh Helyon. It is not improbable that it was the effigy
made for Sir Hugh's own funeral some time in the fourteenth century. There was a similar observance at Clifford
Church where the effigy was that of a priest.

A superstition that I have heard nowhere else (though
there are similar and more uncomfortable ones with regard
to other spring flowers) is that bringing the first snowdrops
into the house will prevent the successful hatching of the
first brood of chickens.

Sin-eating, traditionally, is a custom of Welsh origin. Perhaps its nearness to Archenfield accounts for the fact that

there are later and more satisfactory accounts of this happening around Ross than anywhere else, either in Herefordshire or in Wales.

A poor person, understandably, was chosen for a sin-eater "for a trifling compensation to pawn his own soul for the ease and rest of the soul of the departed.

"One of them"—this was in 1821—"was a long, leane, ugly, lamentable poor Rascal, I remember, lived in a cottage on Rosse highway."

The usual dole was a loaf of bread and some beer. The beer was drunk out of a mazard bowl—made of maple—and there is a tradition of certain families who kept a mazard bowl for the use of the sin-eater.

At the beginning of the nineteenth century these were the "Officers of Police for the Borough."

> Sergeant at Mace
> Four Constables
> Two Searchers and Sealers of Leather.
> A Fish and Flesh Taster.
> Two Market Keepers.
> A Hayward.
> Two scavengers.

A curious record exists, as in Ledbury, of the days when people took (and had to take) the outward observances of religion more seriously than they do to-day.

Philips Price, Vicar, in 1646 granted licences "to invalid and lying-in women to eat flesh on Fish-Days and in Lent."

Ross is unique in one other particular besides the possession of its Man. It is the place where Charles I spent no night at all when he came to Herefordshire.

Charles Dickens came here, though. He and Forster, his biographer, stayed at the Royal Hotel and here they discussed the details of the American reading tour. How Dickens must have loved the Man of Ross. As benevolent as the Cheeryble brothers—and much more solid.

The town sees plenty of traffic. It is on the main road into Herefordshire and Wales. But so many of its visitors laugh at John Kyrle and break the journey to go to Symond's Yat.

I don't think I'll go there after all.

PART II

COUNTRY

Chapter VI

WOOD AND STONE

IN SPITE of its close and ancient kinship with Wales
there is hardly a county in England that strikes the visitor
as so typically English as Herefordshire. This is particularly
noticeable on coming down from the hills. On the Welsh
side of the Border are stone houses, long, low-built, most of
them whitewashed, and often, where they are old and small,
of that peculiar Welsh type with living quarters and farm
buildings all under one roof, the former at one end, the latter
at the other. And then suddenly it is different. One delightful
village succeeds another. They straggle alongside the road-
way by which they have grown up, a broken string of lovely
jewels recklessly scattered across the countryside, most of
the older houses or cottages being in the black-and-white
style; magpie houses, as they are sometimes called.

It is these timbered buildings that give the villages their
charm, and for once that overworked word is not out of
place. There are other counties in England that have the
same kind of dwelling. After all, it was a simply planned
structure that was going up all over England from Tudor
times onwards, when the dark, bad Middle Ages had come
to an end and a man felt he could sleep safely under his own
roof and need not for security attach himself to any great
nobleman and so find quarters in a strong stone castle. But
though the timber-framed house was widely built it was nowhere built so widely or so well as it was along the Marches.
That is generally accepted, and I think it was due to the fact
that it was in the Marches that insecurity stayed longest, an
unwelcome guest, and while in quieter places domestic building had felt its way gradually over a long period of years,
in these borders it developed more quickly and—relative to
the number of houses—much more building went on in a
shorter period of time.

The timbered dwelling was admirably suited to the district. There was plenty of excellent wood, generally oak. Elm seems to have been used sometimes for floors; I have seen an elm floor hundreds of years old, though it was so dark and so highly polished that I should not have been contradictory if they'd said it was oak. Roughly speaking, a framework of oak beams was put up, a sort of skeleton house, and the spaces were filled in. The framework was strong. There is no doubt about that. Anyone can see it for himself. The filling was of different kinds: plaster and lath (or wattle and daub in the small house), sometimes brick. And then for decoration the framework was coloured black and the obvious choice to go with black was white. Brick and timber dwellings are not, as a rule, such a happy combination. Bricks are, even when they are old and mellow, poor companions for wood. I rather think the blackening of the timber work must have begun as a preservative— tar, perhaps. Then it grew into a tradition. It is not in every case that the timbers are black. In one of the loveliest houses in Herefordshire the woodwork is a fine dark grey. Perhaps it should be black—it certainly was not the last time I looked at it.

The rich soil and the genial climate are great allies in giving the county its peculiar Englishness. Every cottager in Herefordshire seems to be a gardener. You don't only see villages of fine black-and-white cottages, but even the smallest cottage has a garden, and a front garden at that, and there is sure to be a fine clematis by the door, or some roses; and from early spring until late autumn there are flowers in the garden, always flowers that seem a little better and a great deal earlier than one's own. Sometimes, when enthusiasts have planted winter-flowering jasmine or some other of our winter-flowering shrubs, they have flowers *all* the winter as well. Delightful to look at, but very annoying if you have a garden of your own in a much colder climate. Such a village is Eardisley. Peter Aquablanca, a very unpopular Bishop of Hereford, was imprisoned in the medieval church here in 1263. He died "exhaling a detestable odour of sulphur," but as he died in Savoy the sulphur did not hurt the Eardisley flowers.

Of course, charm from outside is all very well, but what the average sensible person wants to know is what these old houses are like to live in. The answer is that a lot of them are good. I don't mean the big ones like the Ley at Weobley —perhaps the most famous building of its type along the Border (though rather out of the way if you are looking for it for the first time)—or the Red Lion at Weobley, dating originally from the thirteenth century—or the Grange at Leominster—or the Old House at Hereford, which really might have been placed in a happier, more congenial spot and still attract as many (or more) visitors. These, and dozens of others, are large or medium-sized houses, their rooms are big enough to be comfortable, their windows wide enough to look through and to admit plenty of light.

But the little places are often good too. In comparison with well-planned and carefully built modern cottages they are bound to have certain disadvantages, but compared with what has been palmed off on the country (and town) as good enough for the money and good enough for the people who will live in them they come out best easily. They are not jerry-built, and they are usually warm and dry. They have the inestimable advantage, most of them, of having been built by craftsmen who took a pride in their job and who were not in a tearing hurry. A lot of them have small windows, uneven floors (as might be expected), and sometimes there are bulges in the walls. But too many houses put up in this century won't even have walls to bulge when they are as old as these cottages. Such amenities as water, electricity, and bathrooms don't come into the question. After all, if you buy a coat and it hasn't a pocket because the tailor didn't know how to make pockets, then the only sensible thing to do is to put in a pocket for yourself.

I don't say there aren't bad black-and-white cottages; but there are a lot of good ones, and those of medium size are nearly always a joy.

Everybody takes a fancy to these houses and the villages they make up. I have known townsfolk to go into ecstasies over them. The townsman has an unfortunate reputation of not being able to live out of the sound of dense traffic, or reach of a cinema. That may be, more or less, a fact, but it is also a fact that the average townsman has an intense love for and pride in the countryside. When he thinks of home he may think of a semi-det., h. and c., el. l. and an asbestos garage at the side—*but* when he thinks of England he thinks of something like the turn of a Herefordshire lane and the village that came in sight—a sort of Christmas card done without (or maybe with) the snow, for our best views are as exaggerated as the Christmas cards. As Turner's sunsets weren't like sunsets, they aren't like views—until you see them.

Make no mistake about it. Our best ally in the preservation of rural England is the townsman—yes, the chap who leaves the empty bottles and the picnic papers, and the cigarette cartons and orange peel and (if such things really did exist) the banana skins. But the bottles can be picked up and the paper will blow away and fall to bits and the fruit skins will rot and the worms will make humus of them. But that chap came there *because he liked it*. He liked nothing so much. If he poked fun at the simple countryman he was also rather proud of him. All the same, I wish he would (or, rather, hope he will, when he comes again) mend his ways. The Romans threw their broken pottery away, but the Romans came to a bad end.

Two out of three countrymen will give their birthright away because they simply have not realized they have a birthright.

The unfortunate thing about Herefordshire is that there seems to have been no really good building since the builders stopped putting up the timber and daub cottages. I am not writing now of the big houses. There have been some unfortunate mistakes among those, but there are good Queen Anne houses, such as Much Marcle Rectory and another which used to be a vicarage at Eye. But the picturesque half-timbered style is much too freely interspersed with unpicturesque nothing-on-earth. The point is, you can't fashion a brick house into a John Abel masterpiece by whitewashing it and painting black stripes on the whitewash. If you have a brick house the only thing is to make the best of it. If it is a good brick house it may be quite a good best, and if it is a bad brick house there are ways in which its russet naked-

94

ness may be suitably hidden. But turning it into imitation half-timber won't help. And if there is very much imitation half-timber work one of the finest characteristics of Herefordshire will be spoiled by comparison for ever.

A lot of people hate bungalows, especially where they grow up around a town. For my part I've seen some very nice-looking bungalows around Hereford. They are clean, not over-ornamental, are not intended to look like something else—and they have the true Herefordshire tradition of lovely cottage gardens in front. If they clash with their setting—which they don't—or spoil a view—which I don't think they do—it's a pity they were ever built and a greater pity they can't be pulled down. Otherwise, good luck to them, and I hope they prove as sturdy as those the builders were putting up a few hundred years ago. But that isn't likely. Good Herefordshire oak isn't cheap enough to use widely nowadays.

I'd hate to have to say which Herefordshire village is the prettiest, and obviously it would be asking for trouble to do so. Some people plump for Eardisland, and it certainly would take some beating. Others say Weobley is unbeatable and I've no quarrel with Weobley except that not all its houses are as good as the best in the village.

A couple of the best houses there were burned down a few years ago, and, sad to say, burned too badly to be repairable, nor, I hear, is there any intention to try to put them up again. One was the old market house and in the house next to it were born the thirty-three children of James Tompkyns, during Queen Elizabeth's reign. Two of these later became famous as the first breeders of the Herefordshire cattle.

Weobley was a pocket borough up to 1832, returning two Members to Parliament. The qualification to vote was that a man should have cooked and eaten a meal there, so voters, transferred by the Marquis of Bath from his Shropshire estates, used to appear the night before an election and make fires in the streets, and boil their kettles over them—from which they gained the nickname of "pot-wallopers," and anyone called a "pot-walloper" in Weobley after that could consider himself insulted.

It is impossible to say where in Herefordshire the best black-and-white houses are to be found. There are good examples everywhere and they have grown, the best of them, to be a very living part of the scenery of the country.

Quite close to Weobley is the little hamlet of Sarnesfield. To-day it is so small, so quiet and retiring, that it has to be looked for. You might pass it a dozen times and, excepting the Court near the church, never notice it. Yet Sarnesfield had its day. It was given by the Conqueror to a de Laci. In Richard II's time its lord was Sir Nicholas de Sarnesfield, one of the retinue of the Black Prince, a witness to his will, and later a knight of Richard II's bedchamber, bearer of the Royal Standard and a member of the Order of the Garter (the lady who owned the Garter, by the way, was a Herefordshire woman, Katherine Grandison of Ashperton). Nicholas de Sarnesfield was in 1382 appointed Chief Commissioner to negotiate an alliance with King Wenceslaus, King of the Romans and of Bohemia, against Charles of France, John of Castile, and Robert of Scotland. So the name of Sarnesfield travelled abroad. But Nicholas de Sarnesfield is practically forgotten, while that of a much more humble man, buried in Sarnesfield Churchyard, will be remembered as long as there is a half-timbered house left standing.

There were half-timbered, black-and-white houses along the Border before John Abel's time, but he brought the building of them to such a stage of perfection that his work had an influence difficult to calculate, right through the district. He could not, of course, build all the best half-timbered work of his day (though he did his share), but his best was so good that where he led lesser men followed. Many of the little houses would have been less admirable but for the example he set.

He was born in 1577, so was a mere boy of eleven when the Armada was scattered. His best work is seen in three market houses, those of Kington, Brecon, and Leominster, though that of Leominster was sold (for ninety-five pounds!), moved, and erected elsewhere and is now known as the Grange. The example of his work most often seen, if not always noticed, is the house standing by itself in High

Town, Hereford, known as the Old House. Though it has always been a town house—it used to be part of Butcher's Row—it looks sad and apart to-day, a house meant to be loved and lived in, and one that should be listening to the wind in its sheltering trees, not the unsympathetic symphony played by internal combustion engines.

During the Civil War—John Abel was a Royalist, of course, like most good Herefordshire men—he was in the city when it was under siege in 1645. He devoted himself to constructing mills for grinding the city's corn, and for that service Charles I gave him the title of the King's Carpenter.

One very important work he undertook was the timber work for the new church at Abbey Dore that Lord Scudamore was building to replace the vanished monastery. He seems to have done nothing badly. His influence on local building and on local craftsmen is incalculable.

At the age of ninety-seven he died (in 1674) and he was buried in Sarnesfield Churchyard. Twice I went to find his grave without seeing it, and at last discovered it to be under the large built-up tombstone to the left of the church door. What misled me was that I'd heard so often of the verse of his own composing that was carved on the stone together with a design of the tools of his trade. But, except for a word here and there, the inscription is illegible, so I'll do as others must have done and copy the inscription from where it *can* be read:

This Craggy Stone a covering is for an Architector's Bed
That Lofty Buildings raised high, yet now lays low his Head.
His Line and Rule so Death concludes are locked up in Store,
Build they who list, or they who wist, for he can build no
   more.
His house of Clay could hold him no longer,
May Heaven's Joy build him a stronger.
   John Abel
Vive ut vivas in vitam aeterrum.

All the same I think Sarnesfield might look after his grave a little better. It is not likely, for many a long year, to produce a more worthy son.

If the houses of Herefordshire are good the churches are

just as good. The houses are handsome, the churches are beautiful; the houses are old, the churches are older still. There is something about an old church that attracts everybody. It's a funny thing, that is one of the first questions people ask about a church: Is it old? If it is an old church you venture inside; if it is new it is not worth visiting.

Nearly all Herefordshire churches are old, some are very old. Of course, many of them have been restored. Kilpeck Church is almost completely Norman. It had to be restored, but the work was done with meticulous care, every stone, even the mutilated ones, going back exactly as they came down. Kilpeck is supreme, not only among the churches in the county; it is doubtful if there is an example to equal it in all England.

Moccas Church is nearly as good, and it was restored as carefully as that of Kilpeck.

A number of Herefordshire churches are curious in having towers or belfries detached from the main building. Three of them, those of Ledbury, Bosbury, and Pembridge, are dedicated to the memory of St Catherine. The one at Pembridge is curious, rather like a pagoda to look at and built mainly of timber.

Bosbury has associations with the Victorian novelist, Edna Lyall. Her real name was Mrs Ellen Bayly. I don't suppose anyone ever reads Edna Lyall nowadays, but her books were praised by Gladstone, and one of her novels was the last book Ruskin read. Bosbury was the setting for her book, *In Spite of All*. Her ashes were buried in 1903 at the foot of the churchyard cross. But Bosbury has a greater claim to fame. It was once, the story goes, much larger and much more important than Hereford. It was taken by a Saxon warrior and his army. "If I can take Big Bosbury," said the chieftain, "I can easily take little Hereford." But Hereford was more than he could manage, and for its valour Hereford became the chief town instead of Bosbury. There is a lovely village in the north of the county called Little Hereford, but it was the county's present capital the Saxon meant.

Aston Ingham has a lead font. These are very rare, there being only thirty-eight in the country. But another of them is in Herefordshire, at Burghill, though this was damaged a century ago when the tower collapsed.

Sarnesfield Church has a unique tower. It is—or was—a dovecote. At Brinsop there is a window in the church in memory of Wordsworth. His wife's relations, the Hutchinsons, lived at Brinsop Court and he paid a number of visits there. Mordiford used to have a green dragon painted on the west wall. This was the famous Mordiford Dragon that lived in a local wood and was eventually killed by a condemned criminal, who, presumably, was pardoned as a reward. A more mundane explanation of the dragon is that it was part of the arms of the Priory of St Guthlac, "Gules, a wyvern passant, wings displayed and tail rowed, or," which had an interest in the church.

The Golden Valley in the south-east of the county may have been so called from the Welsh word *dwr,* meaning water, or from the River Dore, or because of its richness (*d'or*). It certainly is rich in lovely and interesting little churches. There is Abbey Dore Church, built by a Scudamore in place of the ruined Abbey, and planned by John Abel, as fine a church as anyone could hope to find in such a quiet spot. There is Vowchurch, with Turnastone Church not far away, built, so the story goes, by two squabbling sisters, one of whom said: "I *vow* I will build my church before you *turn a stone* of yours." There is Peterchurch with its carved trout having a golden chain round its neck, the image of a real one caught, with a real golden chain round its neck, by some old monk hundreds of years ago.

At Dorstone, in the church he founded, was buried Thomas de Brito, who was one of the four knights who murdered Thomas à Becket. Rowlston's iron candelabra, with their swans and cocks (in honour of St Peter, the patron saint of the church) and *fleurs-de-lis,* are unique in England.

In Bacton there is a monument to, and of, Blanche Parry. Blanche Parry, daughter of an ap Harry—she was the first of the family to use the new and shortened form of the surname, Parry—was the Chief Gentlewoman of the Privy Chamber to Queen Elizabeth. She was in the Queen's service from the time Elizabeth was an infant, until her death in 1589 at the age of eighty-two.

So that my time I thus did pass awaye
A maid in Court, and never no man's wife,
Sworn of Queen Elizabeth's bedd-chamber allwaye
With maiden quene a mayd did end my lyfe.

And that—remaining unmarried—has always been put forward as her chief claim to fame. It doesn't seem a very satisfactory story. We are given only half the facts. So many women remain unmarried all their lives and are thought of none the more for it. How many men wanted to marry her? How many did she love—and turn away broken-heartedly, because she had determined to keep Elizabeth company? If we knew that we could be a little more generous with admiration.

The truth is that Blanche Parry was worthy of respect on much better grounds than not being wife to men she may not have had the chance to marry, and never have wanted to marry. She was a widely educated woman. It was her influence that interested the Queen in Dr John Dee, the Radnorshire-born mathematician and astrologer, and procured for him the Mastership of St Cross Hospital, though whether it was ultimately worth the trouble is doubtful, for the doctor, like worse and better men, was more interested in making gold out of nothing than in anything else. She was related to Lord Burleigh and through him is known to have been a patron of learning. Her body was buried in Westminster Abbey and her bowels at Bacton.

But we have stayed too long in Bacton.

At Cusop what is most interesting is outside the church. The yews in the churchyard were mentioned in Domesday Book and beneath one of them is buried in the Martyr's Grave one of Wesley's followers, William Seward, who was killed by a mob while preaching to them.

St Clodock's Church owes its position to a minor miracle, the sort of miracle that has apparently decided the sites of fully a quarter of the churches in the country. St Clodock, who lived in the sixth century, was a son of a king of Brecon and he was murdered by someone jealous of his saintly qualities. His body was put on a cart, but when they came to the ford over the Monnow the oxen refused to cross, and at this

Elm inside Ross Church
Blanche Parry's tomb, Bacton Church

place it was decided to build a church. The builders did not like the position and decided that a place at Llanwonog, a mile and a half away, would be much more suitable. But as fast as they built in the daytime the work fell down at night, and in the end they submitted to the superior wisdom of the oxen and built the church in the place originally chosen.

St Clodock's Church is one of those known to have possessed dog tongs for persuading dogs out of churches. It was the Puritans who first began the pleasant custom of taking their dogs to church in order to show their contempt for forms and ceremonies. Perhaps it began with hats. The Chamberlain's Accounts at Leominster contain a very suggestive entry in 1573:

"Twelve persons were presented for wearing their hats in church on Sunday, 22nd of November."

Leominster had been in the habit of taking hats seriously. You did not wear just any hat you liked in those days. The style of headgear was determined by one's social standing. The ploughboy wore a cloth cap over one ear; the Etonian, a topper; Harrovians, straw boaters. Something like that; only woe betide the ploughboy who turned out in top-hat or boater!

In the Bailiff's Accounts at Leominster for 1568 there is an entry: "Several persons were fined for wearing caps beyond their station in life."

A shilling was the cost of taking one's dog to church.

"Item, They present that the persons under namyd have severallie incurred the payne of xiid, for that they have permitted there dogges, mastyves to goe and follow them unmosled to the church uppon the Soundays and hollidaies, contrary to the order taken in court."

That was in 1556. By 1624 the masters not having improved their manners, the churchwardens, as their accounts prove, were taking it out of the dogs, and paying for the job.

"Correctinge of the dogges in the church. iijs iiijd."

For "correcting of the dogges" many churches went in for dog tongs. They were like the expanding sugar tongs, known as lazy tongs, that were used for picking up lump sugar, when lump sugar was an everyday commodity, one pair of arms hinged on to another pair, and so on, until they opened

Staick House, Eardisland
Market Place, Pembridge

to the desired length, which was usually about five or six feet. With these it was possible to grab hold of the offending creature—unless, presumably, it belonged to the Squire; one would use discretion—and then it could be thrown out of doors, all without risking a bite. Plenty of churches had dog tongs as well as Clodock, though only one is recorded locally, Peterchurch, which owned a piece of land known as Dog's Acre, or Dog Whipper's Marsh, the rent of which paid the man who threw the dogs out. Clodock dog tongs were in Abergavenny Museum about 1876, but the Peterchurch ones seem to have been in use later than this.

Madley has one of the finest churches in the county, part Norman, part Early English, part Decorated. The bells came from Abbey Dore at the time of the Dissolution.

In Madley Church a woman once did public penance for slander. The account was found written on the flyleaf of a Bible in the church.

"She had a white sheet placed upon her and she walked up and down the aisles of the church and recanted all that she had said. Upon leaving the church she swore that she would never enter it again and she never did, she was over ninety when she died."

The penance doesn't seem to have done her much good. On the other hand, considering the age she reached, it didn't do her any harm.

There was a font in Madley Church made out of one piece of marble, but it was smashed by the Scots when they were here during the Civil War.

The church at Solershope should be familiar to every child. That is if they still study nursery tales, for a Whittington of Pauntley married the heiress of one of the family of Solers, and one of their descendants was Richard Whittington, "thrice Lord Mayor of London," of story-book fame, and "he it was that repaired the church [at Solershope] it being the place of his birth." For that we have the authority of one of the Harleian manuscripts, and other counties with their claims on him must make the best they can of that— but we'll allow them the cat.

Welsh Newton is the church where there are English bells that ring in Welsh. *Efyn cant Enfyn* they go, which means "turnip and turnip pottage," "for the soil here being barren," writes Blount, "the poor people plant much of that root."

Leominster Church has a fine nave of the Norman period. All Saints in Hereford is noted for its chained library—which was once nearly sold. Kingsland Church has by the north porch a rare Volca chamber which may have been the home of a hermit.

The truth is that there is hardly a church in Herefordshire that is not worth a visit. There are bells in them that have been ringing for hundreds of years. There are rare Elizabethan chalices—about fifty in the whole county. Seven churches, including the three mentioned, are peculiar in having detached towers. There are curiosities, carved screens of great beauty, ancient fonts, legends.

Everything—except worshippers.

I was out walking with a friend one day and we came to a Nonconformist chapel and I said I thought I'd go inside.

"Oh, I wouldn't bother to go in *there*," he said. "It isn't worth it. There'll be nothing to look at."

I did go in, however, and he waited for me outside. I was wasting my time, and time was a commodity he couldn't spare. It had not occurred to him that I might have wanted to go in to say my prayers or to perform some act of worship. To be frank, the idea of doing so hadn't occurred to me, either. I went in to be obstinate.

There is no denying the fascination of old churches. They are concentrated history. They are nearly always the oldest man-made objects in the district. Everything that ever was, everything that happened, a thousand lives and more, poor and rich, are epitomized in those stone walls. The churches provided to our ancestors a meeting place, a shelter in times of material or spiritual trouble; they were a promise and a hope to minds that would not accept, or feared to accept, complete obliteration at the end of a brief existence. They belonged to nobody, they belonged to all. They were common ground to a community. The community changed but they stayed unchanged.

There are so many lovely churches. And familiarity breeds contempt. Once they were filled on a Sunday, empty on weekdays; now very many are full every day of the week (of the normal tourist season) and nearly empty on Sundays. And by all the signs they will grow emptier still.

I am not voicing a complaint. I am stating what I believe to be a fact, and, for good or ill, it is a fact. Nowhere is it more noticeable than in these rural communities. The older type of countryman still attends regularly; respectable middle-class people a little less regularly, and the younger ones do so when they are christened, married, and buried, or when someone else is christened, married, or buried. In between these interesting events they keep their visits down to the minimum. The most common attitude is that of a man with an old jacket: here is something that was once good and I'll not part with it though I no longer have any use for it.

I don't know what is wrong; I don't even know if anything is wrong. It is not interest in religion that has declined. That is stronger than ever. Perhaps something that was in the old churches is in them no longer. One thing is certain: they were built for worship and dedicated "to the Glory of God." It may be the fault—if it is a fault—of the age, or it may be the fault of the people who might attend, or it may be the fault of the parsons—or even the fault of all three—but most of us are more interested nowadays in a Norman arch than in a prayer; in a Jacobean screen than the glory of God. We are told that one can worship in the open air as easily as in a church; conversely one might say it is as easy to worship in a church as in the open air.

Perhaps people can't say their prayers in a museum. There is no reason why they shouldn't, but perhaps they can't. People are funny that way.

Chapter VII

CERTAIN CARE: UNCERTAIN PROFIT

T h e Herefordshire scene is essentially pastoral. Wherever one goes, meadows, woods, orchards, gardens meet the eye, with their accompaniment of farmhouses, cottages, sheep, horses, and cattle. This is true farming country. There are no manufactures, no factories, no smoking chimneys, no close-packed towns of mean streets. The wealth of the county lies under its good red earth. The life of the county is linked with the soil.

The area of Herefordshire is 538,924 acres (about 842 square miles). Exact figures are hard to come by, but in normal times—that is, not taking into account the extra wartime ploughing—rather more than a quarter is under crops and rather less than a half is permanent pasture. The remainder is taken up by woods, orchards, rough moorland— most of this where the Black Mountains overlap into the south-west of the county—and, of course, buildings and water.

The principal grain crops are wheat, oats, and barley; roughly speaking, about the same acreage being given to each, though probably rather more to oats than wheat and rather more to wheat than barley. The crops have always been good, the yield of wheat, for instance, being a little lighter than that of East Anglia, but comparing very favourably, considering that East Anglia has all the factors—so far as they may be counted on in England—in her favour.

Three crops deserve special mention: hops, cider apples, and sugar beet. Kent certainly produces a much greater quantity of hops—about three times as much as Herefordshire and Worcestershire combined—but even so the county's hops are no mean part of its wealth.

Sheep and cattle are the chief animals reared. The sheep are mostly Black-faced Shropshire Downs nowadays, but the native Ryelands have not entirely vanished, and, considering the fact that their wool once fetched the highest price of any in England, it might be a good move to encourage the few enthusiasts who still breed them.

The cattle, of course, are the famous Herefords. The origin of the breed seems to be a matter of some uncertainty, but there is little doubt that two of the Tompkyns family from Weobley, farming in the neighbourhood of Kings Pyon, were the first enthusiasts to start Herefords on their road to fame. They are handsome creatures with their red bodies, the head, chest, brisket, and under parts of the body being pure white. Sometimes they have a little red round the eyes and this is looked on with favour in hot countries.

Here is the official description of the breed as given in *Hereford Cattle*, the handbook of the Hereford Herd Book Society:

"The head moderately short, forehead broad, with horns springing straight from the side of the head and slightly drooping and of a waxlike appearance, black tips to the horns being considered objectionable. The eyes full and prominent. Nose broad and of a clear flesh colour. The body thick, deep, and on short legs, well set apart. The top and underline straight. Neck thick with a well-developed crest. Shoulders sloping, but lying well open at the top between the blades. Chest full and deep. Ribs well sprung. Flanks deep. Buttocks broad, with lower thighs well developed and coming down well meated to the hocks. The tail neatly set on and evenly filled between the setting of the tail and hip bones. The hip bones well covered and not prominent. The whole carcase covered with firm flesh. The skin thick, yet mellow to the touch, and well coated with an abundance of thick soft hair of a rich red colour and silky to the touch."

Herefords, though excellent milkers, are primarily beef cattle. They are very hardy and, in the county, with the exception of bulls and show animals, are never housed. One of their most striking characteristics is their freedom from tuberculosis. At the Buenos Aires Quarantine Station 1,744 cattle were destroyed on account of this disease between 1903 and 1941. Of these only 28, or 1.6 per cent, were

Herefords, and from 1926 to 1941 only two of the cattle destroyed were Herefords.

They thrive anywhere, doing equally well on the pampas of South America or the steppes of Russia. South America always did have a liking for Herefords. In the United States of America the Hereford is numbered in millions and exceeds all other beef breeds put together—in Texas they make up 90 per cent of the total cattle population. The U.S.S.R. seemed to wake up to their existence in the nineteen-twenties. They sent an Agricultural Commission to Hereford in 1928 which, after careful examination, bought twenty-six bulls and forty-six heifers. They returned in 1931 to make a much larger purchase, and in 1935 published their first Hereford Herd Book. They also bought other British beef breeds, as well as a large number of Herefords from Uruguay. After every conceivable test and experiment had been made the Russian veterinary experts decided on the British-bred Herefords, and in 1939 the Soviet Government were giving orders for all the Herefords they could get. But before many shipments had been made Hitler unleashed his hell-hounds.

"It is evident," says Mr Harry F. Davies, Secretary of the Hereford Herd Book Society, in *Hereford Cattle,* "that the Hereford Breed will be called upon to help to win the Peace."

The South American trade has always been important and the South American buyers have paid large sums in order to get the bulls they want; quite recently as much as 2,500 guineas was given for Mr R. S. de Quincey's Vern Vanguard, a yearling.

"The bull," says the description in *Hereford Cattle,* "should be of masculine appearance and possess plenty of bone and substance. The cow should be altogether more feminine in appearance. Head and neck less massive, the eyes denoting a placid and docile character."

But the most docile females may be excused a bit of temper if they imagine their children are threatened. At one place a fallow buck strayed into a field where a famous herd of pedigree Hereford cows and calves were pastured. One would not expect heavy cattle to rival a deer in liveliness, but the cows, seeming to think their calves were in danger, charged the buck—and killed it!

Pigs and poultry seem to occupy about the share of the farmer's economy usual in most parts, but there is little specialized pig-breeding, nor are there any extensive poultry farms such as one finds, in normal times, say, in parts of Lancashire.

There are three old Herefordshire proverbs connected with hop-growing, two apparently having been made up by the farmers who grow them and the other by someone who thought the farmers weren't doing nearly as badly out of the crop as they pretended.

"Hops are a certain care but an uncertain profit," sighed the grower; and, a little more hopefully, "Hops make or break." To which was retorted, "If it were not for the hops the farmers would have to hop themselves."

Most of the hops grown in Herefordshire are grown in the south, Ledbury being roughly in the centre of the hop-growing country. They are hardly grown at all north of Hereford, though there does not seem to be any hard-and-fast rule why they should not be, the hop, a member of the nettle family and the only species of its genus, often growing wild in hedgerows, and that as far north as Scotland. When they were first introduced from Flanders for flavouring ale in the reign of Henry VIII there was quite an outcry against them, and Parliament was petitioned to stop the growing of "a wicked weed that would spoil the taste of the drink and endanger the people."

The names beer and ale are not very clear in their meanings, both apparently being ancient words. Even old John Gerard, the Elizabethan herbalist, in his *Herball,* says, "The flowers are used to season Beere or Ale with," adding, "and too many do cause bitterness thereof, and are ill for the head."

Later, however, one finds "the manifold virtues of Hops do manifestly argue the wholesomenesse of beere above ale; for the hops rather make it a physicall drinke to keepe the body in health, than an ordinary drinke for the quenching of our thirst."

From which it seems that ale was the original (though

people were using wild hops to flavour it long before they were cultivated) and, when the general custom became to use hops in brewing, the drink was known as "beere."

The proverb about hops being "a certain care but an uncertain profit" was not said without some reason. "The Hop joyeth in a fat and fruitfull ground," wrote Gerard. Not only that, but it likes plenty of moisture and yet good drainage. A very wet season may spell the ruin of a crop, and equally so may a hot dry one. The yield per acre may vary from two hundredweights an acre (very bad!) to twenty (very good!). Apart from weather, the plant has a generous allowance of enemies, both animal and fungoid. One of the former, the sycamore tussock moth, or pale tussock moth, has almost entirely forsaken hops as a feeding ground, in consequence of the repeated sprayings, and has transferred its affections to the sycamore trees. The hop-fly, or hop-aphis, has not been so considerate. It follows the usual aphis cycle of life, reproducing itself both parthenogenetically and sexually, and, between sap-sucking and exuding honey-dew, on which a black fungus grows, making such a nuisance of itself as only an aphis can. Besides the aphis there are hop-fleas, hop-beetles, ghost-moths, and red spiders. The downy mildew which covers leaves on the underside with black patches, and hop-mould, covering the leaves with white patches of knob-shaped fungi, are fungoid pests. So is red mould, which spoils ripe cones (the female flowers) when they are ready for picking. And there are mosaic disease and nettlehead as well.

Truly, the hop-grower's life is not a happy one! They say they expect one bad crop in every seven, and pessimists put it much more unpleasantly than that.

A crop takes three years to come to maturity; that is to say, a bine is three years old before it bears the female flowers which we know as hops, ready for picking. The plant is dioecious, bearing male and female flowers on different plants, and in a hop-field only one male plant is grown to about two hundred female, and that because it is thought that pollination, which is carried out by the wind, improves the quality of the female flowers (hops).

The hops consist of a cone (*strobile*) of bracts. These

bracts protect the ovaries or seed boxes. Between the kernel and shell of the fruit itself there is a substance called *lupulin*. It is this substance that has a bitter taste and which gives hops their value to the brewers. The hops contain two other substances, a narcotic oil and tannic acid, the latter being of use in helping to clear the beer. Lupulin had its place in medicine, being used in extract of lupulin, and also in poulticing. For this purpose it was extracted from the sweepings of oast-house floors.

In Kent I believe there are still skilled stilt-men who tie the bines to the highest wires of the hop-field, but the Herefordshire custom seems to be to go round the field on a platform erected on a cart which is drawn by a horse. It is pleasant to think that here is one job, at least, in which the tractor cannot supersede the horse.

"The floures of hops," writes Gerard, "are gathered in August and September and reserved to be used in beere: in the Spring time come forth new shoots or buds: in the Winter onely the roots remaine alive."

Hop-picking time in Kent is a London holiday. The same may be said for Birmingham and the industrial towns around it, when the hops are ripe in Herefordshire.

When the hops are picked they are put into bins, the bins being troughs of sacking on a wooden framework. At the end of the day the bins are emptied into pokes (bags) and taken to the oast-house to be dried. In Kent oast-houses are round. In Herefordshire they are usually square but with the same cone and swinging cowl above. Charcoal is the chief fuel because it gives more heat and is not so dusty as coal, and, during the drying, sulphur is added to the fires, the sulphur fumes destroying any insect life or animalculae in the hops, though any of these that survive the drying itself have my sympathy. The dried hops are put into special jute bags known as pockets, are pressed tightly by means of special mechanism, and are then ready to be sent away.

So all honour to the hops and to the men of South Herefordshire who grow them, though they be "an uncertain profit"! And for those who can't sleep at nights, let them try a pillow stuffed with hops. That is better than any number of aspirins.

I often wonder what the brewers buy
One half so precious as the goods they sell.

The praises of English beer and English ale have been
sung too often to need any elaboration. I had my knuckles
soundly rapped in the train between Ledbury and Hereford
for trying to add to the subject, but my companion was such
a jolly, rosy, smiling, Pickwick sort of chap that it never
struck me that a good word for the hops would be amiss.

I couldn't help quoting William Stevenson's *Jolly Good
Ale and Old*.

> I cannot eat but little meat,
> My stomach is not good;
> But sure I think that I can drink
> With him that wears a hood.
> Though I go bare, take ye no care,
> I nothing am a-cold;
> I stuff my skin so full within
> Of jolly good ale and old.
>
> Back and side go bare, go bare;
> Both foot and hand go cold;
> But, belly, God send thee good ale enough,
> Whether it be new or old.

A rough, vulgar, sixteenth-century drinking song, I know.
But it was that sort of evening, with the country warm and
rich and mellow that made one expansive and kind-hearted
and understanding.

And then the vials of wrath were opened and the contents
came pouring on my head, damping my spirits and making
me forget the sun was shining.

I made a very poor show. Yes, I had to admit that a man
who spent on beer the money he should hand over to his wife
is a fool.

I had to admit that the man who drank until his wits were
as far away as his money is a pig—though, I protested, that
was being unfair to a pleasant and friendly animal.

I had to admit—oh, I had to admit any number of things.
I thought I should never score a point. But I did.

"What *must* a man drink, then?"

"What's wrong with tea, coffee, lemonade?"

What was *wrong!* Two nasty drugs, one astringent and one alkaloid. (I tried to forget the tannic acid in hops.) And carbonic acid gas under pressure.

"All you've said may be right," I admitted. "But when you say, 'What's wrong——!' The indigestion-cure merchants ought to subsidize you."

He smiled sadly. "So you don't like tea."

"Of course I like it, but I know it's horrible stuff. I think beer is more wholesome."

"Not the beer you buy nowadays. Got any brewery shares?"

"I've no shares of any sort."

"You try brewery shares." He rubbed his chin thoughtfully and stared at the roof of the compartment.

"Brewing is an ancient and an honourable trade."

"Tell your brewers one thing from me," he said.

I didn't quite like them being called *my* brewers, but I let it pass. "What's that?"

"The finest dividend is a job done as well as it can be done."

I let that pass, too.

I laughed at him when we got out at Hereford. "Now if you weren't tee-total I should invite you——"

He thumped me on the shoulder. "Who said I was tee-total? Come on. What are we waiting for?"

Very likely the men of olden-day Herefordshire celebrated their victories in mead, that nearly forgotten drink of fermented honey in water. Almost certainly they would drink the spiced kind of mead known to them—Welsh being familiar—as *meddyglyn* (*meddyg*—healing; *llyn*—liquor), a word that has been Englished into metheglin.

Later on Herefordshire had its vineyards; one, at least, in Hereford, another, according to Blount and to the accounts of the Dioceses of Hereford in the reign of Edward III, in the Manor of Ledesbury (Ledbury) and another at Prestbury. From the time of the Romans England had had its own vineyards and made its own wine. William of Malmesbury wrote in the twelfth century that Gloucester vines were "more plentiful in crops and more pleasant in flavour than any in England," and of the wine that it did not "offend the mouth with sharpness, since they do not yield to the French in sweetness." If Gloucestershire was noted for its vines and its wines it is hardly likely that Hereford lagged far behind.

The English cultivation of the vine died out for one reason and another, but Herefordshire had a wine that could nowhere be made better, and the making of which never did die out, nor gives signs that it ever will. This was apple-wine, the fermented juice of the apple, cider.

How long cider has been made in these parts it is impossible to say. It can be made of crab-apples (not very good cider, according to modern tastes, I admit), so may have been drunk even before apples were cultivated, which would go back to Roman times at least. Later references to it are many. John Evelyn wrote that "in a manner of speaking it [Herefordshire] hath become one continuous orchard." John Gerard in his *Herball* was almost lyrical. "The tame and graffed Apple trees are planted and set in Gardens and orchards made for that purpose: they delight to grow in good and fertile grounds: Kent doth abound with Apples of most sorts. But I have seene in the pastures and hedge-rows about the grounds of a worshipfull Gentleman dwelling two miles from Hereford, called Master Roger Bodnome, so many trees of all sorts, that the servants drinke for the most part no other drinke but that which is made of Apples. The quantity is such, that by the report of the gentleman himselfe, the Parson hath for tithe so many hogsheads of Syder. The hogs are fed with the fallings of them, which are so many, that they make choise of those Apples they do eate, who will not taste of any but of the best."

The fourth verse of Chapter Thirteen of the Book of Judges is the warning given to the mother of the still unborn Samson: *Now therefore beware, I pray thee, and drink not wine nor strong drink*. But so important was the wine of the apple in Herefordshire that when Nicholas de Hereford was helping Wycliffe to translate the Bible into English in the fourteenth century he wrote it, *drink no cider*. The translation was none the worse for that. In fact, it has a homely sound. There is a copy of one of these Bibles in the chained library in the Cathedral.

There was a book published early in the seventeenth century, *Herefordshire Orchards, a Pattern for all England,* which gives a good account of the extent of apple-growing and cider-making in the country. Now Devon has its songs about cider, and, again according to a song, Somerset is "where the cider-apples grow." But the final test of good cider is in the drinking, and the author of this book, claiming a life's experience of the apple-wine and its making, and a knowledge of all the English varieties, said that, in his opinion, and in that of all good palates, Herefordshire cider was the best. So, songs for those who like them, but the last word surely rests with "all good palates."

Any kind of apple won't do for the best cider-making. The right type are known as bitter-sweets (horrible things to eat!), apples rather smaller than the average dessert fruit, which contain more sugar and less acid than eating or cooking apples, and a higher percentage of tannin. Since many bitter-sweets have the word Norman as part of their name (Cherry Norman, Strawberry Norman, White Norman) they are probably of French origin; and, since the French have for centuries been expert cider-makers, it is quite possible that the first French settlers in Herefordshire, friends of Edward the Confessor; and later the Conquest and the subsequent coming of the Lords Marchers to the district; may have given a leg-up to a local habit—one can hardly call it an industry so early—when they were not busy cutting each other's throats.

But, on the whole, the Normans would have stayed loyal to their French wines. It was the fourteenth century before cider made its next stride forward. The Hundred Years' War meant practically an end to the importation of wine from France, and the making of wine from English grapes being on the decline, cider was a good substitute, and, along the Border, ready to hand.

By the sixteenth and seventeenth centuries the industry was, as Gerard records, in a very healthy state. It continued so until the time of the Napoleonic wars and then one of the other Ws of Herefordshire toppled it right off its pedestal.

Wheat was such a precious commodity that men grew wheat anywhere they could. Even up in the hills I have been shown ridged land where nothing but bracken ever grows now and been assured that crops of wheat were once grown on it. If it was money in a man's pocket to grow wheat on poor, thin soil, what was it to grow it in good rich soil like that of Herefordshire? The inevitable happened; orchards had to take second place, or fifth or sixth place, and, one after another, they were grubbed up to make way for a crop more in demand, and commanding a higher price.

From this blow cider took a long time to recover. Loyal Herefordshire men like Knight of Downton Castle planted new orchards and tried to revive neglected ones. But foreign wines and cheap spirits were imported (the latter being the real "demon drink") and the cider merchants adulterated what they bought from the makers.

Of course, it continued to be made, but chiefly for home consumption; and some of the making was none too clever. At times the cider was good and at other times it was bad. The principles of fermentation were not properly understood, cleanliness was not invariably considered important, and there was a good deal of hit-or-miss, especially in the matter of temperature, which is of the utmost importance. Practically every farm of any size had its cider-press, the crushing usually being done by stone rollers, turned by hand, or by a horse, but what they made was what they wanted to drink themselves. Cider-apples not used at home were hardly worth selling and many farmers rolled them into the ground so that they would rot more quickly.

It was quite largely due to a delicate boy, son of the Rector of Credenhill, near Hereford, or perhaps to the good advice his mother gave him, that the industry ever regained its feet. He was not strong enough to enter one of the professions and when he asked his mother's advice on starting a business for himself she suggested "something to do with eating or drinking, because they never go out of fashion." So in the autumn of 1887 H. P. Bulmer made his first two casks of cider.

Herefordshire cider is now known everywhere. In fact, not enough apples are grown to supply the demand, and before the war apples actually had to be imported from France. French apples to help make Herefordshire cider! Not quite good enough. But that will not last. The firm of Bulmers are encouraging Herefordshire farmers to grow suitable apples for Herefordshire wine, by a scheme in which they supply the right trees at cost price. Tens of thousands of trees have been planted in recent years and presumably more will go in in the future. So that should be all right. Between thirty and forty thousand tons of cider apples were used every year before the war—Bulmers were crushing over twenty thousand tons—so it may be judged whether cider-making is important or not.

There are two subsidiary interests that go cheerfully hand-in-hand with cider. The need for the complete pollination of the cider-orchards gives bee-keeping a chance to expand; and from pomace, the residue of the apples when the juice is pressed out, pectin, a jelly used to make jam set, is extracted.

The pectin industry is young, but bees have been kept in Herefordshire from the earliest times, though at present bee-keeping in the county seems to be mainly the concern of cottagers. There is a reference in Domesday Book to ninety-six men of Archenfield who paid forty-one sestiers of honey, and another to the King's Manor of Leominster where the men gave seventy-five shillings' worth. There is a record in the Pipe Rolls of the see of Hereford of a hundred shillings for honey in 1166–67.

Cider-making as a home industry, is perhaps a dying one. I do not think it will die out altogether for some time. Working men's taste seems to be for "hard" cider; the factory-made product is too refined for them, often too sweet. Personally I find I cannot manage hard cider in any quantity; perhaps I don't work hard enough. I remember sitting outside the back door of a farm—that is, in the garden—with a mug of it in my hand. It was about as much as I could do to drink it all, but you can't slap hospitality in the face, and I had said incautiously that I liked cider. I was just congratulating myself on my empty mug when the farmer's wife came out with a jug and refilled it! I felt I could do no more. When I was alone I took a careful look to see no-

body was about and then gave my second mugful to a dyspeptic-looking sunflower languishing in the bed against the wall. The plant expanded into sudden life and a sunflower shot up like a jack-in-the-box, and punched me in the eye. Or did I dream that? If it didn't it should have done, it was a powerful brew.

One may see some pretty good orchards in Herefordshire and one may see, also—if he travels about the county—some pretty poor ones. No doubt they were good once, but it was a long time ago. "Mossed cottage trees" are all right in a poem; they ought to be reserved for the use of poets.

What Gerard wrote in his *Herball* over three hundred years ago is as apt to-day as it was then, and it was written expressly for Herefordshire men.

After mentioning the part already quoted that even our pigs are choosey as to which apples they will eat, for they "will not any but the best," he goes on: "An example doubtlesse to be followed of Gentlemen that have land and living: but envie saith, the poore will breake downe our hedges, and wee shall have the least part of the fruit; but forward in the name of God, graffe, set, plant and nourish up trees in every corner of your ground, the labour is small, the cost is nothing, the commodity is great, your selves shall have plenty, the poore shall have somewhat in time of want to relieve their necessitie, and God shall reward your good mindes and diligences."

He couldn't have spoken more fairly, and never did he advise more wisely.

So, "forward in the name of God"!

The old cider presses are languishing on most farms nowadays. There are a few that go round in the season, moving from farm to farm and making a few barrelfuls for each from their own apples. A pity to see the old presses drop out of use. Another home industry passing.

Herefordshire men drink cider at their work. But most of them seem to prefer beer in their leisure hours. The happiest-looking roadman I have ever known told me that he and all the large family of which he was one were raised on cider. He did it credit. But he had a pot of beer in his hand as he spoke.

Hop Picking
Packing Hops

I have had a sort of proprietorial interest in the growing of sugar beet ever since I raised the only crop grown in my own part of the country. The field was at the height of over a thousand feet, with a light well-drained soil, and faced north-west. I was told they would not grow, but I persisted. There were other crops growing in the field, and they were good crops, but the sugar beet was by far the best of the lot, and all the local farmers used to come on September Sunday afternoons to look at them.

This was in 1940 and the idea was that we should make a kind of syrup from the beet to help out the sugar ration. The idea was dropped because the method of syrup-making seemed tiresome and messy, and, besides, people told us that it would have a filthy taste. So in the end I took home a few sackfuls and told John Price to give the remaining cartloads to his stock, which he did. The few I had for myself I gave to the hens to eat, and once they had found they liked the flavour I had only to throw them down raw in the fowl-run and they promptly ate them, and throve on the diet. Every year since I have said I would grow more, and every year sowing some sugar beet is one of those things that does not get done. But the idea remains sound.

The plant seems to have no history much except as a feed for stock, and for this purpose it was grown first in Silesia, until the wars against the French at the end of the eighteenth and the beginning of the nineteenth centuries, when Napoleon encouraged its culture on the Continent in order to replace the sugar that was no longer coming from the West Indies.

Gerard mentions a beet that may be sugar beet, almost certainly was, though I have no note to that effect.

"The common white Beet hath great broad leaves, smooth and plain: from which rise thicke crested or chamfered stalks: the floures grow along the stalks clustering together, in shape like little stars, which being past, there succeed round uneven prickly seed. The root is thicke, hard and great."

That sounds like sugar beet; but the old herbalist was more interested in a novelty "brought unto me from beyond the seas, by that courteous Merchant Master Leke . . .

leaves very great, and red of colour, as is all the rest of the plant. . . . The juyce conveighed up into the nostrils doth gently draw forth plegme, and purgeth the head."

After all, Gerard was a doctor. He had no time to spare for cattle food.

It is impossible to talk of sugar beet without running into the prickly question of the sugar-beet subsidy. It does seem commonsense to grow in one's soil what can profitably be grown and not something that cannot be raised without an extra payment, whether it is lemons, oranges, bananas, or sugar beet. At the same time there is a large percentage of sugar in this root and sugar is important. Before the war of 1914–18 the world production of sugar from beet nearly equalled that from the sugar-cane, and now it may be much higher. Obviously it is a good thing to have one's own sugar at one's doorstep in time of war, but then it would be a very much better thing to have no war—and no need to have one's sugar at one's doorstep.

Most farmers do not like growing sugar beet as a crop. Some grow it because they have to, and some grow it for the sake of the subsidy. The chief objection to it (subsidy apart) is that it takes a lot of labour. Conversely, its chief virtue is that it's a grand crop for cleaning the ground. Keeping the crop clean and clear of weeds takes a lot of work, and so do the lifting, cleaning, and topping in the autumn. When the plants are topped the crown of the root is cut off as well as the leaves because there is no sugar in it, and it contains a colouring substance that would do the sugar no good. Sugar-beet tops are a fine feed for animals, a crop being as nourishing as a crop of turnips or half the same acreage of mangolds. The leaves can be used for silage, but I believe silage is not, at the moment, a popular subject with many farmers.

The part of the county growing most sugar beet seems to be the southern half, like the hop-growing area, roughly with Ledbury as its centre. As one comes north the acreage appears to decrease, though from my own experience, I judge it can be grown almost as well on hill-land as in deep rich soil. And my roots were quite as good as I've seen in truckloads on the railway. But I admit one swallow doesn't make a summer. Perhaps I had green fingers that year.

As long as sugar beet has to be grown I expect Herefordshire will produce its share. But I don't doubt also that, once *He maketh wars to cease in all the world,* the sugar beet will cease, too.

For a couple of thousand years whenever there has been a rural community there have been rural craftsmen. Their evolution has been slow, so slow sometimes as almost to be stationary. As an example, garden tools have hardly changed during the last seven hundred years, or maybe much longer. They may never have changed materially since they were first thought of. Even the plough has not altered very much, considering how long it has been used. The hook, or sickle, is pretty well what it was in Anglo-Saxon days and the flail, still in use in a few isolated farms on the Herefordshire borders, lasted from the same time until its comparatively recent dismissal. Men have been thatching roofs—there are still a few thatched roofs in Herefordshire; and still a few thatchers—for hundreds and hundreds of years, and their methods have not altered appreciably, and though the hedgers and ditchers may have been less in demand under the open-field system, their method of pleaching is materially what it was when it was called, in Middle English, *pleche.*

Herefordshire villages have their craftsmen, men who have learned their craft from an earlier generation, as they did from an earlier one still, and so on, back into a dim, misty past. It is not Herefordshire alone, it is the same wherever the land has been supreme. And the long continuous chain is breaking at last. No, that is wrong. It is broken. The petrol engine has gambolled wildly across it, and where it has not snapped already it is showing signs that it will shortly do so. Once, the man who worked in metal or wood or straw would have taken his son to learn the craft, or, failing sons, would have taught somebody else's son. But a man will no longer teach his son a trade at which he himself can hardly earn a living, and no other man's son wants to be fooled that way either.

The two chief craftsmen in any village were always the smith and the carpenter. Sometimes, if the villages were small, they served a little ring of them. But the twentieth century has treated them badly. The carpenter will get along for a time because, whatever happens, people will die, and he has always made their coffins. But the smith had nothing like that to fall back on. He depended on horses, and horses, for thousands of years man's only means of transport and his only means of doing tasks he could not perform by his own strength, are now being ousted by the tractor. Historians look back a century at the Industrial Revolution and point this lesson and that lesson. But there is a revolution taking place now under our noses and most people are either not seeing it at all, or finding it very jolly.

It is all happening a great deal too quickly.

It is not a new complaint. In a scrap-book in Hereford Library I came across a paper that had been read to the Agricultural Society of Hereford on October 19th, 1816. It was entirely directed against machinery. During the war new machinery had come into use, and soldiers and sailors returning home after whipping Buonaparte found there was no work for them on the land.

What would the speaker have thought of the petrol engine?

Of course I know we never, *never* make the same mistakes twice . . . but in those days the chief culprit went to a comfortable, even luxurious, exile on St Helena, while the men who had fought him came home, many of them, to starve; or, if they stole a sheep so that they should not starve, went to a gaol that was neither comfortable nor luxurious—or else were hanged.

Craftsmen, of course, enjoyed something of a respite during the war. There was work for every man. Things were wearing out and could not be replaced. Carpenters and smiths had their hands full. But is that going to last long? A few years perhaps, a few decades . . . and then?

Herefordshire farms are going to be fully mechanized. Of that I feel sure. It is ideal country for mechanization. Back in the hills the old ways may last a while; a century perhaps, perhaps more. Before the war the tractors were already replacing the horse—and a lot of labour. The war quickened the process.

One can't blame the farmers. One cannot blame a man for doing a job in one day rather than taking three over it. One can't blame a man for getting something done for a penny instead of threepence. In fact, there doesn't seem to be anything anyone can do about it; and, candidly, very few people want to do anything about it. The smith will disappear, the carpenter will disappear, so will the thatcher—though he's practically unwanted by now, anyhow, poor silly fellow, except by a few people with artistic fancies, and the artistic reason for having a thatched roof is the worst there could be. The hedger and ditcher and the roadman—no, they should last a little longer—until someone invents a bulldozer to push up walls of cement to replace our pleasant hedges.

It's Progress. Why all the fuss?

The fuss is this. That the rural life, the life of the land, is a way of life as well as a way of making a living. The way of life was that a man wrestled with the soil and the soil in return for the struggle gave him a living. Men never thought of it like that, of course; nobody is so prosaic as your typical countryman. But you couldn't snatch; you couldn't be greedy. You couldn't grow two crops of corn a year from the same field; you couldn't keep a hundred cows where there should be only fifty. Life was slow and made a rhythmical pattern. It was the most satisfying pattern in the world, seemingly everlasting. And on those who break the pattern Nature has a funny way of getting her own back. The men who formed the Dust Bowl of America thought they were being clever. They were sowing where they did not reap (for when a man sows he sows more than seed). The end was disaster.

People who believe in the kinship between man and the soil sometimes wonder where the mechanization is going to end. It is in its infancy. If one man can do the work of two or three or four, is there any reason why he should not, someday, when more and even more wonderful machinery has been invented—is there any reason why he should not do the work of a whole farm single-handed? Or twenty farms? Or a hundred? And where are the men to go who had their living by the soil? They will go, as so many have already gone, to the towns, to the factories and workshops, to help turn out more of the machinery (and "you ain't seen nothing yet") that displaced them. Already there are six cottages where twelve once stood, small-holdings have vanished by the score. Never did men so long for the country as they do to-day—and never was there less chance of their becoming a part of it. Their hearts are urging them to the fields, but their bellies will drive them to the towns.

Much of the old way of rural life was bad. There were poverty, low wages, bad housing, more than a little petty tyranny. But there was good as well as bad. Unfortunately both will, unless we are very careful, or very lucky, go in the scrap-heap, together.

In David Smith's *No Rain in Those Clouds*[2] he has a chapter entitled "The Village Scene" in which he mentions such matters as women and their families stone-picking, at the rate of a penny farthing a bushel, and gleaning [called "leasing" in Herefordshire] and children pig-tending and sheep-tending. And he concludes the chapter with these words:

"I was talking to an old village woman not long ago, and what she said is, I think, the best epitaph on what I have tried to describe as 'The Village Scene.'

" 'We were all so happy then,' she said."

But David Smith is a farmer. You would expect him to have a feeling for the old way of agriculture. Let one of our foremost English novelists speak the final word.

"I do not believe that I am influenced only by an illusion natural to the man of letters to think that the best pattern of all is the husbandman's, who ploughs his land and reaps his crop, who enjoys his toil and enjoys his leisure, loves, marries, begets children and dies. When I have observed the peasantry in those favoured lands in which the earth produces her plenty without excessive labour, where the pleasures and pains of the individual are those incidental to the human race, it has seemed to me that there the perfect life was perfectly realised. There life, like a good story, pursues its way from beginning to end in a firm and unbroken line."[3]

[2] *No Rain in Those Clouds,* by David Smith (Dent.).
[3] *The Summing Up,* by W. Somerset Maugham (Heinemann).

Chapter VIII

THINGS THAT GO BUMP IN THE NIGHT

THE first ghost story I heard in Herefordshire came through giving a man a lift. I was driving along the Hereford–Eardisley road one evening. It may have been late spring or may have been early summer—I know it was daylight—and just beyond Bridge Solers there was an old man waving a stick at me. I pulled up a few yards beyond him. I had a three-wheeler at the time, and he came hurrying along to the side of the car.

"You going through Kington?" he demanded fiercely.

"Yes." I pushed the door open. "Want a lift?"

He clambered in awkwardly, grunting a little, and not appearing very grateful, and I drove off.

"Going to Kington?" I asked him.

" 'Tween there and Eardisley. Bin to see my darter down Bridge Solers, I 'ave. Told me 'er were ill. Ill!" He sounded very cross about it all. "Warn't a thing wrong with 'er. 'Whatever be come for to-day, Father?' she ses when she see me come in. ' 'Eard you was about dying,' I ses, and 'er laughed at me. 'Me?' she ses. 'There ain't nothin' wrong wi' me. Never bin better in my life!' " He turned to spit over the side of the car, which, luckily, had no side-curtains. "Real disgusted, I were," he said. "Thinkin' to find 'er bad and 'er right as rain."

He contemplated his disappointment at his daughter's health.

"Then I goes an' misses the ruddy 'bus," he added.

I didn't say anything and for a while we fell into silence.

He was rather a picturesque old villain. He might well have been eighty, but he had clear eyes, a fine curving hawk-beak nose, and a greyish-white beard. His cheeks were rosy.

By the way he spoke I knew him for pure Herefordshire. There is very little dialect, considered purely as such, spoken now in the county. An unfamiliar word is heard now and then like "pitch" for hill, "oonty tumps" (molehills) and "frum" —in the Kington district. But the intonation is very noticeable. There is the soft, burred, drawly speech of the south Saxon, less broad than one finds farther south in England (Wiltshire or Devon), yet with no hint of the hardness that will appear going north towards the Black Country. Add to this gentle drawl (which is not too respectful of the letter *h*) the sing-song, rising sharply at the end of the sentence, that is a gift from the Welsh part of Hereford ancestry, and the result, if it could only be "Herefurd" instead of " 'Erefurd," is distinctly pleasing.

It is generally the older people who "talk broad." On younger people, though the soft drawl and sing-song are not entirely absent, the influence of the cinema and the B.B.C. have made themselves felt. In outlying villages the children still speak as their grandfathers and great-grandfathers did, but on the main 'bus routes dialect has often faded into such richness of language as "Sez you!" "Oh yeah!" and "O.K., baby!"

My passenger was fidgeting a bit.

"Queer dam' contraption, this!" he remarked.

I thought he meant one of the instruments on the panel. I wasn't particularly pleased to realize he meant the complete car, for a car I considered it.

"Just the same as goin' backwards in a wheelbarrow—and it goes a sight too fast, I reckon."

I was, or had imagined I was, in a hurry. But a hurry is the silliest thing in the world to be in, so I took my foot up and we eased down to a comparative crawl.

"What would you have done if I hadn't given you a lift?" I asked. This was a gentle rebuke for "queer dam' contraption."

"Had one off somebody else. Or walked."

"Walked! Twelve miles or so?"

"That's nothing. I could do that easy. I've walked forty before now."

I nearly said "Not for a long time," but realized he might take it unkindly. He added himself, however, "When I was younger."

"How far are you going?" he asked.

"Radnorshire."

"Live there?"

"Yes."

"What part?"

"Near Rhayader."

He cackled derisively. "Know what we used to call Radnorshire people down this way?"

"No, what?"

"Radnorshire sheep-stealers."

I grinned. "You should come and tell them that in Rhayader."

"So I would. I ain't afraid of no man. It was the truth, too, mind you, that name. Set of damnedest sheep-thieves you ever see! An' poachers! Poach a salmon, that lot, if 'twas their own brother."

"Do you know anybody up there?"

He spit over the side of the car again. "Not me. I went to Newbridge Horse Fair once. And I did come to know one of them hill-farmers, but he got 'isself hung."

I thought he was serious. "Is that a fact?"

"Yes. For killing his granny. Found out 'er'd got a tooth with a gold stopping in it, see? Come like second natur' to 'it her on the 'ead then." He sniggered at me. I think he thoroughly despised both me and the vehicle I drove. He was the sort of old pirate who would despise anybody unless they punched him on the nose.

"Do you know what we call Herefordshire people up in Radnor?" I asked.

"No."

"Herefordshire apple-smashers."

He cackled again. "Ar, I've heard that."

He was a liar. I'd made it up then on the spur of the moment.

"Had a name for everybody, us did," he confided: "Gla'ster long-eared 'uns. And Wiltsheere moonrakers."

"Why that?"

"Wiltsheere—that's where they tried to rake the moon out o' the pond. Thought 'twas a cheese, see? One of'm 'as 'is boy along. 'Do'ee rake agin, Dad,' the boy kep' sayin'. 'There's another cheese there.' "

"What about Monmouth?" I asked.

"I never did 'ear one for there. But Warwickshire is where they milk the cow by the tail, and in Wu'ster they cuts beans in blow because they'll never look prettier." He changed the subject abruptly. "What you do for a living?"

"Nothing," I lied. "I'm a millionaire's cousin and he sends me fifty pounds a week."

He gave me a sharp look and only just didn't call me what I was. "Why the 'ell don' 'ee send a 'undred?"

"Well, that's a funny thing," I said. "I never thought of it. I'll have to ask him. But I don't think I could spend a hundred."

He grunted. "Been to 'Erefurd?"

"I came from there. I've been to Weobley."

He chanted:

> "Poor Weobley, proud people,
> Low church, high steeple.

"So I've heard," I said.

"I knows another like that. Even been to Cowarne?"

> "Dirty Cowarne, wooden steeple,
> Cracked bell, wicked people."

"They are very nice people in Cowarne."

"Well, it's a saying-like. There's wicked people anywhere." He sang tonelessly:

> "Lusty Tarrington, lively Stoke,
> Beggars at Weston, thieves at Woolhope!"

He was silent for a while.

"Do you know any more of those old rhymes about places?" I asked.

"There's one, but I misremembers it." After a minute he chanted:

> "Dinglewood Common and Molesey mere
> Are the coldest places in Herefordshere.

"Know anybody in Weobley?" he asked suddenly.

"A few."

"You ought to ha' knowed the Colcombes. There's the chaps would ha' told you rhymes, and riddles—all sorts of stories, I reckon. There was a Colcombe in Weobley, but he may be left or dead, I don' know. I ain't been to Weobley this long time. The Colcombes is about the oldest family in 'Erefurdshire. Been here hundreds o' years. Not gentry, mind, working people like you and me. [He'd forgotten my fifty pounds a week.] They do say as you won't never find a Colcombe outside of this county." He had a habit of switching abruptly from one subject to another. "There was used to be a haunted house in Weobley."

"Where was that?"

"Well, it wasn't rightly in Weobley itself. It was a farm there. Old Griggs's ghost, they used to call it. Griggs was the farmer, see? He was very tight on his family, kept 'em hard at work and short of money. So what did they do? They said they'd get rid of 'im. They couldn't think what way to do it 'cause he was a wise old devil. If he spotted what they was up to there'd be hell to pay. They was afraid of him, mind you. Anyhow they thinks up a way in the end. The ol' chap was right fond of his belly. Eat like a horse, an' something tasty he liked better than his own mother. So his sons caught some toads and killed them, and one of the daughters, 'er cooked it up lovely, spiced and what not so you'd never know what it was, an' give it the old boy for his supper.

"He et it real hearty.

" 'What's this?' he asked. 'I haven't tasted it afore.'

" 'Chickens' livers,' says the gel, 'er 'aving killed some fowls to sell that day.

"Well, nex' day she cooks more toads. 'Chickens' livers,' she says again, and he eats it up.

"That's how it went on and nat'rally in a couple o' days he was dead."

"I didn't know toads were poisonous," I said.

"Well, they are. Griggs died of 'em. You try."

Not exactly a kind invitation.

"What happened?"

"Went as merry as a wedding-day at first. Plenty of money and not too much work. Only sons and darters there was, see? The mother was dead.

"They was having a nice time an' then one night something funny happened. Feasting an' merrymaking they was in the house and thinking how clever they'd bin and suddenly one of them quieted the others.

" 'Listen,' he said. 'There's a calf got out.'

"They could hear a calf bleating close by the window.

"The funny thing was they hadn't got no calves. But they thought it was one of somebody else's, so one of them went out to put it in a building. He come back after a bit looking white in the face.

" 'Where was the calf?' they asked him.

"He said there wasn't no calf. He'd seen it by the window and when he went near it it vanished.

"Well, they laughed at him summat odd, but they wasn't laughing long. Because soon they heard the calf again, only this time it was in the parlour. The one that had went first wouldn't go again, so in the end they all went out. When they got in the parlour they would see the calf plain, but when they got near it vanished.

"Well, they didn't have no peace after that. By day things was peaceful enough, but come night and there would be the calf bleating. Out in the yard, they'd hear it; in the buildings; up and down the house. They'd not be in bed of a night before it would start, perhaps outside the bedroom door. No peace at all.

"They soon guessed who it was. It was old Griggs's ghost."

"What was the end of it?" I asked.

"Well, it was fair sending them mad and at last they tried to sell the place. But others had come to hear of the ha'ntings and none 'ud buy it. They split up best they could and went their ways. I never heard of no good coming to them."

"And did the hauntings stop?"

"No, they never did. The place had to be took down. I did hear somebody had the ghost laid in the end. Can you swim?"

I thought he was changing the subject again.

"Yes."

"You know Garnstone?"

I said I did.

"Well, there a pool in Garnstone Park. You swim to the bottom of that you'll find a silver snuff-box. But I 'udn't open it if I was you, not lest you wants to have a calf following you about the rest of your life. That's what they laid old Griggs's ghost in."

"I think I'll keep out of the pool altogether," I said.

"How'd you like to live in Weobley?" he asked after a while.

"I would—only I'm comfortable where I am."

"You don' want to live in Weobley. Any time you wants to live in 'Erefurdshire you go to Orleton. That's the place to live."

"Any special reason?"

"Yes, there is, then. Orleton's the place where the Resurrection Day is going to begin, see?"

"Is that so?"

"Yes. In the old days lots of people had theirselves buried at Orleton so's they'd be nice and 'andy. There was a man left a lot of money to Orleton, only they had to bury him close to the churchyard gate with his feet towards it."

"Why?"

"So's he could get out first, o' course, when the Last Trump sounded. He was buried there, too, like he said, but I d'know what 'appened to the money. Parson or squire got their claws on it, I war'n."

A question came into my mind. I've always wanted to find out for certain about the sin-eating.

"Look," I said, "have you ever heard anything about sin-eating?"

"What's that?"

If I'd told him he might have made up a story. He was quite capable of it.

"Have you ever heard of it?"

He hated to admit it, but he hadn't.

Then I explained it to him.

"I d'know nothing about that," he said. "But I'll tell you

what. I knew a man that helped turn somebody in his grave."

I'd heard of such things metaphorically.

"Actually turned him?"

"That's right. He was lying in his coffin on his back. They put him to lie on his belly."

"Whatever for?"

"So's his spirit could rest easy. It's been done many a time. This chap, the one I know, was turned, he was ha'nting or something. They say his missus was courting again and that did lie heavy on his spirit. So they dug'n up and turned'n. But it didn't do no good. He wouldn't rest and the widow had to give up her sweetheart 'cause he was a fellow said he couldn't sleep comfortable three in a bed."

"Where did this happen?"

"Some place in the Golden Valley, I think."

We were through Eardisley by now and going up the hill. He took out an old charred pipe.

"Got such a thing as a bit of bacca?"

"No." I opened my cigarette case. "Have one of these."

He eyed them with disgust. "Can't abear they faddling li'l' things," he growled.

"Break one up and put it in your pipe," I suggested.

He took one gingerly and looked at it. "Reckon I'll need two," he said, and helped himself to another.

When we came to Kingswood Common he asked me to set him down.

He stood by the car-door a minute. "You tell 'em in Rhay'der what I said."

"What's that?"

"Radnorshire sheep-stealers!" He grinned wickedly at me like one who has had the last word, the light blue cigarette-tobacco smoke curling round his face, and then turned and stumped off up the lane on the left.

I only saw him once again. He was coming out of the Tram Inn in Eardisley. I waved to him, but he took no notice of me. He ought to have recognized the three-wheeler but perhaps he disdained to know a man who on fifty pounds a week couldn't manage one more wheel.

One of these days I'll meet him again when he's missed the 'bus. I'd rather like to.

I enjoyed company in the car. Remembering my derisive friend and his chatter, I stopped on another occasion to give a lift to a very similar-looking gentleman who was waiting on the same road, apparently for a 'bus.

He was going to Kington and accepted the ride gratefully.

But he was of a different quality. All I had out of him were two words repeated over and over "There's another!"

As he was getting in the car a big chauffeur-driven limousine went past, with two women in the back. On the luggage grid was tied, of all things, a large sack of potatoes.

We caught up with the limousine quite soon, and then my companion noticed something.

"They'm losing their taties," he said.

They were, too. There was a smallish hole in the sack and every now and again a potato would fall out of the sack and bounce and roll across the road in front of us.

"There's another!" the old chap would squeak.

"There's another!" A quarter of a mile, "There's another!"

I hooted and I tried to pass, but the chauffeur thought I was trying to show off and kept me behind. The road through Letton and beyond is narrowish and winding and I wasn't passing on bends in a three-wheeler to save anybody's potatoes.

"There's another!" went the song by my side. "There's another!"

We were nearly in Kington before they realized what was happening. Perhaps one of the women looked back at one of the crucial moments.

I slowed up to speak to the chauffeur as he tied up the half-empty sack.

"If you want your potatoes they are lying at intervals of two hundred yards between here and wherever you got them," I told him.

My passenger apparently had forgotten all his words except "There's another," and he had no more use for those.

I was always being warned that my habit of picking up all sorts of queer customers would bring me to a sticky end. But I was only nervous once. I was on my way to a Home Guard lecture and gave a lift to a girl hiker who had signalled

THE·SITE·OF·S͓T·ETHELBERT'S

for one. She sat in the back and she chattered, and she had the most obvious accent (Central European—Austrian at a guess) I'd ever heard. Invasion was considered to be "when," not "if," at that time and I had the horrifying visions of being held up, and even more horrifying visions of how my platoon would love reading the headlines: "Home Guard Officer Tied Up and Left in Ditch by Girl Spy."

There are other ghosts in Herefordshire. The Wye is haunted near Goodrich by the ghosts of Alice Birch and Charles Clifford, who were drowned while escaping from Goodrich Castle when Colonel Birch and his Roundheads were besieging it during the Civil War.

On the Black Mountains there was a ghost that more than once guided lost people to safety.

Pembridge had its ghost, a troubled spirit, that of the wife of a minister, Dr Breton, who came back wanting to restore land she had stolen from the poor.

But these are old stories, faded and half-forgotten. They are wraiths from another age, pale and misty, by the side of the ghost of Callow Hill. And the ghost of Callow Hill is not the ghost of a person, it is more substantial, more terrifying; it looms heavily over the pleasant Herefordshire landscape, grim and forbidding. It is the ghost of a house.

It has been seen. Yes, in the prosaic, mechanical twentieth century it has been seen in broad daylight. For all I know it may be seen to-day. I've been told there is an old book that has in it a woodcut of the house, and even in that it frowns darkly.

It does not stand on Callow Hill any more. A mound in the grass, perhaps; a vague outline which might have been anything. But a few have seen it for all that—and have felt far from happy at the sight.

The house was still standing about the beginning of the nineteenth century. Two fields away was the inn, a coaching inn, where the travellers from the north used to stay the night. What pleasant memories that conjures up. Shades of Dickens and Washington Irving! Jolly, Christmas-card scenes. Glowing fires and laden tables and full bottles of wine in the candle-light. Stamping hooves and the smell of

Norman Doorway, Kilpeck Church
Harvest Time in the Wye Valley

straw and horses and harness oil. Laughter of women and the voices of men growing louder over their second bottle.

Perhaps it was like that. But if it was, it was only half the picture. Night came, the candles were out, the fires burned low, their merriment smothered under grey ash; the gentlemen, having emptied three bottles now, snored lustily. Outside there was only the sound of a horse that pulled at its head-stall, the cry of an owl, perhaps the melancholy piping of a lonely curlew in the valley.

And then in the darkness figures moved, vague indistinguishable figures, stealthy and silent, that carried something large and limp and ungainly between them. A dead hand trailed through the dew in the grass as they crossed the fields to the house on the hill. Presently they returned, walking erect, carrying—nothing.

And in the morning the coach went on with a passenger less. An old man was fatigued with the journey and had decided to stay a few days; a woman, so obviously alone last night, had found friends in the neighbourhood and wished to visit them; that silly young man who had thrown his guineas about with such abandon had hired a horse in the early hours and galloped away.

It came out in time what had been happening. And when it did they had only to go to the ugly house nearby to find the travellers who had broken their journey.

They had not merely broken it. They had come to its end.

The house fell empty. People eyed it askance. It was the sort of place you hurried past, without looking too much. A house, like a man, grows up, mellows or turns sour, develops a personality. You can go into a house and feel its friendliness, its wholesomeness; and into another and know nothing but an unexplainable discomfort. The house on Callow Hill had sheltered cruelty and evil. It was a bad house. So in the end they pulled it down.

But it may still be seen—exactly as it was when it housed murdered travellers.

A fairy-story! But it is not.

I heard Robert Gibbings mention it. This was in his Montgomeryshire cottage (there is an engraving of it in *Coming Down the Wye*) where he had come to work on his book,

Lovely Is the Lee. He said that a friend of his had seen the house, not once, but continuously, over a period of years, and though the sight of it, for no reason she could understand, filled her with vague horror and depression, she did not find out it was not a real house until one day it was no longer there. Then she began asking questions and discovered the whole uncomfortable story. There was no doubt about her seeing the house. She was able, he said, on going over the site with a native of the place, to point out just where the front door had been and that was where nobody would have expected it to be, because at some time during the century the road had been altered to a different course altogether from the one it followed when the house was standing.

Well, the parsons laid Black Vaughan's ghost. I'm wondering how they would manage this one.

Chapter IX

CHARMS AND CURES

T w o fears have had an immeasurable effect on man's life down the ages, fear of death and fear of illness. There are other emotions—the desire to mate, for instance, and hunger —that can be more powerful for a short time, but appetites of any sort wax and wane. These two fears are constant. To them are very largely due the folklore and superstitions that are the inevitable heritage of country people. I say country people deliberately, for town life has never been productive of the richness in folklore as life in the country was. These folk-tales and superstitions are, in certain ways, a concentration of old wisdom. What has not stood the test of time or has proved unattractive for some other good reason has died away and is forgotten. The rest remains—or until the twentieth century it did largely remain. The folk-tales lasted, not because they were necessarily true, though they may once have had some basis in fact, but because they were an amusement. The lore, such as "red sky at morning, shepherd's forewarning; red sky at night, shepherd's delight," lasted because on the average it proved to be true. Country medical lore stayed either because it was basically sound (very often it was) or because fear forbade disbelief.

Townspeople have always had a chance to be in a crowd. They could talk, not in couples or in small groups, but in large numbers. They had a lot to talk about; they heard the news of the world; they were in touch with what went on. And much of their talk was gossip about events.

The Herefordshire countryman, up to a century or so ago, was cut off from what he would have called the great world. Roads, for the most part, were shocking affairs that we would not consider good cart-tracks; communication was difficult, in winter often impossible. People spent their whole lives within a few miles of the place where they were born and where they would die. Their knowledge was intense, but it was local. It was passed from one to another, ale-house talk, winter-fire talk. Their beliefs were bounded by their horizons, coloured by their earth.

And the Old Red Sandstone soil was, in this respect, as in others, a fertile one.

It was the fashion at one time to portray the typical un-educated countryman as a fool, a kind of gaping wretch with a silly grin on his face and straws in his hair. The better-off countryman was a slightly superior idiot; "Farmer Giles," stubborn and stupid.[1] A funny idea to grow up when both, if not quick and ready of speech, had a wealth of specialized knowledge at their finger-tips.

The town is favourable to the growth of knowledge. So is the progress that has taken place during the last fifty years. The countryman now gets to town and shares the knowledge, and, picking up knowledge, throws away some of the ancient lore.

All very right and proper. But is it? Knowledge has come but not always wisdom in its train. A man may have read the Encyclopaedia Britannica from beginning to end, but if, at the end, he is still susceptible to the hypnotism of the scream-ing flood of advertising that was a feature of the pre-war years, then I say he is still a bigger bumpkin than his grand-father who never saw a train in his life (nor an aeroplane, lucky fellow!) and tied his stocking round his neck when he went to bed to cure his sore throat.

Where, for instance, is knowledge, as knowledge, more respected than in America? And where, whatever popular magazine you pick up, from the cheapest pseudo-scientific shocker to the most sophisticated journal, could you find so many or such attractive traps for fools, prepared with the obvious belief that the quarry would fall into them? But we needn't look at America. We were running a splendid second.

It is usual to laugh at the old country beliefs. And yet a lot of our grandfathers' remedies could be used to-day as widely as they ever were, given the right opportunity. For in-

[1]Giles was a character in Robert Bloomfield's poem, *The Farmer's Boy,* first published in 1800. The poem was immensely popular at the time, and the name caught people's fancy.

stance, there was a belief common in parts of Herefordshire
that an eel's skin worn as a garter below the knee prevented
cramp. I don't know whether it does or it does not. I have
never tried it, and anyhow I don't suffer from cramp, but I
do say that if a man, to-day, had a sufficiently large store of
eel-skins, and employed a really first-rate advertising agency
to push the idea that eel-skins cured—oh, almost anything
you like—*and* he were willing to pay for an extensive advertising campaign, he could sell all the eel-skins he had, or
could get hold of.

Witchcraft did not come to an end in Herefordshire when
they stopped sentencing the witches to death.

"There'll always be nine witches from the bottom of Orcop
to the end of Garway hill as long as water runs," goes an
old saying, and since the water is still running there may still
be the nine witches. Only much more respectable than they
used to be.

In its earlier history there is little doubt that witchcraft
was a bad business. There were Black Masses, Witches
Sabbaths, and much obscene and cruel ceremonial. Serious
students have ascertained so much. But mixed up with the
supernatural was a lot of pure humbug. And it is not easy
to know how much was beastly and how much was humbug.
The Central European countries (more of them then and
most of them smaller than they are to-day) took witch-find-
ing more seriously than it was taken in England. There were
wholesale denunciations, confessions—and more denunciations—made under torture, witch-burnings. Hundreds of
people—perhaps thousands—went to the stake. The whole
business became a beastly carnage, with the majority of the
sufferers innocent of any evil intent. There are a few very
telling burnings of witches in the *Fugger News-Letters* for
those who care to be made sick in this way, and the confessions of Walpurga Hausmännin of Dillingen in 1587 are
perhaps the most astonishing examples of the heights to
which the imagination can rise under "kindly questionings
and also torture."

But the later story of witchcraft in England is a comparatively mild one. There were no doctors, so they did the

doctoring; there were no veterinary surgeons, so they doctored the animals as well; they were midwives and fortune-tellers; they were feared because of the harm they could do, and respected because of their knowledge. Little by little they gave up their less pleasant ways, such as "witching" the pigs into getting swine fever, or spitefully stopping the butter coming, and attained respectability by being known as white witches and conjurors.

In their earlier and more malevolent aspects they were given credit for possessing considerable supernatural powers. One was the power of changing themselves into animals. This power seems to have been credited to witches in almost all countries; it accounts for the legends of werewolves. In England the hare was usually the chosen form, and even to-day there are country people who consider it most unlucky for a hare to cross their paths.

"Could I help it if the hare crossed my path? Could I help it?" cried Prue Sarn's mother sadly. She knew from the moment she saw the hare that Prue would be born with a hare-lip.

A witch in the form of a hare was safe from the hunter's gun. Only a silver bullet could hurt it.

There is a folk-story about the witch masquerading as a hare—or, occasionally, a fox—that is common all over England and Wales. This is the Herefordshire version:

Some men who were out hunting one day caught sight of a hare and set the hounds on it.

In the excitement of the chase somebody could hear a little boy screaming, "Run, Granny, run, the dogs be arter 'ee."

The hare would have escaped easily only that in going through a hole in the hedge it got caught and took some time to get free. Just as it was escaping one of the foremost hounds bit it on the leg. Then they lost it. There was a cottage near and the men went towards it to see if there was anyone who could tell them which way the hare had gone. There was nobody about the cottage, so one of the men opened the door and looked inside, and there was an old woman bathing a newly made wound in her leg.

Witches, this earlier, to-be-feared kind, were afraid of a whip made either of elder or of mountain ash. It was a common practice to nail an elder branch over the door to keep away witches, and just as common to have a small piece of elder wood let into churns, to prevent witches spoiling the butter.

The one person who could control the actions of witches was a "maister o' witches." This would be a shrewder, and perhaps more popular, member of the fraternity, or sister-hood. A maister o' witches could undo their work, or make them undo it. There was a very famous one who lived years ago somewhere between Hereford and Bromyard and he was in great demand, both for removing spells and for find-ing lost or stolen property. Unfortunately he seems to be forgotten, or only exists as a name. Billy of Dormer was an-other "wise man." "Wise man" or "wise woman" sounds better than "witch" and was in use wherever the person in question was respected. There was a wise woman living at Weobley Marsh many years ago; and, judging by the stories told about him, a Dr Coates, who lived in Hereford a hundred years ago, had magic at his finger-tips.

Witches and wise men (or sorcerers; later they were more commonly known as conjurors) did in the country districts most of the work done to-day by the doctor and the parish nurse; and in minor ailments they were undoubtedly success-ful in a great many cases. They had two methods, or a mix-ture of both. In the first they worked purely through the supernatural; through spells, a few of which have come down to us as "charms," and presumably, if the patient had faith —and nothing seriously wrong with him—he recovered. In the second case curing was done by herbs, or "yarbs." Herbal lore again was of two kinds. One was governed by what is known as the Doctrine of Signatures. This was best expressed in the words of one of its principal practitioners, William Coles, in his *Art of Simpling* (1656.) "Though Sin and Sathan have plunged mankinde into an Ocean of Infirmities, yet the mercy of God, which is over all His workes, maketh grasse to grow upon the Mountaines and Herbes for the use of men, and hath not only stamped upon them a distinct form, but also given them particular Signatures, whereby a man may read, even in legible characters, the use of them."

Briefly, whatever the disease, there is some plant that

shows by its shape, colour, or some other characteristic that it is good for that disease.

Not entirely unmixed with the Doctrine of Signatures, yet having a definitely different basis, was healing by vegetable drugs, known as Herbalism. No doubt if an herbalist were stumped he would turn to the Doctrine of Signatures to help him out, but good herbalists would not need that help very often. They had a wide knowledge of the values of plants as medicine, though there are surprising gaps in their knowledge. Gerard, for instance, dismisses fox-gloves, from which we get digitalin, one of the most important drugs in certain diseases of the heart, "Yet are they of no use, neither have they any place amongst medicines."

Quite likely the cures that appear so ridiculous to the twentieth century had some sort of reason for themselves when they were first used, though tracing these reasons is no longer possible. For instance, a Herefordshire cure for fits was to wear a ring made of a shilling that had been put in the offertory in church. There does not seem any reason why people should believe that, but in the neighbouring county of Radnor people still wear silver rings to prevent nose-bleeding. There may be some connection.

The use of an eel-skin garter as a precaution against cramp has already been mentioned. Eel-skins are used in different ways by people in difficult places. I know a man who swears by them—and uses one if he needs it—to cure sore throats.

The Hand of Glory, the mummified hand of a hanged person, was a powerful talisman in witchcraft; so was a candle made from the fat of a person who had died in this way. The halter with which a man had been hanged was said to cure headache. The rope was placed to soak in water and the sufferer had to drink the water. An unwholesome business, but hardly more unwholesome than gloating over a collection of hangmen's ropes that have been used in actual executions—and I've seen more sophisticated people than " 'Erefurdshire volk" doing that.

For approaching baldness the remedy was much more pleasant and much more picturesque—a wreath of ivy leaves had to be worn, and it was said to be an infallible recipe. In parts of the country adder-skins were used to draw thorns, a remedy of vital importance this in the country, for in the winter when hedging is carried on it is quite common to find hedgers suffering from poisoned fingers, and hands where thorns have gone in and started a festering sore. Hedgers accuse blackthorn of being the worst offenders; they are much more poisonous, they say, than the thorns of any other bush or tree, a statement I can corroborate, for the only trouble I myself (an amateur but enthusiastic hedger) have had after hedging was when a blackthorn spine got in under my wrist-watch strap.

The split-tree cure for rupture has been practised in Herefordshire. The cure is a direct descendant of the Doctrine of Signatures: like cures like. It is mentioned, among other places, in Gilbert White's *History of Selbourne*. The method was to split a young tree down the trunk. The ruptured person was then passed through the cleft. Next the tree was bound together and plastered over. As it grew together— *if* it grew together, and no cure was expected unless it did— so was the rupture supposed to do the same. There was a certain amount of simple ritual, the person—it seems to have been done principally with children—being passed through the tree in the direction of the sun; that is, clockwise. Cures were definitely reported, but perhaps the patient rested in bed until the tree grew together, in which case the tree can hardly claim all the credit. Ash was the tree generally used, and an ash was used at Waterstone, at Thruxton, and at Broxwood. But at Eardisland it was a willow, the only time I have heard of this tree being used. I cannot get at the date when this was last practised in Herefordshire, though I have the details of a successful cure worked in Devonshire as late as 1876.

Herefordshire mothers in many villages—I think Letton was one—hung a bag of live woodlice round their babies' necks to help them get through their teething easily. Rather hard on the woodlice!

As witchcraft toned down and gradually became respectable, the spells became charms, and the art of the charmer is not altogether unknown to-day. The worst of charming, if you want to find out anything about it, is that, like all the best medical practice, it is carried on in secret; and neither patient nor practitioner will talk. To be frank, I don't think I should talk myself if I had an ailment charmed. One must play fair. The only bit of charming I've ever seen was the removal of a particularly obstinate wart (not mine). "I can get rid of that for you," said a woman, and she caught hold of the offending thumb a moment. I don't know what she did or said, but the wart went very soon afterwards. She told me she was the seventh child of her parents. That may have had something to do with it.

There were written charms as well as those to be performed. Here is one from Weobley, typical of the needs of the countryman in that it was to get rid of a thorn.

"At Bethlehem our Saviour Jesus Christ was born, and at Jerusalem was crucified with a cround of thorns and it did neither wrinkel nor swell and I trust in and through the name of our Lord and Saviour this thorn it will go well. In the name of the Father and of the Son and of the Holy Ghost. Amen."

I have come across another cure for one pricked by a thorn, and though it is not from Herefordshire (it is Cornish) it may be found interesting as typifying the need of countrymen of all parts to have some sort of remedy against thorn wounds.

> Happy man that Christ was born,
> He was crownéd with a Thorn;
> He was piercéd through the skin,
> For to let the poison in:
> But his five wounds, so they say,
> Closed before He passed away;
> In with healing, out with Thorn;
> Happy man that Christ was born.

All the thorn cures refer to Christ's Crown of Thorns. And who knows, the psychological effect of one of these charms written on a much-fingered bit of paper, together with a lot of faith, may have saved many an old hedger from a poisoned hand.

Toothache is another ailment that had, understandably, a host of country remedies. With dental surgery at its present height of perfection, little as anyone enjoys using it, we can hardly imagine the terror toothache was to those who suffered from it a century ago. There were tooth-drawers here and there, and no doubt doctors were able to perform extractions. But without an anaesthetic. No wonder people preferred to trust to luck and a charm of some sort.

Herefordshire country-folk used all the popular talismans. A double nut carried in the pocket was supposed to be the best of them, but carrying a potato was a help.

An old notion commonly held was that toothache was caused by a worm gnawing its way out of the tooth. That is the explanation of "the worme shall die" in the following charm against toothache:

"Christ met Peter and said to him, Peter, what is the matter with thee?"

"Peter said, Lorde, I am tormented with the pain in the tooth.

"The Worme shall die and thou shalt live and thou that shalt have this in writing or in memory shall never have the pain in the tooth.

"Therefore believe in the Lorde your God."

Gerard mentions these (supposed) worms when he recommends henbane root for toothache.

"The seed is used by Mountibank tooth-drawers which run about the country, to cause worms to come forth of the teeth, by burning it in a chafing dish of coles, the party holding his mouth over the fume thereof: but some crafty companions to gain mony convey small lute-strings into the water, persuading the patient that those small creepers come out of his mouth or other parts which he intended to ease."

Mistletoe was highly esteemed by the old herbalists, very largely because they never quite understood its growing on other trees in the way it did. It "doth not increase himself of his seed, as some have supposed; but it rather cometh of a certain moisture and substance gathered together upon the boughs and joints of the trees, through the bark whereof this vaporous moisture proceeding, brings forth the Misseltoe."

Naturally, mistletoe, growing, as it does, in nearly every orchard in the county, was made use of in local medicine. Mistletoe tea was good for almost any sickness. The herbalist Johnson says it was made from "a few of the berries of the Misseltoe bruised and strained into oyle and drunken." Taken thus, it cured the stitch. But it was for curing epilepsy that mistletoe was most highly valued, and it was considered potent against any nervous maladies. I have been told it was quite a good general tonic as well.

There was a country method of curing an illness that depended not at all on other people, whether witch or conjuror, but entirely on the patient. This was to drink water from a holy well. On the face of it, it does not seem a method in which one could have as much faith as in those in which something was said or done by somebody else, or perhaps something was given to be swallowed. "A bottle of stuff from the doctor" is as highly respected in the twentieth century as a bottle of something made up by old so-and-so was in any of the centuries that preceded it. But the fact remains that the healing wells of our ancestors were an important factor in their lives, as anything that holds out hope of renewed health must be important to those who feel they have no reason to hope. For the comparatively doctorless ages that have gone there was always, as a last resort, if it had not been resorted to earlier, the well, a drink of whose waters would put an end to suffering and pain.

Wells were the patent medicines of those printless ages.

Now, I have a great respect for healing wells. I was once persuaded to drink of one in a remote country churchyard, and a few days later found a cure for an ailment that had made my life tiresome for years. I have written the story elsewhere and will not repeat it. The water did not cure me. I had no faith in it, nor did I in the least expect the miracle that followed. But I did drink of the well and I did find a cure. It could only have been a silly coincidence, but so far as I am concerned the well may have the credit for the coincidence and my blessings also.

Hereford has lost its three wells, though the site of St Ethelbert's is still there. From this when it was cleaned years ago was taken a large quantity of pins. Pins seem to have been the payment made by people who came to be cured. There must have been a superstition that it was essential or

lucky to throw something in the well and a pin suggested itself as a suitable currency. Kington had its crooked well—
still in existence—and in this it was usual to throw a crooked
pin, hence its name. Whether it was for some particular
reason or just to be different from everyone else is not
known. St Ethelbert's Well, of course, owed its powers to
the victim of Offa's ambition. It was supposed to be especially good for sores and ulcers.

The other two wells in Hereford were St Pippa's Well,
which became shortened to Pipewell, and Bridewell, but both
have disappeared.

Cae Thomas Well (*Cae Thomas* is Thomas's Field) at
Llanveyno was probably a mineral spring like those found
comparatively near at the Central Wales Spas. Its water has
been analyzed and it definitely did have some medicinal
value. But as a rule the dissolved minerals did not matter;
people would go to drink, and then come away and hope and
pray for the best. Spa cures have never been a hobby of cottagers—unless perhaps they lived at the Spa *and* (which is
not always the case) the water happened to be free. No, a
little of the wonderful was worth a lot of mineral. At St
Anne's Well, Aconbury, which still exists, the water would
suddenly bubble up and smoke at midnight on Twelfth
Night. The first bucketful had to be bottled then and there
and it worked wonders for eye troubles. St Peter's Well at
Peterchurch was another one good for bad eyes, and may be
yet, since it is still there. This was also a well where quantities of pins have been found. There were three springs altogether, two for eye troubles and one for rheumatism.

In the Golden Well at Dorstone was caught the fish with
a gold chain round its neck. This is the fish whose representa-
tion in sculpture may be seen in Dorstone Church. Oh happy
angler, to catch such a fish and to have such ecclesiastical
backing for his truthfulness!

Many of the old wells have vanished. A spring does not
necessarily remain a spring for ever. It may become choked
and come out at another spot; it may dry up; or a slight earth
movement may send its waters elsewhere. But Higgins Well
is still at Little Birch, though it once justified people's indignation by turning up in a most inconvenient place.

Higgins, from whom it takes its name, was a churlish fellow who was irritated by the people who came to it, so he had it filled in. That night as he sat by his fireside, no doubt feeling very pleased at what he had done, there was a gurgle and a rush of water and up came the spring at his feet. He did the only thing possible, opened the well again. If he was not pleased he was the only person who wasn't.

Herefordshire was particularly rich in healing wells for I have particulars of fifteen, apart from those mentioned, that have either vanished or of which I have not been able to find any evidence that they are still in being. One of these, Dragons Well at Brinsop, is where St George killed the dragon. It was in a field known as Lower Stanks, a suggestive name because the Radnorshire word for a dam across a stream is a "stank." Laugh Lady Well in Laugh Lady Dingle at Brampton Bryan was another well that bubbled up at certain times, and it was also one of those wells where a pin was dropped in as payment. From near Lady Well at Thornbury there was traditionally an underground passage leading to Thornbury Camp. Sap's Well at Wormesley would cure ulcers if they were dressed with ointment mixed with its water. St Cosmos and St Damien's Well, another that seems to have gone, was good for the eyes, and so was Eye Well at Bromyard.

Heavenly Well at Vowchurch has a lovely name. It was good for anything, and may still be tried. St Margaret's Well at Urishay is another that still offers the sufferer a chance, Walm's Well on the Herefordshire Beacon also, and St Edith's Well at Stoke Edith.

St Edith's Well was the result of a miracle. St Edith was a daughter of King Edgar. She was made Abbess of Wilton when she was only fifteen years old. She died at the age of twenty-three on September 16th, 984, and the annual wake in her honour used to be held on the first Sunday after September 8th. When the church was being built she carried the water for mixing the mortar. The task was too much for her, however, and when she could carry no more she sank to her knees and prayed. In answer to her prayers the water gushed out of the ground at her feet.

One can hardly wonder at many of these old wells vanishing. I suppose wells are out of fashion. But they are not to be laughed at. My young friend who made such fun at my wanting to find a certain well and at my stories of them carries a bent threepenny bit with him wherever he goes, and if you stole it from him I don't believe he'd live twenty-four hours, so great would be his fear of the disaster he would consider inevitable. I remember another sophisticated modern who spent the morning before an examination hunting anxiously for a four-leafed clover. He found the clover but made a shocking mess of the examination.

Farm near Dorstone
Spring in Herefordshire

CHAPTER X

THE DEVIL IN HEREFORDSHIRE

I T I S impossible in the case of old country beliefs and customs to put one's finger on any particular one and say: "This came to an end at such-and-such a time."

The fairies are a case in point.

Once they inhabited the whole of the country, but as invasion followed invasion they retired slowly westwards (where there are still a few if all I am told is true), many crossing the sea to Ireland. It was only natural that some of them should stay along the borders, and Herefordshire had its share.

I know only one person, a woman of intelligence and culture, too, who openly claims to believe that fairies still exist, but I have noticed once or twice that old men who have laughed the notion to scorn have presently gone on to relate something extraordinary that happened to their grandfathers or grandmothers and that was capable of no rational explanation at all—unless, of course, there happened to be fairies in those days.

In Herefordshire the fairies were known as Pharisees, and there is a story told of an old man who, hearing of the Pharisees in the Bible, believed them to be the same creatures. People living around Kenchester, the Roman station of Magna Castra, and not understanding to whom the ruins were due, thought they must be something to do with the fairies.

"Here then," wrote Leland, "yet appear ruins or buildings of the whiche foolish people caull one of the King of Fayres Chayre."

The Roman coins, often dug up in the neighbourhood, were known as "dwarfs money," and among the ruins where the legions had stood on guard the little folk were supposed to dance on moonlight nights.

Medieval Cottages at Mansel Lacy
14th Century Buildings at Weobley

People had a respect for them, a respect slightly tinged with fear, for they could do mortals harm as well as good, and it was best to keep on the right side of them. In some places—in Foxley, little farther back than living memory—there were people who left their doors unbarred at night and food on the table so that fairies could come in and feast if they were so minded.

Indeed, one of my own vivid childhood memories is of an old woman who lived in a lonely wood in a Pembrokeshire village and she would never on any occasion have her door fastened at night. I went to her cottage often, and have been since she died, though now it has fallen down and the brambles have taken possession. Looking back, I have no doubt at all it was on account of the fairies that she would have no truck with keys or bars.

It was not everyone who could see fairies. According to some authorities, nobody could see them unless they had a certain ointment, which, applied to one eye, gave the necessary power of vision.

The existence of this ointment was apparently known in Herefordshire, but the recipe, so far as I can find, has been long forgotten. Strangely enough, I already knew it, though I have not gone to the trouble of trying it. It dates from about 1600.

"A pint of sallet-oyle, and put it into a vial-glasse; but first wash it with rose-water and marygolde water; the flowers to be gathered towards the East. Wash it till the oyle becomes white; then put it into the glasse, and then put thereto the budds of hollyhocke, the flowers of marygolde, the flowers or toppes of wild thime, the budds of young hazle, and the thime must be gathered neare the side of a hill where fayries use to be; and take the grasse of a fayrie throne; then all these put into the oyle into the glasse, and settle it to dissolve three dayes in the sunne; and then keep it for thy use."

Perfectly straightforward, you will observe. Unless you didn't happen to know "where fayries use to be." No particular difficulty about that. Try Kenchester for a start.

Fairies do not like being visible to mortals. Few people

get further than hearing their bell-like voices and their silvery laughter—few ever get as far. Anyone who saw fairies was wise if he kept the fact to himself. Once they found out, one of them would be asking with disarming friendliness:

"Which eye do you see me with?"

"This one."

And the next thing would be a quick stab with a bulrush and the loss of an eye.

Fairies had an unpleasant habit of stealing mortal babies and putting changelings in their places. These changelings were a trial, lacking the tractable and docile temperaments of human children. Fortunately, once suspected, they were easy to identify. All the worried mother had to do was to brew beer in an egg-shell, within sight of the suspected child. The changeling's curiosity was never proof against this.

"I am old," it would say, "ever so old, but never did I see anyone brew beer in an egg-shell before."

That gave the show away and the mother would "go for it." The changeling would run away and presently the mortal child would be returned.

I have sometimes wondered if the dislike for, and cruel treatment often given to, cretins and the mentally deficient in other times were caused by the widely believed stories of changelings.

At Aymestrey in older days there was a wood called Poke-house Wood (Puck's House Wood) inhabited by Puck. One dark night a man venturing to try to find his way home through the wood was misled by the fairy and tormented until daylight. He never forgot the experience and when he died left a piece of land, the rent of which was to pay a man to ring one of the church bells for a certain time every night in order to point the way to travellers led astray in the wood.

They no longer ring the bell in Aymestrey to lead travellers out of the fairy's clutches, but there is still in the north-east corner of the bell-ringing room a hole for the rope of the bell that was rung nightly to outwit the Pharisees.

Folk-tales have a habit of turning up in slightly varying forms in different countries, in different parts of the same country, even in different parts of one county. The stories of the Mermaid of Marden and the bell, Great Tom of Kentsham, for instance, have quite a lot in common.

The Mermaid of Marden must have had her home in the River Lugg. There she had charge of a bell that by rights should have been in the church. Only in one way could the people of Marden get the bell from her. They must attach a rope to it, and the rope must be yoked to twelve white heifers, and they would be able to pull it out of the river. But while this was going on nobody must say a word.

The method was followed, the rope fastened to the bell, and the heifers began to pull. It was a mighty tug-of-war, for the mermaid had magic to aid her. But it was not good enough magic for twelve white heifers. Slowly they began to strain forward, the bell to move. When it came as far as the bank one of the teamsmen could contain his excitement no longer. " 'Tis coming, 'tis coming," he cried, and his voice broke the spell. The rope parted and the bell rolled back into the water.

Very similar is the story of Great Tom of Kentsham, only in this case it was being brought by sea, giving endless trouble, and it was an oath sworn by the captain of the ship that caused the bell to fall overboard.

The story has also an obvious relationship with similar ones in other countries. The details are almost those of the return of Eurydice from Hades and that one fatal, backward glance of Orpheus.

Fairy-stories, of course, yet there must have been some tradition of a lost bell at Marden. In 1848 one was found there in a pond, said to be the place where Ethelbert of East Anglia was buried before his body was taken to Hereford. The bell is now in the Hereford museum. It was probably a *bangu,* a bell once kept in all Welsh churches for announcing deaths.

In olden days the church bell was of great importance to the country people. When rung at some set hour, like the curfew, or the five o'clock morning bell at Kington, it was often their only way of telling the time, and when they died it welcomed them sadly along their last earthly journey,[1] and showed, by the manner of tolling, their age and whether it were man or woman.

Folk-stories in which animals talk and generally behave as human beings do have always been popular in the country. Herefordshire has an example from the Longtown district in which two crows betrayed murderers, two brothers who had killed a shepherd and buried his body. They were overheard talking about the murder they had watched, and discussing the improbability of the body ever being found as it had been buried so well and so secretly.

But John o' Kent (Kentchurch) is Herefordshire's own property. Undoubtedly he did once exist, but who he really was nobody knows for sure. Some say he was Owen Glyndwr, shorn of his glory and his armies, but with his magic powers unimpaired. Some say he was Sion Cent, the Welsh poet; others profess to believe he was Sir John Oldcastle, Herefordshire's Lollard martyr. He may quite easily have been none of these, but just John o' Kentchurch.

He had a great appetite for playing tricks; simple, homely, countryman's tricks. But they never failed; astonishingly, because the person he nearly always played them on was the devil.

They built a bridge over the Monnow once, or rather John o' Kent started, and had to call the devil in to help because what John built in the daytime fell down in the night. The devil's price for his help was that he should have the first passenger to pass over the bridge when it was finished. John agreed and then, the moment the bridge was completed, threw across it a bone that he had kept in his pocket and a hungry dog standing by darted after it.

Another time John and the devil went to market to buy pigs.

"How are we going to divide them?" asked John.

"Oh, I'll take the ones with straight tails," said the devil.

"Agreed," said John, and then as soon as they had decided which pigs they would buy he gave them a good feed of beans. As a result of this all their tails curled beautifully

[1] At Ocle Pychard all the bells are chimed when the funeral procession comes in sight of the church, a custom known as "ringing him home."

by the time they came to drive them home, and the devil had none for his share.

Next time he thought he'd do better.

"I'll have the ones with curly tails this time," he said.

"Suits me," said John, and got the lot together and drove them all through water and their little tails stood out like ramrods because they were cold and wet. The devil came off worse again.

He always did. He never seems to have learned anything. He went into partnership with John o' Kent on a farm once.

"What part of the crops d'you want?" asked John. "Tops or butts?"

"I'll have the butts," said the devil, so John sowed the farm down to wheat, had all the grain for himself, and the devil got only straw.

"Now then, tops or butts?" demanded John when the time for sowing came round.

The devil wasn't going to be caught again.

"Tops," he said promptly.

John sowed turnips this time, with the result that he collected the roots and the devil had the leaves.

When haymaking time came John went out in the night and planted harrow tines in the part of the field the devil was having for his share. As the devil was mowing next day he kept notching his scythe on the tines and John told him the stuff wasn't worth the trouble of cutting because it had burdocks in it. In this way he was again able to get most of the crop for himself.

At last they came to threshing (perhaps a year when the devil had managed to harvest a bit of grain).

"Tops or bottoms?" asked John.

"Tops," said the devil.

John arranged hurdles for them to thresh on; the corn (John's share) fell through to the floor and the devil's share was straw.

Perhaps the devil, who doesn't seem to have been a very intelligent fellow, depended on the proverb that he who laughs last laughs best. But he really should have had more sense; one is almost tempted to feel sorry for him at times. Even in dying John o' Kent cheated him. He sold him his soul whether he were buried in or out of church. So he had himself buried in the church wall and won the last round. Perhaps the devil got John's liver and lights—if they were any consolation for losing his soul—for those organs, when he was dead, were to be put on some spikes on Grosmont Church. But I think it must have been a last gesture of defiance.

The devil seems to have had a fancy for Herefordshire. Whether the company suited him, or whether the people were so good he just had to try for one here and there, like an angler will try for the fish he knows he hasn't a chance of landing, is not clear, but there is hardly a parish where he hasn't played his pranks at one time or another.

All his playfellows hadn't the mother-wit of John o' Kent, either. At Stoke Edith, a friar saw him in a wood disguised as a badger, and, according to the story, the badger ran away with the friar.

At Kington a dissolute tailor made a suit for the devil, but at the last moment he saw his danger and refused to take any payment. The fright did him good for he repented of his bad ways and was a model of good behaviour afterwards as long as he lived.

A man called Jack of France was on his way home one night. It was the Eve of All Souls and he had to pass Dorstone Church. He could hear something going on in the church, so he went into the church porch and peeped through the keyhole. There was the devil, in the church, reading out the names of the people who were to die during the coming year, and one of the names John heard was his own. He had been rather a bad character and he tried reforming his ways, but it was too late. He died even as he had heard he would.

Weobley was a place where, if you were so minded, you could see the devil. At midnight you had to walk slowly seven times round the preaching cross in the churchyard, saying the Lord's Prayer backwards. At the end of this performance the devil would appear.

He turned up on one occasion at Weobley, when his presence was probably most unwelcome. The schoolboys there in their master's absence got hold of his books and, finding in one of them a method of raising the devil, decided to try it. To their surprise it worked. They raised the devil, and, incidentally, a commotion as well. They had, as amateur practitioners are apt to do, omitted to discover, before raising him, a method to lay him. Eventually the master returned and got rid of the visitor. We aren't told, but probably the master then raised the devil again. But rather differently.

You could see the devil at Stoke Edith also, only there it was round the church one had to go seven times, and then he could be seen on looking through the keyhole in the church door.

The Demon of Burton appears to have been not the head of the faculty but lesser fry. It was a poltergeist, the sort that amuses itself by throwing furniture about, and haunted a farm in Burton, in Weobley Parish, about the end of the seventeenth century.

Even Hereford Cathedral was liable to invasion. A devil, if not the devil, paid it a visit about the year 1290.

"An unheard of and almost impossible marvel occurred in the Cathedral Church of the Hereford Canons. There a demon in the robe of a canon sat in a stall after matins had been sung. A canon came up to him and asked his reason for being there, thinking the demon was a brother canon. The latter refused to answer and said nothing. The Canon was terrified, but believing the demon to be an evil spirit put his trust in the Lord and bade him in the name of Christ and St Thomas de Cantilupe not to stir from that place. For a short time he bravely awaited speech. He at last went for help and beat the demon and put him in fetters. He now lies in the prison of the aforesaid St Thomas de Cantilupe."

Rather a vulnerable devil. If only those of the twentieth century could be handled as easily!

Perhaps the devil still pays a visit to the county, on one day of the year, at least.

Sir Robert Harley of Brampton Bryan was one of the few Herefordshire gentlemen of importance to be on the Parliamentary side during the Civil War.

Brampton Bryan took its name from Brian de Bramton, but the last Bramton, Margaret, had married a Harley in

1308. A castle was built—there are still the ruins of it—and here was born later Robert Harley, first Earl of Oxford, whose collection of papers, the Harleian Manuscripts, are in the British Museum, and who gave his name to Harley Street.

Brampton Bryan Castle was of some strategic importance by being on one of the roads into Wales. At the beginning of the war Sir Robert was in London, and not able to leave. In charge of the castle was his third wife, Lady Brilliana, a woman of spirit and courage. In 1643, from July 26th until September, Lady Harley defended the castle against a siege by Royalist forces under Sir William Vavasour and Colonel Lingen. She not only opposed the King's forces, she beat them, and they had to withdraw. Unfortunately the strain of defending the castle was too much for her health and very shortly afterwards she died. The siege was renewed in the spring of 1644 and in the end was surrendered to Sir Michael Woodhouse.

Sir Robert Harley was one of those who opposed the execution of Charles I and on this question he quarrelled violently with Oliver Cromwell. At Cromwell's death the devil, to spite the Harleys, dragged him through Brampton Bryan Park. And ever since, on one day in the year the devil rushes through the park, though whether he still takes Oliver Cromwell with him is questionable. Sir Robert saw the beginning of this annual trip. He wrote, "I wish the devil had taken him any other way than through my park, for not content with doing me all the mischief he could when alive, he has knocked over some of my finest trees in his progress downwards."

Here and there in Herefordshire are found stones, or groups of stones that evidently were put in place by the hand of man countless ages ago. The most famous is Arthur's Stone, a cromlech, near Dorstone in the Golden Valley. It is the only cromlech in the county, and this is rather strange, for in the Welsh hills so near at hand are many carns or garns, mounds and tumps. It makes one wonder if the chieftains of the Stone Age, for only important chieftains would merit such lasting graves, lifted up their eyes to the hills when they thought of death, and had their remains taken to them for burial. Or perhaps the people "down-country" were less respectful to the resting places of their remote ancestors than were the hill-men. And on the hills the cromlechs and carns are lonely and often not very accessible.

Arthur's Stone is, traditionally, the grave of King Arthur, another link between him and Herefordshire, since it was St Dubricius who crowned him, and one of the most important Knights of his Round Table was Brian Vraich-Vras (Strong Arm), a chieftain of Cradock.

The Wergin Stone, between Hereford and Bodenham, is said to have been used for an annual ceremonial payment of money. The Hoarstone, Delamere, has marks on it that are supposed to be the footprints of stolen horses, by which they were traced; while Colwall Stone was even more wonderful as an old story says that it turns round in the night when the clock strikes twelve.

Another of these stones is the Whetstone, on Hergest Ridge at Kington. The name may have originally been Wheatstone and have had something to do with the sale of that grain.

What is interesting is the fact that all these old landmarks seem to have been on very old routes, or trading roads, or, as they are sometimes called, leys. Apparently, the Ancient Britons (to use a rather loose term for pre-Roman inhabitants) made their tracks between important points as straight as they could. Local tracks, in hilly country at any rate, would probably follow the line of least resistance, perhaps paths made originally by animals in search of pasture or of water, and so would grow the winding lanes. But the trade routes, to fetch a commodity that could only be obtained at a distance, were made as short as possible, and the old stones, like the Wergin Stone and the Whetstone were used as sighting marks in getting the line of a ley. Certainly the stones always seem to be on a straight line between important points, and in the hills, where the carns are more common, it is not unusual to be able to line up quite a number of them. It was suggested to me that *delay* was the fate of one who strayed from the straight, and doubtless often narrow, path, but I can find no etymological justification for that claim.

Two old Herefordshire customs were concerned with the laws of inheritance.

The first concerned the city itself. In Hereford citizens were entitled to leave property "so that they be of such an age and no less that they know how to measure a yard of cloth and to know and tell twelve pence."

Ultimogeniture or Borough English, whereby inheritance was by the youngest son (instead of the first, as in primogeniture, or division, as in gavelkind), was the rule in four Herefordshire manors: Barton and Tupsley, Hampton Bishop, Homer and Shelwick, and Ledbury.

There were a number of interesting heriots and peppercorn rents in Herefordshire. In its original sense (from an Old English root) the word heriot meant the rendering to the lord of the manor a payment, usually the best live beast or the best chattel, by a tenant's heirs on that tenant's death. The peppercorn rent, in many cases, was a rose.

The Hereford family (from which came that Nicholas de Hereford who said Samson's mother should drink no cider) held land in the manor of Mordiford by the payment of a pair of gold spurs on any occasion when the King of England should ride over Mordiford Bridge. In 1304 this was changed to an annual rent of a pair of gilt spurs of the value of six pennies. They had to be paid at Michaelmas. But prices rose even in those days. By 1387 the value of the spurs had risen to three and fourpence.

A rose was what Thomas Gelons paid in the sixteenth century to Isabel Gardiner, Prioress of the convent of Aconbury for a stable in Hereford. He was a citizen and mercer to the convent, and he paid his rent—a red rose at that—on the Feast of St John the Baptist. For this pleasant fee he had a lease for ninety-nine years.

It seems a trifling business, this payment of a rose, but no doubt it was a way of rewarding a service by allowing the use of land or buildings and, at the same time, keeping them in the possession of the original owner.

Thomas Walwyn of Much Marcle had to keep an eye on his roses for he had to deliver one—also payable on the Nativity of St John the Baptist—for messuages he held at Ledbury of the Bishops of Hereford.

In the reigns of Edward III and Richard II seventeen acres of land at Marden were let in return for a slight, if peculiar, fee, the carrying of a cord to measure the site of any castle in the Marches which the Crown might be thinking of rebuilding.

Domesday Survey records that the only service payable by the tenants of the Manor of Kington was to carry game from the King's forest at Treville, which is near Kington, to Hereford.

At Tupsley also the tenants had a service to perform. Tupsley was part of the episcopal manor of Hampton Bishop, and they had to put in two days' work every week in the harvest season, weeding the lord of the manor's corn, mowing, making hay, and carrying it. For this they were paid by the Bishop a halfpenny farthing.

The Manor of Chabnor was held by Thomas de Chabbenour in Edward I's reign in return for the service of one man with bow and arrow at the Bridge of Clifford.

John de la Hay, in the reign of Edward IV, held of William Barneby, Lord of Laysters, "a parcel of land, rendering therefor 20d a year and a goose fit for the Lord's dinner in Michaelmas."

It was not only the greater nobles who collected these dues. The Rector of Eaton Bishop used to have a claim to the right shoulder of every calf killed by any of his parishioners in his own house, or of his own breed. The Rector of Leominster, in return for officiating at the chapels of ease at Stoke and Dockelow, was entitled to Trug Wheat, a trug being a twelfth of a horse-load of corn. The name trug for a large garden basket may well have come from this word.

The heriots in the Manor of Kingsland were either the two best beasts in the tenant's possession or the best chattel or jewel in his house at the time of his death. As late as 1716 there is an entry in the court rolls stating that the bailiff of the lord of the manor had seized one black and one brindled bull on the death of a certain tenant.

In the Manor of Orleton the heriot was the best chattel within or without the manor.

The lord of the Manor of Pencomb had the privilege of claiming a pair of gilt spurs from the estate of any Mayor of

Hereford who died in office, and on one occasion at least the claim was made and settled.

All along the Marches from time immemorial there have been parish wakes or feasts. Usually they were held on the festival of the patron saint of the parish church. Here was one day in the year when the humblest village came into prominence. Visits were paid, games were played, children who had left home to seek work or their fortunes, if they had not strayed too far away, came home to see their parents and their friends.

Perhaps St Augustine had something to do with the establishment of the wakes. Something, but not, I think, very much. His instructions from Pope Gregory were to utilize the pagan customs he would meet and turn them into Christian channels. But along the Border of Wales and England people were already Christians. Yet the heathen Saxons can hardly have given him a worse headache than the British bishops he came to meet, as many claim, in Herefordshire, and at which a Bishop of Hereford was present. (Augustine's oak, where they met, was still standing in 1753.) It was the English of whom the missionary had had such bad accounts in southern Gaul that he had sent messengers back to Rome for permission to give up the whole project. He must have wondered when he met the leaders of the Celtic church (it *may* have been at Aust in Gloucestershire) why he had heard nothing of these stormy petrels. If he suggested turning any heathen customs to better use he would have had a shock. The men of the west were proud of their established Christianity and would have answered stonily that they had no heathen ways to make use of. But it was over the question of fixing Easter that the conference broke down (as conferences do have a way of breaking down), so that for years some people were joyfully celebrating the Resurrection while others of their countrymen were still in the solemnities of Lent.

The wakes went on right through the summer months, and lasted into the autumn. At fairs one may still be pelted with confetti, or perhaps hit by a soft paper ball stuffed with sawdust which returns on a strip of elastic to the thrower

when it has done its duty. Our forefathers were more lusty
—and they had no elastic. A man must have something to
throw when he is enjoying himself, and if he has somebody
to throw at so much the better. What, in Herefordshire,
could be more appropriate than apples? Crab wakes, they
were called in the Golden Valley, and they had them over
the Border in Wales, and in Shropshire as well, and many a
labourer on wake day must have gone into the orchard, or,
if the apples were gathered, to the hedges, for crabs, to
stuff his pocket with windfalls to throw at the girl of his
choice. Love expresses itself in queer ways, but a clout on
the side of the head with a hard little apple couldn't very
well be ignored.

So next time a sawdust ball hits you on the ear as part of
the fun of the fair think of the crab wakes of Herefordshire
where such pleasantries originated and be thankful it is not
something harder.

In a county where apples were such an important crop it
is no wonder that they attained almost the importance of
corn. For fallen corn the poor people went gleaning—
though along the Marches, and far back into Wales, it was
known as leasing. There was, to follow the leasing, Gooding
Day, St Thomas's Day, December 21st, when good-hearted
farmers gave a quartern of corn to each leaser who asked
for it to add to her leasings. The apples were treated with a
similar respect (though there was no Gooding Day for
apples). Gleaning, or leasing, the small apples that the well-
to-do scorned to pick up was known as grigging, and many
a barrel of good cider must have been made by small cottagers out of their griggings.

Nicholas de Hereford might easily have tripped up, as he
did in Judges, in the Book of Ruth. He did not, though. A
pity.

CHAPTER XI

HEREFORDSHIRE, SHEELD AND SPERE

The propyrte of every Shyre
I shal you telle, and ye will here.
Herefordshire, sheeld and spere.

F o r thousands of years the people here were warriors, not from choice but from necessity. Nobody could have lived on the borders of Wales without learning to handle weapons. Yet nobody, either, could have lived on this fertile soil and not wanted at times to hang up the sword and feel in his two hands the handles of a plough. The men of the hills were shepherds, and shepherding can leave time for fighting; the men of the kindly lowlands were farmers at heart all the time, and they had to make time to defend what they grew and raised. Perhaps the actual words "Taffy was a thief" were not always on their tongue; the thought must have been in their minds.

But for three hundred years the sword has been allowed to rust, and farming instruments have taken on a higher polish. The ordinary man—they were almost all countrymen —was a farmer, a shepherd, a cattle-raiser, ploughman, waggoner, or hedger. If he was not one of these he was a craftsman whose craft was dependent on agriculture: smith, carpenter or wheelwright, a maker or mender of tools, builder or thatcher. In some way, direct or indirect, his living came from the red soil.

And what of the richer men, the men of good or great (not necessarily synonymous) family? The men of leisure and culture?

There were plenty of these in a land so fertile of everything. But on the whole, just as the county itself tagged along on the margins of history rather than tumbling uncomfortably in it, so its best-known men and women played their parts without often taking the lead. They were of the play, but not the principal actors.

It is one of those things impossible to state with absolute certainty, but so far as one is able to judge, the history of England would hardly have been widely different from what it has been if the Herefordshire actors had sulked at never having the leading parts, and had stayed at home. There is no Nelson here, no Shakespeare or Milton, no Wellington or Marlborough, no Oliver Cromwell, no Queen Elizabeth, no . . .

But wait a minute. Queen Elizabeth. Perhaps . . . perhaps one man did alter history. If he had not acted as he did things might have been very different.

When the French took Calais from us, one of their prisoners was William, Lord Grey of Wilton. In the pleasant manner of the time they told him that it would be no compliment to fix his ransom at anything less than twenty thousand marks. A Herefordshire gentleman was perhaps worth more, but at twenty thousand they left it.

Now twenty thousand marks do not grow on gooseberry bushes. If they did, Lord Grey knew of no such garden. Something would have to be sold. And, looking round, he decided that his Manor of Peterstow in the county of Hereford would have to go.

He found a purchaser in his own nephew, Charles Brydges, the second son of Lord Chandos. And he was the man, perhaps—no, almost inevitably—to whom is due the fact that our history books are written as they are and not entirely differently. He had been Deputy Lieutenant of the Tower of London and to him had been brought King Philip's warrant for the execution of his young sister-in-law, the Princess Elizabeth. Brydges would have none of it. He might have been a time-server, anxious to ingratiate himself with the Queen's husband; he might have been a servile fellow who would take orders from a Spaniard; he could have seen the young lady safely out of English history. But he was not servile and he would not have any execution without very much better authority. So the Princess lived to become Queen. And, whatever her faults, the English story without Queen Elizabeth is unimaginable.

164

The Post Office at Perrystone Hill
Vowchurch

If Lord Grey of Wilton had to leave good English money in France it was only tit for tat.

Rowland Leinthall was a man of not particularly distinguished lineage, but being a favourite of Henry IV, holding the post of Yeoman of the Robes, he presently married the King's cousin and gained for himself the position his ancestors had not left for him, and good lands into the bargain, some of them in Herefordshire. By 1415 Henry IV was dead and Henry V on his way to France, Leinthall going with him. The share of the army he provided consisted of a retinue of eight lances and thirty-three archers. And the archers from the Border were the best in Christendom. They could shoot an arrow through a three-inch board, and one of their favourite pastimes was to shoot a horseman through the thigh, pinning him to his horse. Presently there was Agincourt and in time Rowland Leinthall came home (and, I hope, his eight lances and his thirty-three bowmen also to tell in Leominster alehouses the stories of their doings). With him he brought good French gold, the ransom of the many well-born prisoners he had taken at Agincourt. He had been knighted for his share in the battle, and presently he built his mansion of Hampton Court.

There are always ploughmen, but great families come and go. By the sixteenth century Hampton Court belonged to the Coningsbys—and it no longer belongs even to them—who bought it from Rowland Leinthall's great-grandson, Baron Burford.

Sir Thomas Coningsby was at the siege of Rouen in 1591. He founded Coningsby Hospital at Hereford "in thankfulness to God for His defence and protection as well in travel by sea and land as also against malice and practice at home." He bought the hospital of St John (which order had been suppressed in 1540) for his almshouse, which was for "a decameron of decayed soldiers or sailors and servants, under a corporal, and a chaplain, the Vicar of Bodenham," and they were to be known as "Coningsby's Company of Old Servitors."

This Coningsby was said to be a great humourist and he was something of an eccentric in dress as well—his decayed soldiers were for a long time dressed out in red, by the way

Cross commemorating death of 315 people of the Plague, Ross Churchyard
A Herefordshire thatched cottage

—and he was the model on which Ben Jonson based his fantastic knightly character, Puntarvolo, in *Every Man Out of His Humour*—a character he loved to recognize as himself when he saw it played.

His son, FitzWilliam Coningsby, defended Hereford for the Royalist cause, and, like many of King Charles's followers, suffered great losses.

A later member of the family, Thomas Coningsby, saved William III's life at the Battle of the Boyne, staunching with his handkerchief the blood from a wound the King took. The handkerchief became an heirloom in the family of the Earls of Essex.

This Thomas was a queer customer. In many ways a fine character, he indulged in quarrels and lawsuits and at one time was imprisoned in the Tower of London.

Not all Herefordshire men like to be reminded of their kinship with the not-always-reputable, wild Welshmen, though the influence worked both ways and Radnor lost its Welsh tongue two hundred years ago. But the Border is fixed, Hereford is English and proud of it, and for hundreds of years they and the Welsh fought on opposite sides and cut each other's throats with the best will in the world.

One of the Coningsbys, however, knew what was good in Wales. It is not often you hear a Welsh harpist nowadays, more's the pity. But there is an account of a party at Hampton Court: "We were entertained by my Lord Coningsby at his seat at Hampton Court. At dinner time one of the ancient bards in an adjacent room played to us upon the harp and at proper intervals threw in many notes of his voice with a swelling thrill after a surprising manner much after the tone of a flute."

This is the Coningsby whose heir, by his second wife, was choked by a cherry stone and died at Hampton Court. He is buried at Hope, nearby. Coningsby erected as a memorial a monument showing the child with a cherry in his mouth and blood on his cheek, a grim reminder of the tragedy and hardly the sort one would have expected. But eccentricity seems to have run in his veins.

Next to Coningsby Hospital the Bargate Almshouses in Leominster are probably the best known in the county. Those

four almshouses were erected in 1736 by Hester Clark, not
altogether wisely, for in building them she was doing what
country people call "giving the loaf and keeping the crust."
In other words, she could not afford it, and as a reminder
there is over them a figure of a man holding a hatchet in his
hand, and under it this couplet:

> He that gives away all before he is dead
> Let 'em take this hatchet and knock him on ye head.

One of the Conqueror's followers who came to Herefordshire was Ralph de Toni, who had been the standard bearer
to the King at the Battle of Hastings, but, apart from found-
ing a Benedictine cell at Monkland, which was attached to a
Normandy abbey, he left little impression.

Another of William's knights to come here was William
FitzOsbern, who was made Earl of Hereford. To him was
given Ewyas Harold and he surely deserved it, for he had
supplied no less than sixty ships for the invasion. When the
King went to Normandy he was left joint ruler, with Queen
Matilda, of England. He was killed in Normandy where he
had been sent to help Matilda govern the country.

The Normans who did make themselves felt in the
Marches were the Mortimers. These, perhaps more than any
other Herefordshire family, truly had a lively finger in the
historical pie.

The first to come was Ralph de Mortimer, and for his
subjection of Edric the Saxon the King made him grants of
land around Wigmore. For the next four hundred years
Herefordshire and the neighbouring counties had to reckon
with the Mortimers. Wigmore became their headquarters.
It is quiet enough to-day, yet in its time men-at-arms came
riding to its castle. There were monks and abbots at Wigmore Abbey, which was built by a knight called Bernard for
Oliver de Merlymond, seneschal to "that valiant knight
Hugh de Mortimer," while de Merlymond was on a pil-
grimage to the shrine of St James at Compostella. There
were visits from knights and nobles and lovely women; there
were plotting and scheming.

Hugh de Mortimer from his castle here defied Henry II.

Here came Prince Edward after Roger de Mortimer had rescued him from Simon de Montfort.

All dust. The castle a ruin; the abbey gone. In November 1538, Abbot Skypp and his ten monks surrendered Wigmore Abbey to the King's Commissioners, the bells were taken away to be sold for their metal, and the buildings began to fall into decay, helped, no doubt, by any farmer who wanted building stone. "Back to the land." Perhaps, after all, it was poetic justice that made buildings and barns of the tumbling ruins where eleven Mortimers were buried.

Blount records that "among the outbuildings contiguous to the highway leading from Leintwardine to Wigmore town there is an alehouse which they say was heretofore the Abbey prison for malefactors."

About five miles from the place his family had dominated for so long the last great Mortimer, Edward, met his enemies at the Battle of Mortimer's Cross.

There is a memorial stone, erected in 1799, on the site of the battlefield which summarizes all that happened.

"This pedestal is erected to perpetrate the Memory of an obstinate, bloody and decisive battle fought near this spot in the civil Wars between the ambitious Houses of York and Lancaster on the 2nd day of February 1460 between the Forces of Edward Mortimer, Earl of March (afterwards Edward the Fourth) on the Side of York and those of Henry the Sixth on the Side of Lancaster.

"The King's Troops were commanded by Jasper, Earl of Pembroke. Edward commanded his own in Person and was victorious. The Slaughter was great on both Sides, four Thousand being left dead on the Field and many Welsh Persons of the first distinction were taken Prisoners. Among whom was Owen Tudor (Great Grandfather to Henry the Eighth and a Descendant of the illustrious Cadwallader) who was afterwards beheaded at Hereford.

"This was the decisive Battle which fixed Edward the Fourth on the Throne of England who was proclaimed King in London on the fifth of March following."

On the morning of the battle the Yorkists observed a natural phenomenon known as parhelion or mock sun, a spot on the solar halo at which light is intensified. Three suns they saw and they took it for a good omen. But did not the Lancastrians see it too? And was it such a good omen after all? The Mortimers had climbed to their zenith. From this time they declined, and their name causes no man in the Marches to tremble any more.

The only Mortimer I ever knew was a farmer, and a happier man, I warrant, than any of his great ancestors.

Two other battles, as cruel and as bloody, were fought in the district, one in the county, and the other, in which Herefordshire men fought, and suffered heavy loss, just outside it.

Pencoyd, a Welsh name meaning Head of the Wood, was the first. According to the Harleian Manuscripts, the Battle of Pencoyd was fought in the time of King Ethelred when the Mercians, who had come as far as the Wye, tried to extend their conquests over the river.

The other was fought just over the Border at Pilleth in Radnorshire. Here in 1401 a Welsh army under Rhys Gethin (the Terrible), Glyndwr's lieutenant, defeated Edmund Mortimer (uncle of the Mortimer who was to win Mortimer's Cross), the larger part of whose forces were the men of Hereford. Eleven hundred of them were slain. What happened to them and to their enemies who fell with them we may guess from an occurrence hundreds of years later. At Pilleth there was always a great mound marking the site of the battle. For years it remained untouched and then an ambitious farmer decided that he would plough some of it. But when he took the plough over it he could not go on for the multitude of human bones he turned up. The mound was the graveyard of the Battle of Pilleth. Trees were planted on it and so it remains. This was the battle reported to Henry IV:

> There came
> A post from Wales loaden with heavy news;
> Whose worst was, that the noble Mortimer,
> Leading the men of Herefordshire to fight
> Against the irregular and wild Glendower
> Was by the rude hands of that wild Welshman taken,
> A thousand of his people butchered.

Mortimer was captured in this battle and presently he married one of Glyndwr's daughters.

the great magician, damn'd Glendower,
Whose daughter, as we hear, the Earl of March
Hath lately married.

But whether it is true, as Shakespeare made him say, "My wife can speak no English, I no Welsh," one may take leave to doubt, for Glyndwr was an English gentleman before ever he was a Welsh leader—"For I was trained up in the English Court."

Glyndwr was not a Herefordshire man, yet his story touches the county heavily—eleven hundred local men dead in one battle! How many limped home maimed and broken? And Pilleth was not all. For ten years there was always the fear that the Welsh magician, a master of swift military movement, was on his way. And more than once he came, as Leominster well knew. Where Glyndwr went he destroyed, even in Wales. A wiser man could have made better use of his victories. That he was a patriot there is little doubt, but for all his vaunted powers he was as little foreseeing as a mole.

Two more of his daughters married Herefordshire squires, one a Scudamore and the other a Croft, and, according to tradition, it was in Herefordshire that he ended his days, deserted, a Samson shorn of his strength—and without a Gaza to die in. Monnington-on-Wye is said to have been his refuge, and for hundreds of years there was a stone in the churchyard (and still is) under which he was supposedly buried. It was opened in the last century, but of Glyndwr relics there were none. Hardly surprising, for Monnington-on-Wye in his day was the property of the anti-Welsh Audleys, and it was at Monnington Straddel, just outside the Golden Valley, where lived the Scudamores, and his daughter who had married one of them.

To mention one battle brings others to mind, and it is probably in consequence of a battle fought in Herefordshire that the legend grew up that St Paul once visited this country. I want to interfere with nobody's favourite stories. If people can believe that Alfred burned the cakes, or that Canute sat wetting his feet at the edge of the sea, or that our Mercian lady, Godiva, rode naked through the streets of Coventry,

170

all honour to them! Those who begin by believing little end by believing nothing. But there is no evidence that St Paul ever came here.

What did happen was that the Silures—and the Hereford men were of those—under their leader Caractacus, being slowly driven back by the Romans from the line of the Malverns, stood and fought Ostorious and his legions (if Tacitus was right) at Coxwall Knoll near Brampton Bryan. The legions won; most of the Herefordshire as we now know it ceased to be a part of Siluria, and the British leader was taken prisoner and, with members of his family, was sent to Rome. Whatever part Caractacus played in a Roman triumph, he was eventually treated well, and his daughter Gladys, later known as Claudia, became the wife of a Roman Senator, Pudens Pudentinus. Claudia and her husband Pudens were both well-known to St Paul. *Eubulus greeteth thee and Pudeus and Linus and Claudia, and all the brethren.*

Is it a very wild guess to imagine that at some time Claudia talked to the Apostle of her home, of the wild dark frowning hills of Radnor, the pleasant Wye, and the green pastures of Herefordshire?

St Paul, of course, was not the only one of the first Christians said to have made the journey to England. Joseph of Arimathea came to Glastonbury, and on his arrival there on Christmas Day thrust his staff into the ground, whereupon it miraculously took root and burst into flower. And from that staff all trees of the Glastonbury thorn are descended. Nowadays anyone may plant a tree of *Crataegus praecox* and in a mild season have flowers on it right through the winter. (It usually flowers again in the summer.) Herefordshire, with its kindly winter, was just the place for the holy thorn to flourish, and years ago when it was more rare, though one can hardly call it common to-day, people used to walk miles at Christmas to see it in flower at places where it grew. Eaton Bishop was one of these places, but there were many in the county.

As the Mortimers dominated the district for hundreds of years after the Conquest, so did the family of Scudamore come into prominence from the sixteenth century onwards.

The two families had this in common: that they were originally enriched by gifts of property that did not belong to
the givers.

John Scudamore, Esquire of the Body to Henry VIII, was
made Receiver (or surveyor) "of divers abbeys within the
county of Hereford, and others appointed to be suppressed."
Occupying that post, it would have been a wonder if he had
not grown richer. He was given grants of confiscated land
and property, and after a time he built Holm Lacy. Holm
Lacy had been the property of the de Lacys, the first of
whom, in England, was William de Lacy, or de Laci, who
had fought like a hero at Hastings. It had passed to the
Scudamores through marriage with a de Lacy heiress in the
fifteenth century, but it was John Scudamore, and monastery property, that made it the finest house in Herefordshire.

John Scudamore did his work well, and he had his reward,
but I have often wondered if he was ever troubled by conscience or superstitious fears. Not all men who were enriched in that way invariably got happiness from their
wealth. Plenty, of course, took what was going and seemed
to do pretty well for themselves and to the devil with old
wives' tales. But there were others who were uneasy when
misfortune came. It was a superstitious age, and they had
only to look at the example of their master, for Henry VIII,
surely, was the most unhappy man in history.

For the next two generations Scudamore heirs died before
their fathers. John Scudamore's son, William, married
Ursula, daughter of Sir John Parkington, but he died while
his father was still alive; and the estate descended to his,
William's, son John.

This was the Scudamore, devoted courtier of Queen Elizabeth, of whom Spenser, a friend of the family and a visitor
to Holm Lacy, wrote high praise in *The Faerie Queene*.

John Scudamore's eldest son, James, was knighted for his
gallantry at the siege of Calais, but again the family history
repeated itself and he was survived by his father.

James's son, John, was made first a baronet and then a
peer, becoming Viscount Sligo. Did he begin to wonder if
there was a curse on their inheritance? I have never heard it

suggested—curses are for those who believe in curses—but the fact remains that it was he who began to return to the church what had come from the church. He was an intimate friend of Archbishop Laud, and Laud visited him at Holm Lacy once, at least. He is said to have had some prickings of conscience about retaining the church property acquired by old John Scudamore, and he consulted the Bishop of Bath and Wells on the question of restitution and was advised in favour of it.

He began by building, or re-building, on the abbey site, a church at Dore in the Golden Valley. He built a rectory there and endowed it with tithes from his property, and presented ground for a churchyard. The church, complete with seats, a magnificent—some say too magnificent—screen by John Abel, Communion plate, and bells, was dedicated to the Holy Trinity on Palm Sunday, March 22nd, 1634, by the Bishop of St Davids; Wren, Bishop of Hereford, being then chaplain to the King.

Did Lord Scudamore sigh with hopefulness or relief when his new church was finished?

He went on to restore the tithes of the churches at Aconbury, Bosbury, Bredwardine, and Little Birch. He united Bolston and Holm Lacy churches and to Holm Lacy he later left in his will the Communion plate which had by that time been removed during the Civil War. He endowed a church in Gloucestershire (Hempstead) and added to the endowment of that of Leominster. He was liberal, more than liberal, in his help towards the repair of Hereford Cathedral after the war; and, during the Commonwealth, was generous to clergy who had lost their livings, though he himself had suffered great losses in the same cause. Finally, money that he left for the poor in Hereford was used to build and maintain the city schools that still bear his name.

His benefactions are said to have amounted to £50,000.

They served the Stuarts well, the Scudamores. Barnabas, brother of Lord Scudamore, held Mordiford Bridge against the Scots. When Leven started a flanking movement he withdrew to Hereford and held it until relieved by the King. For this he was knighted, but later he had to surrender to Waller and was taken prisoner to London. It was while he was in

London that the King stayed a night at Holm Lacy on September 17th, 1645.

Lord Scudamore's interests were not confined to his county. He was a friend of the Duke of Buckingham and in 1634 was Ambassador to France. It was while he was in Paris that he was able to do John Milton a favour.

"The noble Thomas (sic) Scudamore," wrote Milton (in 1638), "King Charles's Ambassador to whom I carried letters of recommendation received me most courteously at Paris. His lordship gave me a card of introduction to the learned Hugo Grotius at that time Ambassador from the Queen of Sweden to the French Court, whose acquaintance I anxiously desired and to whose house I was accompanied by some of his lordship's friends."

At peace Lord Scudamore was a farmer, as all good Herefordshire men are. He did a lot to help agriculture in the county, and perhaps his most notable achievement was the introduction of the Red Streak Pippin, the best cider-apple then and for many a year afterwards.

> Yet let her to the Red-streak yield, that once
> Was of the sylvan kind, uncivilised,
> Of no regard, 'till Scudamore's skilful hand,
> Improved her, and by courtly discipline
> Taught her the savage nature to forget—
> Hence called the Scudamorean plant, whose wine
> Whoever tastes, let him with grateful heart
> Respect that ancient loyal house.

Not excellent poetry, but the praise was well deserved.

Lord Scudamore, or Viscount Sligo he was by then, died in 1671. If his conscience had once been uneasy over the behaviour of his ancestors surely no man could have done more to make amends.

There was one more misfortune to fall upon the family. James, the third Viscount, "fell from a horse riding hastily to Hereford about some electioneering business which impaired his understanding and at length caused his death."

Fortunately his grandfather was beyond worrying about such affairs.

Sir Robert Harley, who has been mentioned earlier, was as staunch a supporter of the Parliament side in the Civil War as the Scudamores were of the King. He was Member for Herefordshire in Parliament in 1625 and again in 1640. I don't think he could have been very popular with Herefordshire folk. They liked a randy, a bit of merrymaking, a maypole, a morris dance, and their sympathies were with the old religion. Harley was sincere, but his piety was of a sour and austere sort. He was very active about such business as abolishing superstitions in the way of pictures of saints in church windows, and the use of copes, surplices, altars, and crosses, ensuring that Sunday was properly observed and suppressing the games that people enjoyed on that day, for the old-fashioned Sunday is no more than a Victorian crest of a wave. The real old-fashioned Sunday was a holiday and *in it thou shalt do no manner of work* was interpreted freely as an injunction to play as much as you liked, even Sunday fairs being still in fashion in many places.

Sir Robert maintained lecturers, Puritan preachers, to take the place of parsons who had lost their livings, in many of the parishes round his home, and was always ready to help them if they were in trouble with the Courts of High Commission or Star Chamber.

The debt was freely acknowledged after his death in 1658. Thomas Froysell, the "florid preacher of Clun," gave the funeral sermon.

"If other saints are candles, he was a torch. If others are starres, he was a starre of greater magnitude. He made his outward greatnesse but a servant of the exercise of his graces. He was a copy for all great men to transcribe in all descending ages. He was a man of desires: a saint in great letters, famous (I think) throughout the land, one where or other, for his graces. To my knowledge eminent ministers did most eminently praise him. Sir Robert Harley was a sweet name upon their lips."

One of Sir Robert's descendants, Thomas Harley, third son of the Earl of Oxford, was Member of Parliament for Herefordshire for twenty-five years. He came into the public eye when, as Member for the City and Sheriff of London and Middlesex, he had to burn Number 45 of *The North*

Briton, and the mob smashed the windows of his carriage.
He beat Wilkes in the election for Mayor, which led to more
window-smashing, Wilkes's supporters venting their annoy-
ance on those of the Mansion House. He bought Berrington
Park at Eye and died there.

After the Mortimers and the Scudamores and the Harleys
the gentlemen of Herefordshire are village worthies rather
than national figures. Some achieved passing fame, some a
little fame that has endured, and some notoriety.

Of the last there was Thomas Kidderminster of Tupsley
at Hampton Bishop who got himself murdered at White
Horse Inn, Chelmsford, in April, 1655, a crime that went
undiscovered for nine years and undetected for many more,
Moses Drayton, an hostler, being executed for it in 1667.

John Hoskyns of Harewood, compiler of a lexicon, was
imprisoned in the Tower with Sir Walter Raleigh and Henry
Percy, Earl of Northumberland, and there is a monument to
him in Abbey Dore Church. Camden and Donne were among
those who sang his praises.

His grandson, Sir John Hoskyns, became President of the
Royal Society. Evelyn has an entry in his diary:

"30 Nov. (1682) I was exceedingly indangered and im-
portun'd to stand the election (for President of the R.S.)
having so many voices, but by favour of my friends, and regard of my remote dwelling, and now frequent infirmities, I
desir'd their suffrages might be transferr'd to Sir John
Hoskins, one of the Masters of Chancery; a most learned
virtuoso as well as lawyer, who accordingly was elected."

From Much Marcle came Richard Walwyn, Esquire of
the Body, who was knighted by Queen Mary for suppressing
a Herefordshire rising in favour of "Queen Jane." Surely
never was knighthood more easily earned. It was for Queen
Mary that Herefordshire men were throwing up their caps
and lighting bonfires in the streets.

To Much Marcle also belonged the Fells, who lived at
Hall Place, the best known of whom was Dr John Fell,
Bishop of Oxford from 1685 to 1686. Here is a man every
child has heard of. A sad business. The one Herefordshire
man everybody knows. And not one likes him.

I do not love thee, Doctor Fell
And really why I cannot tell
But this I know and know full well
I do not love thee, Doctor Fell.

But Much Marcle has a much better claim to fame than
Sir Richard Walwyn, and even than Dr Fell. On the 17th of
February, 1575, Marcle Hill moved, overthrew a chapel at
Kinnerton, and came to rest on the 19th. That was something
like a landslide.

Camden describes it in these words:

"Near the conflux of the Lugg and the Wye, eastward, a
hill which they call Marcley Hill in the year 1575 roused
itself, as it were, out of sleep, and for three days together,
shoving its prodigious body forwards with a horrible roaring
noise and overturning all that stood in its way, advanced
itself, to the astonishment of all beholders, to a higher station, by that kind of earthquake the which the naturalists
call Brosmatia."

Landslide? Earthquake? I'm sure the good people of
Much Marcle said it was the Last Day (despite the tradition
that claimed it was to start at Orleton) and not a few dis-
appointed when it turned out not to be!

On the whole, Herefordshire will give Devon credit for
producing the better sailors, and be content with beating her
at cider. But even Devon never had a braver son than James
Cornewall of Moccas. He was in command of the *Marlborough* in the action off Toulon in 1743. During the battle
both his legs were shot off but he continued to fight his ship
"upon his stumps." Could Sir Richard Grenville have done
more? Cornewall is buried in Westminster Abbey.

From Withington came two literary men.

John Philips is best known as the author of *Cyder,* a long-
ish, unquotable poem which I personally find tiresome. It
was a worthy subject, and the poet treated it exhaustively,
but the style seems artificial and heavy. He wrote other, and,
I think, better poems. He died in 1708 and was buried in
Hereford Cathedral, a bust of him, and a rather weak
epitaph by Dr Friend, being given a place in the Poets'
Corner of Westminster Abbey.

William Broome was born in 1664. (Though the *Oxford Book of English Verse,* which contains two short poems by him, has a question mark in place of his birth year.) He died in 1745 at the age of 81, and his work was more solid than that of Philips. He was a classical scholar and started to write a *History of Herefordshire,* but he is better known as the man who helped Pope translate the *Odyssey.*

> Pope came off clean with Homer, but they say,
> Broome went before and kindly swept the way.

If puns were still funny that would be a good one.
Broome translated eight of the books and made notes for the whole work for which Pope paid him £500 and a hundred copies.

Hibernian politics, O Swift, thy doom;
And Pope's—translating three whole years with Broome.

In a county where every man is a gardener it hardly seems discreet to praise one more highly than another. Yet three men who lived some hundred and fifty years ago stand out clearly from the crowd. They were Sir Uvedale Price of Yazor, and Richard Payne Knight and Thomas Andrew Knight of Wormesley.

They lived in the days of Capability Brown and his spiritual successor, Repton. Brown, a garden designer of the landscape school, got his nickname from his habit, on first examining a garden, of saying it had capabilities. It became the fashion to have a garden designed by Capability Brown, and though in many ways he was a skilful designer, he destroyed much that was beautiful when it stood in the way of his plans.

> Lo, he comes!
> The omnipotent magician, Brown, appears!
> Down falls the venerable pile, the abode
> Of our forefathers. . . .
> He speaks—The lake in front becomes a lawn;
> Woods vanish; hills subside, and valleys rise,
> And streams, as if created for his use
> Pursue the track of his directing wand.

Now this was all very well when making a new garden. On old estates features that should never have been touched were vanishing.

The two Knights and Sir Uvedale, each in his own way, opposed Brown strongly, and each was to some extent responsible for a saner outlook in garden designing.

Richard Knight in a poem, *The Landscape,* addressed to Sir Uvedale, describes "the melancholy spectacle presented by some of the stately houses surrounded by the stiff and unreal 'natural landscape' substituted by Brown."

> Oft when I've seen some lovely mansion stand
> Fresh from the improver's desolating hand,
> 'Midst shaven lawns that far around it creep
> In one eternal undulating sweep;
> And scatter'd clumps, that nod at one another,
> Each stiffly waving to its formal brother:
> Tired with the extensive scene, so dull and bare,
> To Heaven devoutly I've addressed my prayer;
> . . . .
> Replace in even lines the ductile yew,
> And plant again the ancient avenue.
> . . . .
> Some vary'd tints and forms would intervene
> To break this uniform, eternal green.

To Sir Uvedale Price gardening owes a still greater debt. It was he who, with the help of Sir Joseph Banks, organized the Horticultural Society in 1804, which five years later became the Royal Horticultural Society. This society was planned to be the stimulus to horticulture he felt was needed, and time has proved how right he was. His fellow-countyman, Thomas Andrew Knight, became President in 1811 and the Society prospered and expanded under his rule.

I suppose, if it were so minded, the county could claim a share of one of England's greatest warrior kings, Henry V. True, he was born in the neighbouring county of Monmouth, but it was at Welsh Bicknor, in Herefordshire, that he was nursed by the Countess of Salisbury.

But no one can claim any share in Richard Hackluyt. He came of an old Herefordshire family, some of whom were

settled at Leominster, and some at Yatton. Richard Hack-
luyt was born in 1552, went to Westminster School and
Christ Church, Oxford, and later took orders. His interest,
however, was in geography. Drake was his friend, and Philip
Sidney, Humphrey Gilbert, Howard of Effingham and
Walsingham; friends to stir the blood of any man whose
dream was of travel and distant lands. In 1598 he began to
publish his writings under the title of *Principall Navigations,
Voyages, Traffiques, and Discoveries of the English Nation.*
Hackluyt's *Voyages* is a living book. Perhaps of all Here-
fordshire men his name will last longest.

Unless it is Dr Fell!

Farmers stick to their fields, their ploughs, their barns
and stack-yards. And the farmers' wives can be found in
their kitchens. But there are Herefordshire women, too, who
will not be forgotten. Blanche Parry was a most exceptional
woman; to remain a maid apparently being in the nature of
a miracle in Elizabethan days. Something has been said, too,
of the mistress of Treago—once a Border fortress, having
two walls, an outer and an inner, between which animals
could be kept during a raid—for the mistress of Treago
met the Scots with a dagger in her hand so that they changed
their minds and went elsewhere to seek what they could find.

But what of Constantia, the wife of Grimbald Pauncefote
of Much Cowarne? In 1253 Pauncefote was captured by
the Moors and Constantia gave—literally—her right hand
to ransom him. Until the seventeenth century there was a
monument to her in the church showing her with her hand
cut off at the wrist.

My own interest in Mary Abrahall of Foy is purely a personal matter. There happened to be an old book I was
anxious to get a copy of. And when I eventually got it, it
turned out to have belonged to a descendant of Mary Abrahall, as proved by a genealogical table written inside the
back cover. She was at the coronation of King George I and
wrote a rather amusing letter home describing it.

"My spouse was the finest of all his brethren, haveing a
new sute with silver buttons, he went to St James's where ye
King turn'd twice to look at him.

"We view'd the chair & throne & was within three yards

of ye Princes who was in black velvet, embroidered with gold and silver; she's a jolly woman, pretty tall & plump & pretty fair."

At Westminster Hall, Mistress Abrahall "saw ye King and Princes & Diner with all ye rest at ye other tables, there were at least 900 or 1000 candles lighted; ye Champion ride into the Hall on Horseback in Armour (with ye Earl Marshall, Lord High Steward and Duke of Montague) and gave ye Chalenge. Ye King drank to him in a Gold Cup, he pledged ye King's Health and had ye Cup for his reward and the horse he rode on wch was one of the King's . . ."

But there's the touch I like: "My spouse was the finest of all his brethren." The proud Herefordshire wife! "Ye King turn'd twice to look at him." *Twice!*

I suppose most of the people who think of Elizabeth Barret Browning at all nowadays have had their ideas moulded by *The Barretts of Wimpole Street* on stage, screen, or radio, or all three. Once she was a poet. She was, also, the wife of a poet, a poet greater than herself. But that was before the nineteen-thirties. Now she is the heroine of an Œdipus complex, a beautiful girl who broke away from a tyrannical and overbearing and, perhaps, over-loving father. Whether the play represents her as she actually was, I think most of us have a much greater affection for her than when she was only the woman who had written *Sonnets from the Portuguese* or *Aurora Leigh*.

She was born in 1806 at Kelloe, Durham, and her childhood was spent at Hope End (the house is no longer standing) at Colwall, under the shade of the Malvern Hills. Her father was Edward Moulton, the name Barrett being added later by deed poll.

She was a lively, happy child, and even at this early age was writing poems—mostly about her home here. But when she was fifteen she rode a pony on which the saddle had not been properly secured and she had the fall from the effects of which she never entirely recovered, and from the yoke of which only Robert Browning was able to free her. The Barretts left Colwall when Elizabeth was about twenty years old to go, after an unhappy period in Torquay, to Wimpole

Street. When she left Wimpole Street it was for Florence, where she died in 1861.

"Be the players ready?"

"Ay, my lord; they stay upon your patience."

On the 3rd of April, 1665, Samuel Pepys went to a rather indifferent play. "All the pleasure . . . was, the King and my Lady Castlemaine were there; and pretty witty Nell Gwynn." She was born at Hereford, and was one of the first actresses, for women before this time had not acted upon the stage. If she forsook this profession for one much older who is to blame her? To become a king's mistress was in those days no dishonourable part to play. Though, for a Herefordshire woman of an earlier day, fair Rosamund Clifford, it ended sadly. More highly born women than Nell did not scorn the part, and she kept Charles's affections to the end, as he showed by his plea, "Do not let poor Nelly starve."

The comic actress, Kitty Clive, was the wife of George Clive of Wormbridge. Her friend, Horace Walpole, wrote her epitaph.

The Kembles were Herefordshire people, players descended from players, with acting in their blood, and it was they who were to raise the family from a not particularly exciting strolling company, giving performances in small halls and, as at Leominster in the time of their grandfather, "Ward the Player," the schoolhouses, to the top of their profession.

There were four children of Roger Kemble, John Philip, Stephen, Charles, and Sarah. Stephen, who was born at Kington, was the only one actually born in the county, and he became remarkable for his size. He is said to have been the only actor to play Falstaff without padding. A useful quality when playing Falstaff, but something of a handicap, surely, if he wanted to take a slighter part.

All four had ability, but it was the sister who was to shine most brightly. Comparisons are not merely odious; they are, over much length of time, impossible, but there is no doubt at all that she remains one of the greatest tragic actresses the stage will ever see.

She was born at Brecon on August 5th, 1755, and from

her earliest days was in her father's company. Barnstormers they may have been, but there was no better school for acting. Her name first appears on a playbill in the part of Princess Elizabeth in Havard's play, *Charles the First*. This was on February 12th, 1767, when she was twelve.

Six years later she was violently in love with Siddons, one of the players in the company, and, in spite of her parents' opposition, married him at Coventry in November 1773.

It is strange to think how little is remembered of Siddons, though his wife was to take his name so completely that one almost forgets she was a Kemble; it needs even an effort to recall her Christian name. She was hall-marked by greatness. She was Mrs Siddons.

She was first engaged in London by Garrick, and appeared at Drury Lane as Portia on December 29th, 1775.

She was a complete failure.

Recalling the heights she later reached, it is difficult to realize that; but for the next six years she was touring the provinces. Her next London engagement did not come until 1782, when she appeared at Drury Lane again, this time to stay.

Eleven years later she went to Covent Garden to act with her brother, John Kemble, and from then until her farewell performance as Lady Macbeth on June 29th, 1812, she was acknowledged to be without equal.

The daughter of the Herefordshire strolling players had achieved greatness. The Kembles had reached their zenith.

She died on June 8th, 1851, and was buried in Paddington Cemetery.

Only Charles's children were to carry on the stage tradition. He had become Licenser of Plays, and this office his son, John, held after him. John was more scholar than player, however; something of a writer, too, though his best work, *The History of the Saxons in England,* he left unfinished.

Charles's daughter, Fanny, was a tragic actress, but probably the glare of greatness reflected from her famous aunt kept her from reaching the first rank. She married an American, later divorced him, and toured America for many years, giving Shakespearean readings. Her sister, Adelaide, struck out in a new direction and became an opera singer, a career she forsook to become an authoress.

Herefordshire boasts one other actor of the first rank. David Garrick was born at Hereford where his father was an army captain. He went to Lichfield Grammar School, and was later a pupil of Samuel Johnson. The stage was not his first choice of a career. He tried the law and the business of wine-merchant first. But once on the stage, he was supreme for almost forty years.

It is a queer business the way names change in a district. The families who were great—whether, as the Mortimers, in intrigue and national affairs; or as the Kembles, in an art—seem to climb to a height and then their descendants are heard of no more. Names that were once whispered with awe, and sometimes with terror, have become those of the ordinary countryman.

There is nothing new in it.

"The author can particularise lineal descendants of our most ancient existing Duke who are or were Mechanics and Day-labourers," wrote the author of a book on Ross a hundred and twenty years ago.

The old families die out, people say. They are rotten, or weak, effete, feeble. They've gone, the old gentry, the old nobility.

I don't think it's like that. Apart from the fact that a good labourer is as worthy of respect as a good Lord Marcher (if there were any good ones).

To me it seems that families are like the blackthorn. In the hedge the old stump is dying. It is hollow, powdery, a home for woodlice and earwigs, ready to snap off at a touch. But far out in the garden, perhaps so far you'd hardly recognize it for the same plant, young, strong blackthorn suckers are pushing their way up. They can be transplanted to take the place of the old tree that has gone, and in front of them stretch years of health and strength and usefulness.

CHAPTER XII

THE GOODERE TRIAL

O N Wednesday the 28th of March, 1770, the citizens of
Hereford were in a stir. It would be, unless the day has been
changed since, a market day, but the streets were crowded
more than was usual even on market days. Throngs of
people from the villages round about had come in to make
a holiday and there were strangers in town, too, many of
them riding shaggy mountain ponies, strangers who jabbered
quickly to one another in a language not often heard in
Hereford in those days—in Welsh.

The inns and ale-houses did a roaring trade in beer and
cider, to say nothing of spirits. Voices rose, both in Welsh
and in drawling Herefordshire. There were arguments,
probably a fight or two.

It was not every day a town could offer the luxury of a
murder trial.

On the 28th of March, 1770, William Spiggot and eight
other men with him "were tried . . . at Hereford before
the Honourable Mr Baron Perrott and Mr Justice Yates
for the inhuman murder of William Powell of Glanareth in
the county of Carm, Gent."

What made the trial notable was not that Welshmen were
once more in an English Court of Justice, but that a number
of the nine men accused could not speak a word of English.
They gave their evidence in Welsh and an interpreter had to
be used.

The murder had been a piece of callous, clumsy brutality.
Of the guilt of some of the nine men there was no doubt;
the point seems to have been to decide which, if any of them,
had had no part in the murder. In the end six were found
guilty and hanged, and three were acquitted. Spiggot, the
ringleader, and another were hanged in chains, and the

bodies of the others were given to the surgeons for dis-
section.

Murder seems to have a fascination for mankind not
equalled by any subject on earth. "All the world loves a
lover" may be true. Equally well it may not. All the world
certainly seems to love a murder. It is a strange phenomenon.
Death is seldom pleasant to contemplate. Violent death
never is. Perhaps it is this taste, aberration, call it what you
like, that is responsible for the popularity of stories classed
vaguely, but not very accurately, as thrillers. Yet between
the deaths in the thriller and death in reality there is no connection whatever. In the thriller the body lies conveniently
in the library or the shrubbery or behind the door of a locked
room. The detectives, and perhaps one or two others, look
on it unobtrusively, but never often enough to get on one's
nerves. I know what I'm talking about because the first book
I ever sold happened to be a thriller.[1] It was an early venture and I was lavish with murders—with convenient out-
of-sight murders. Very gentlemanly, and nothing to make
anybody sick. I wrote some more thrillers with more murders in them.

And then one day I came face to face with real tragedy
in a shooting accident. That day I remembered the light-
hearted deaths I had invented. I don't mean I was suddenly
ashamed of what I had written, or that I never wanted to
write the same sort of pleasant rubbish any more, but the
difference between the fictional and the real thing impressed
itself deeply on my mind.

Real murders would seldom do for fiction. In the Spiggot
case, for instance, the culprits were traced by one of the
gang leaving bloodstains right up to his own house *in the
snow*. The most casual murderer in a book would never do
that. Perhaps because the real murderer has a conscience
while the imaginary one has had that inconvenient instru-
ment painlessly removed.

No doubt the citizens of Hereford were the more excited
about the Spiggot trial because they had been cheated out of
the trial of the man who was known all over the country as
the Bristol Fratricide. There was a murder, clumsy and ill-

[1]Published under another name.

planned though it was, that must have had the whole county talking. A Herefordshire gentleman had murdered another Herefordshire gentleman—and his own brother at that. They were both well-known locally. Their father had been Member of Parliament for the county. Their home was in the county.

All England was interested in the Goodere Trial; at least two contemporary accounts of it were published, one "taken in Short Hand by order and Direction of S. Foot of Worcester College, Oxford, Esquire, and Nephew of the late Sir John Dinley Goodere, Bart." If England was interested how much more was the Herefordshire corner of it?

When I first became interested in this old story of horror and woe I thought it would make a good theme for a book. I don't think so any longer. The public likes its murders watered. So do I. The Goodere murder is neat, unadulterated nastiness. The sort of thrill it gives is not the kind wanted in fiction.

Sir Edward Goodere, Bart. of Burhope, Wellington, for some time Member for the County, had three sons. The eldest stayed at home to become fitted for his inheritance, and the other two, John and Samuel, joined the navy and went to sea.

I know very little of the early history of the Goodere family, but at this time they seem to have met nothing but misfortune. The first sad blow was when the son who should have become the next baronet and squire of Burhope was killed in a duel in Ireland.

The second son, John, who was serving in a ship called the *Diamond,* was sent for as he was now the heir. He seems to have been a thoroughly unpleasant character, eccentric and intractable. His father had no illusions about him. "You are more fit," he told him soon after his return, "for a bo'sun than to enjoy the title of a baronet."

But a baronet he did become and inherited another estate as well from a Sir John Dinley, upon which he added Dinley to his name, and became Sir John Dinley Goodere, Bart.

His baronetcy made him no more attractive than he was before. He married, but the marriage was completely unsuccessful. He had a son and, when the child was old enough, he crowned neglect and unkindness by apprenticing him to a saddler. He disliked his wife and encouraged her, so it is said, to be unfaithful to him. Then he accused her of misconduct with a friend, Sir Robert Jason, and at a trial was awarded five hundred pounds damages. It has been suggested since that the accusations he made against his wife and her supposed lover were completely false, and that the evidence on which he won the case was all carefully arranged (and perhaps well-paid) perjury.

Later he brought further accusations against his wife that she was conspiring attempts on his life, and again he won his case and she was sent to prison for a year. But by now someone began to doubt the reliability of his witnesses, and when he petitioned the House of Lords to grant him a divorce, they refused it.

Samuel Goodere was still in the navy. He was quite different from his brother and they detested each other thoroughly. When they met they quarrelled, and it only needed one to take a side on any question for the other to join the opposite side. Samuel appears to have been the popular member of the family, the handsome younger son. To make the setting complete, he was as poor as his brother was rich.

But he was a Goodere, and, whatever may have been their virtues in the past, the Goodere blood at that time was tainted.

Then his prospects improved considerably. Sir John's son, weak and neglected, the country squire who had learned nothing but the trade of a saddler, died, and Samuel found himself heir to Burhope and the baronetcy. About this time, also, he was given the command of a man-o'-war called the *Ruby*. He must have imagined that Fate was on his side at last.

But Sir John had a fine taste in being unpleasant. It was in his power to cut off the entail, and this he now proposed to do in favour of their sister, who had married a Mr Foote of Truro, and whose son, Samuel Foote, was later to become famous as a dramatist.

The scene changes to Bristol. On the 23rd of January, 1742, the Goodere brothers both dined at a house in Rope

Walk. The house belonged to Mr Smith, an attorney, who had done some business for Sir John, and possibly for Samuel as well. Mr Smith got them together to see if they could not be reconciled, and he was so far successful that they seemed on better terms than they had been for a long time, and they parted, apparently, good friends.

Samuel, it came out at the trial, had that morning ordered a dinner for six at the White Hart, College Green. Six sailors turned up for the dinner, and, a fact that struck the landlady as particularly queer in sailors, they drank *tea*.

Samuel was the first to leave the house in Rope Walk. He joined the men who had come out of the White Hart and then they waited. Presently Sir John left Mr Smith's house and as he came walking along his brother pointed him out to the six men and they surrounded him and began to drag him along. They were joined by twelve more men and between them they dragged him to the riverside at Hot Wells where a boat was waiting.

The queerest part of the whole business at this point is the complete lack of secrecy. Eighteen men to kidnap the Baronet for a start! There were onlookers. An old picture of the event shows women staring in dismay at the struggling mass of men. Captain Goodere was directing them and the Baronet shouting for help and crying "Murder!" When he cried out that he was Sir John Dinley Goodere, his brother clapped a hand over his mouth. He explained to some of the people who watched that they were taking a thief and murderer who had escaped from a ship; to others he said the poor fellow was a madman and they were taking him aboard a ship to save him from gaol (this word is spelled "goal" all through the fullest contemporary account).

When one considers what was yet to happen in the light of this practically public kidnapping there is only one possible conclusion.

Captain Samuel Goodere was mad.

They got Sir John in a boat, most of the men were dismissed after receiving a guinea apiece, and they rowed out to the *Ruby*. On the way Sir John said he knew they meant to murder him and he begged them to do it there and then, but his brother quieted him, and a few minutes later they were on board. Sir John was taken to an empty cabin and shut in and a guard put on the door.

That evening Mr Smith, the attorney, accidentally heard of how a man had been forcibly taken to a ship and he guessed part of what had happened. His thoughts hardly took him as far as murder. He went in the morning to see the Mayor and asked him to send a search party out to the *Ruby*. The Mayor agreed, but when the constables came to the ship Captain Goodere was already a prisoner. Lieutenant Berry, one of his officers, and the cooper had gone to his cabin when they saw the law-officers coming, and secured him.

Sir John was dead. He had been strangled.

Two other men, Matthew Mahony and Charles White, were arrested as well.

The trial took place at Bristol on the 26th of March. "The Trials of Samuel Goodere, Esq., Matthew Mahony and Charles White for the Murder of Sir John Dinley Goodere, Bart. (brother to the said Samuel Goodere) on board His Majesty's ship the *Ruby*." Captain Goodere challenged two of the jury and got them changed. His defence was that his brother was insane, which may have had some part of truth in it, and that he committed suicide by strangling himself—which had no truth in it at all.

A defence on any grounds was out of the question. Three people had actually seen the murder. They were Lieutenant Berry, the cooper of the ship, and the cooper's wife. They were in the next cabin and through a crack in the boards had been witnesses of the whole brutal business.

Apparently the guard had been sent from the door. At five o'clock in the morning the Captain, Mahony, and White had gone into the cabin. Sir John pleaded for his life, offering them money, but they took no notice of him. The Captain had a sword in one hand and a pistol in the other and he stood on watch while Mahony and White did what they had been hired to do. It does seem here that the watchers might have interfered. They may have known quite well that Captain Goodere was prepared to shoot the first person to interfere, and Mahony and White were unpleasant customers, but a number of remedies for that come to mind. The fact remains that they did not interfere.

Mahony first tried to strangle Sir John with a handkerchief, but, after failing with that, he used a cord the Captain took from his pocket, and with the cord was more successful. White helped, and as he helped to hold the unfortunate man he took his watch and eight guineas from his pockets. It was a part of the bargain. Mahony was to have two hundred guineas, White a hundred and fifty and the victim's watch and the contents of his pockets.

The watch became an important part of the evidence, for White gave it to a woman to mind for him, and she became frightened at the arrests and hid it in a privy, where it was found.

The trial dragged out. Witnesses were called—Herefordshire witnesses these must have been—to give evidence that Sir John was obviously insane; witnesses gave evidence as to Samuel Goodere's excellent character; others to Mahony's; others to White's. But there could be only one end to it all. What Berry, the cooper, and the cooper's wife had seen closed any avenues of escape. The three men were sentenced to death. And with them—an odd, pitiful touch, it seems to me—was sentenced a poor devil of a woman, Jane Williams, for killing her bastard baby.

And another thing seemed strange, too: the coincidence that Sir John was called home from sea in the *Diamond* to return to it to be murdered in the *Ruby*.

As to the men who seized Sir John, they escaped lightly. Only three of them came up for trial and they were fined forty shillings each and sent to prison for a year.

The Captain would not give up hope. He did all he could to get a reprieve, and when that failed tried to engineer a rescue by some colliers. When all chance of escape was gone he became resigned and before he was hanged made a confession.

The three men were hanged in sight of the place where the *Ruby* lay.

According to one version, they were hanged there in chains. Perhaps that was so in the case of Mahony and White. Captain Goodere, if a murderer, was still a gentleman, and he had influential friends. His body was kept for a day to prevent any attempt at reviving him and then was surrendered to his family.

Soon afterwards Herefordshire cottagers may well have waked in the night and wondered at the sound of a coach driving by. If they peeped through their windows into the darkness they saw a funeral coach drawn by six horses. Samuel Goodere was being brought home to Burhope to be buried among his ancestors and near the brother he had murdered.

The old accounts of the trial are illustrated with curious engravings. Some are of Captain Goodere, a pleasant, genial-looking man; "the gentlest creature that ever walked a quarter-deck," said one of his officers, giving evidence. There are pictures of ill-fated Burhope, of the abduction—a tame, innocent-seeming affair with no life in the figures; Mahony and White in shackles in prison; the murder itself—by someone who had never been aboard a ship, for the cabin is large and very lofty; and the unfortunate Baronet looking, for a man who is being strangled, singularly placid, the only sign of disarray being his wig which has tumbled to the floor.

Samuel Foote was, as he might well be, very distressed at the murder. He was a man who did not have much sympathy for other people's ghost-stories and he "overwhelmed Johnson with ridicule for his belief in the Cock Lane ghost." But he declared that on the night of the murder he was awakened by the sound of strange unearthly music, and, naturally, when the news was brought to him he connected the eerie music with what happened.

The Goodere family was not yet extinct. Samuel had had two sons, neither of whom married. The older died, but the younger lived until 1809, one of the Knights of Windsor, a sinecure that had been given him out of pity, a poor, silly, shabby old man, what country-people would describe as "not all there." The last Sir John Goodere of Burhope in the County of Herefordshire, Bart.

Burhope was said to be haunted. Haunted or not, it was hardly a house in which anyone could be happy again. A Mr Turberville, the last owner, sold it for the materials in it and it was pulled down.

Wasn't it Dr Johnson who said it will be all the same in a hundred years' time? Not always true. There are people and doings worth remembering over a thousand years. But the Gooderes are forgotten. A vague story told by an old man by the inn fire. That is as it should be.

CHAPTER XIII

UNDER THE GREENWOOD TREE

T H E only place in Herefordshire where nothing will grow
is on Stanner Rocks, near Kington, and this is not the fault
of the county, but the fault of the devil. He has his garden
there and in it nothing grows at all. One would think he
would have at least *something:* a choice mixture of poisonous plants, say; or a collection of berries to glow temptingly
in the watery sunshine of a dying autumn day—black bryony,
deadly nightshade, cuckoo-pint, fetid iris, and mezereon
could make a handsome nucleus—but there is it, everyone
to his taste, and in the devil's garden nothing grows.

The spot must be unique in the county, for with its genial
climate and fertile soil there seems to be nowhere else where
something does not grow.

Two wars have reduced the number of trees grown, though
the fact hardly strikes the visitor. Everywhere are woods
and copses, and the little hills that rise here and there are
almost always tree-clad. Before the war of 1914–18 the
amount of timber grown was actually on the increase. Dr
Bull mentions that about a fifteenth of the county was taken
up by woods. That was about 1880. By 1911 the proportion
had risen to a twelfth, and did not take into account the
orchards which occupied, roughly, another eighteenth.

The trees of the hill-country thin out as we come down
into Herefordshire. There are not so many of the birch,
mistily purple in the spring, or gleaming palely against the
russet of the fern all winter. For the alders and the willows
one must now look in the river valleys, and even there they
are scarcer as the Wye and its companions broaden out and
become tamed. Of the little mountain willow there are no
more to be seen unless it is on the edge of the Black Mountains thrusting into the county in the south-west, and the
mountain ash or rowan is no longer everywhere in sight.

But the larger forest trees are growing to perfection. The only part where I have seen finer beech trees is in the Chilterns, and the oaks and elms, at their best, are not surpassed anywhere. I don't know of any Herefordshire oak that can beat the Cowthorne oak with fifty-four feet of girth, but a tree at Eardisley is some thirty feet round the trunk and there must be many approaching this, some perhaps surpassing it.

A curious fact is that though there are excellent specimens of both oak and beech they are trees which are poor company for each other. The oak has a deep tap-root and a deep spreading root system (the reason one so seldom sees them blown down), but the roots of the beech are shallower and wider. As a result, where oak and beech grow together—though I suppose no forester would plant them together—the beech takes, as it were, the cream of the salts washed down by the rain, and the deeper roots of the oak are in the position of Mrs Hubbard's famous dog.

The cultivation of oak trees suffered when wooden ships ceased to be built, and following that blow came a fashion for walnut in furniture-making, and then for mahogany and satinwood. The effects of these changing tastes are slow in making themselves seen in the woods. The oak is hardly mature from the timberman's point of view until it is about a hundred and fifty years old. Timber-planting in recent years seems to have been mainly of the quick-maturing conifers. The man who plants oak, like the man who plants pears, "plants for his heirs." *His children shall rise up and call him blessed.* That man is practising one of the most delightful forms of unselfishness known to us. *Verbum sapienti.*

The oak, a full-grown hearty, English oak tree, is host to some five hundred different species of insects. But, bless you, it can put up with it!

The common elm is not a native, but was introduced by the Romans. Though elms grow everywhere it cannot be called a popular tree. There is no "hearts of oak" ring about the name to stir one's emotions. Perhaps its unpleasant habit of shedding a bough occasionally, entirely without warning, has something to do with it. Or is it because its chief use has always been for making coffins? As a carpenter's wood its tendency to warp proves something of a drawback, though I have seen some excellent elm floors. For outdoor use, wheelbarrows, garden doors, tool handles, elm is excellent and durable. When its greatest enemy, Dutch elm disease, is conquered perhaps the elm will be better behaved and better liked. After all, nobody can be expected to have a deep affection for a tree that at any moment may drop a branch on his head. For good or ill it is certainly a permanent part of the English scene, and, though it sets seed uncertainly, bearing good crops only once every few years, it propagates itself freely by suckers. It is not a greedy tree, and other vegetation will grow beneath its shade, a fact that makes it excellent for park-land.

The elm has some distant relationship with the common stinging nettle, another Roman introduction. A strange thing is that all members of the tortoiseshell butterflies feed on the nettle, except the large tortoiseshell, and that makes itself at home on the elm.

Both the common elm and the wych elm grow in the county, but I have not noticed the weeping variety of the latter anywhere. The wych elm, though a native, is much less often seen.

People who have any affection for trees—and that must be nearly everybody—want to see them covered in leaves. Yet it is a fact that trees, when they have shed their leaves, are still beautiful and, in many cases, it is only then that their real character and grandeur are revealed. And if it is a question of identification, the tree in winter is, at a glance, a much easier proposition than when it is fully dressed.

These two elms are a case in point. Looked at side by side, of course, it is easy enough to tell one from another; when each stands alone with none of its cousin's seeds, or leaves, or bark handy for comparison, it is quite easy to be confused.

But studied bare—the merest glance is enough. The full-grown common elm stands top-heavy, many of its lower branches gone, and the others starting halfway up the trunk and spreading out umbrella-fashion. The wych elm outlined against the sky is like a river into which many tributaries hurry; or a giant hand with an abnormal number of pointed

196

fingers, for all the branches start low down and fan straight out.

I can hardly think of a common tree that cannot be found growing somewhere in Herefordshire. The crabs and wild pears, like the rowan and the birch, are seen much less than they are in the hills. Chestnuts are plentiful. I know one walnut, having picked and eaten its nuts, and no doubt there are plenty more. The conifers grow, all kinds of them, where they are planted, but they are overshadowed in beauty by the deciduous trees. There are yews everywhere, many of them venerable giants of an enormous age. There seem to be geans in every copse, and blackthorn and hawthorn too, and hazel, though I have never seen the hazel here as in one or two places in the hills where they have grown, single survivors of a forgotten hedge, perhaps, nearly to the dimensions of a forest tree.

As a nurse to other and slower-growing trees there is nothing to beat the sycamore. It is not a carpenter's tree for the wood is not tough or durable enough (though the cabinet-maker has uses for it) and it does not live to a great age as a rule. But it certainly grows nearly anywhere—there are good specimens in many places along the banks of the Wye—and it has a most remarkable power of procreation. I don't think there is any tree—no tree I know—that has so many of its children at home as this member of the maple family (plane tree to Scotsmen). Under every sycamore grow dozens, sometimes hundreds, of seedling trees. They do not survive unless they are growing in a suitable spot. Anybody who fancies tree-planting—any kind of tree—should visit an old sycamore in spring. He may take a young forest home with him and nobody will mind. At least I hope they won't. I've done a bit of transplanting on my own account. I have a very nice sycamore that any efficient Sherlock Holmes could, with his microscope and bit of scratching for the red soil (if there's any left) under the bole, identify as Herefordshire in origin.

Sycamores only came to England in the fifteenth century, but they have settled down very nicely and (as has been mentioned earlier) they were adopted by the "hop-dogs," the caterpillars of the pale tussock moth, when the "hop-dogs" were driven, by spraying, from the hops.

Good Hereford timber
A farm near Orleton

Flowers, like trees, grow in sheer abundance, both in quantity and variety. The flowers of the sea-shore, thrift, samphire, sea-lavender, naturally, are absent; and so are those few like the butterwort that prefer the boggy hill-tops of Radnor and Cardigan. The heaths and lings can be found on the Black Mountains, and there too are found whortleberry, cowberry, and the crowberry. I believe there are even a few winberry hills within the county boundary. There are certainly plenty of them a mile or two outside.

With its acres of woodland, its hundreds of miles of hedgerows, in addition to the natural fertility of the soil, Herefordshire is a Paradise of wild flowers. Species favouring any of a dozen localities from the riverside up to the hill-tops have everything in their favour. Rarities have been found, such as the orchid *Epipogium aphyllum,* and there are plenty of flowers not commonly found wild, such as snowdrops, monkshood, and lily of the valley, though it is possible that some of these have escaped from cultivation. The county is so rich in its gardens that it would be a wonder if there were not a number of escapes.

Flowers like the pasque flower that have a liking for chalk are missing and so are such plants as the bird's-eye primula that need semi-bog. But primroses grow in masses in every hedge during March and April and I have seen a field so yellow with tall cowslips that I gasped in delight, thinking I had come on daffodils growing wild.

There is no natural lake in the county, so that bars out both the yellow water lily (brandy bottle) and the native white water lily (both of which grow wild not far away, in Welsh lakes) and a number of other water plants as well, but in the shallow parts of the Wye the water-crowfoot makes a white carpet over the water in summer.

When we first started wandering about in Herefordshire, I was in the first throes of about as bad a case of gardening fever as anyone ever had. I once knew an old woman who was bringing up her orphaned grandchild and that woman would do anything, *anything,* to get a ha'penny or a bun or an orange or a sweet for that horrible child. I was in a similar fix, only it was my garden I was trying to scrounge for. Wherever we went I always had my eyes open for something I could beg, something I could transplant, seeds that could be taken home. From the garden of a ruined house in Carmarthenshire I brought an old-fashioned, but excellent, anchusa. In another in Pembrokeshire I found an uncommon monkshood; in another the gnarled stumps that were to make the finest bushes of cabbage roses I have ever seen. I brought thrift home from Devon, mesembryanthe-mums from Cornwall. I dug black poplar suckers out of a London lawn and hunted—vainly—for pinks in the Cheddar Gorge. I got sedums from all sorts of places, and thymes, lings, and heathers in hearty chunks of peat from our own hills. The number of plants I "won" by begging from houses I passed, it fills me now with shame to think of. I believe the only plant I really resisted was the winter heliotrope I found in flower on Christmas Day along a Pembrokeshire shore—but I'd been warned about that sweetly scented spreading pest!

And yet in all the time I've known Herefordshire I have brought home only one wild plant, a cowslip that I dug out of a hedge near Pembridge. I planted it in my own garden hedge and it still flowers and has seeded itself freely into the bargain.

I don't know why I treated Herefordshire with this con-sideration. There were surely some flowers I could have transplanted. Looking back, I wonder why I never grew mistletoe, for there is mistletoe in nearly every orchard and I know some that grows on elms by the roadside and even one on a hawthorn. It is fairly easy to grow if the seeds are smeared or stuck on to the branch of an apple tree, when they are ripe, which is about March, *not* at Christmas. But I never even tried.

Perhaps the wild flowers of Herefordshire are to look at, not to pick. *Primula farinosa* (the bird's-eye primrose) and pasque flowers and autumn crocuses, these are the flowers that tempt the garden planter. The glory of wild cherry and foxgloves, bluebells and hound's tongue and wood anemones cannot be moved. The flowers are just right where they are.

There are two memories I have brought back with me from my journeys and perhaps they will serve me longer and better than the flowers themselves could have done, the more because I can renew them any spring or summer. The

first is coming up the hill out of Eardisley towards Kingswood Common on an April evening. Above the road is a
field and a house and trees. And in the field literally thousands,
probably very many thousands, of little daffodils. I suppose
they were planted at some time; I don't know what the
species is, except that they look to me smaller than the Tenby
daffodil, *Narcissus obvallaris,* and yet are much larger than
the real miniature daffodils. All I know is that they look
lovely and the sight of them gladdens me.

The other is near Garnons a few miles from Hereford. A
deep ditch outside a wood and suddenly we see that it is
smothered with the blue periwinkle. I have periwinkles in
the garden at home, a white one with variegated leaves, and
a small double purple one. But good as they are, they do not
approach this wild flower for colour or beauty.

I don't know why I didn't transplant a bit of that. But if
I've given the idea I was unscrupulous in my plant-collecting
it was, to use contradictory words, a conscientious sort of un-
scrupulousness. I was collecting, not spoiling. And the periwinkles are mine as much as anyone's. Any day they are out
I can go and see them. That's where a hedgerow gains over
a garden. You don't have to ask before you can look.

Our wild animals are, as in all England, many, but not,
on the whole, of a size to be readily noticed. Field-mice and
dormice and pigmy shrews are interesting if you really get a
good look at them, but most people do not, and a dead shrew
by the roadside does not convey to one person in ten the
tremendous battle that took place. Yet the animal is, size for
size, about as fierce—when fighting over its females—as
any in existence. It has given its name to quarrelsome females and there are in existence recipes for cures for the
bites of "savage shrew mice."

The worst of our small native animals is the difficulty of
observing them. The water-vole (the field-mouse is really
a vole), or water-rat as it is generally called, is to most
people little more than a "plop!" and a spreading arc of
ripples in the river on a dusky evening.

Nobody is much interested in moles except the farmer,
and he, short-sightedly, thinks only how to be rid of them.

Nobody, so far as I know, has yet adopted the plan suggested by W. H. Hudson of dividing a mole-infested meadow into two parts, letting them have their way in one half and excluding them from the other and then letting "the grass crops of the two portions be compared as to weight and quality for a period of four or five years." Sensible people know the mole to be more of a friend than a pest. The others try to kill them off. They have a long fight ahead. The mole has hundreds of thousands of years of history behind him.

Hares are not common, though there are plenty in the Black Mountains and on Radnor Forest, but rabbits, of course, are plentiful. It is sad to have to write "of course," but it is the truth. "The rabbit always dies in debt," is also the truth. It does more harm to crops than any other animal or any bird (or, I daresay, any number of them combined) that we have. The rabbits' friends are the pheasant, the partridge, and the gamekeeper. The pheasant and the partridge are pleasant to look at and good to eat, but as long as the keeper is thinking of them he will be on the safe side and shoot the weasel, the stoat, and the badger, to say nothing of owls and any hawks, large or small, he may see.

Which is all very good for the rabbit.

The wild-cat, which was once an article of food in the county, has completely gone; the stoats and weasels put up some sort of running fight against the keepers, and their cousin the polecat (foumart or fitchett) has taken himself up to the hills, where he is almost common again, and returns only for a visit.

I don't think Herefordshire will get rid of its badgers as easily. No harm in trying, though why anyone should want to try is a mystery. Brock is a gentleman, clean, retiring by disposition, good to his family, faithful to his wife. Can all Christians say as much? His unobtrusive ways give most people a mistaken impression that he is nearly extinct. But the truth is that he *is* unobtrusive, not that he is not there.

I rather admire the badger and make a point of asking after his health.

"Any badgers about here?"

"Oh, one or two," or "There were some a few years back," or some such answer.

You are very seldom told they do not exist. Herefordshire, barring the presence of the gamekeeper, with its
numerous woods and copses, is an ideal home for badgers.

People have tried to clear them out. I've never yet heard
of any who succeeded. Some years ago the gamekeepers on
an estate in County Wexford tackled a badger sett in which
one tunnel alone was over a hundred yards long. A couple
of years after the poor animals had been exterminated they
were back again. Queer!

Even funnier was the Battle of Cumberland. A few years
ago the *Manchester Guardian* printed a leader, "The Badger
Badgered," in which it pointed out how stupid it was to try
to exterminate our wild animals. The point was that the wartime agricultural authorities in the county had schemes for
dealing with the badger as a pest. In other words, they
meant to get rid of their badgers.

Not long ago in the same paper the feature called "A
Country Diary" started with these words from Cumberland:

"The badger is becoming as common a beast as the fox."

So either the Cumberland wartime agricultural authorities
didn't try, or, if they tried . . .

I would like to quote two more sentences from the same
"Country Diary":

"They are very seldom seen, and the only one to be destroyed for many years was a fellow who entered a hen-hull."

The only one I *saw* for many years was one who had got
into a hen-house.

"What interested us most about this colony was that all
the bedding was out to be sweetened by the air."

You don't smell a badger at home. To get the full, over-
powering odour of badger you have to skin him. I happen to
know.

Mind, I'll admit Brock likes a few eggs. But we all do.

The fox is not as shy and retiring as the badger, nor, in
hunting country like this, does he need to be. Wherever there
is hunting the fox is safe; though it sounds ironical to say it.
I've heard people say that but for the hunt foxes would now
be extinct. I doubt it. The case of the wolf is not a good
precedent. I don't know exactly how long it is since there
were wolves in Herefordshire, but in John Cumin's ac-

counts for the see of Hereford for the year 1166–67 there
is an entry: "and for taking three wolves 10/–." The wolf,
admittedly, has gone. But so might elephants if they had
ever lived here. The wolf is much larger than the fox, more
ferocious, much less easily hidden. And every man's hand
would be against him. Not that that necessarily counts for
much. Every man's hand is against the brown rat, and there
is no sign of its extinction. Not all the Rat Weeks in Christendom will finish that gentleman. He is comparatively
small, breeds quickly and easily, and has brains. The rat is
the one animal who hasn't a friend—except the keeper who
shoots the stoats and owls—the one wholly objectionable
creature we have. We must just be thankful that he is not a
native—there are no rats indigenous to this country, both
the brown rat and his rather less hated cousin, the black rat,
being Asiatics—and keep pegging away at him. To get rid
of the rats, failing another Pied Piper, is more than one can
expect; they certainly might be less common than they are.

Up in the hills where hunting is quite impossible the farmers have for years been trying to get rid of the foxes. They
organize hunting parties—this is enough to make hunting
people shudder—with guns! They shoot a lot of foxes and
destroy cubs. But presently there seem to be as many as ever.
I know the hill-foxes much better than I know the hunted
beasts of Herefordshire. It happens that I live a stone's
throw—well, a small stone and a strong thrower—from a
dingle, actually, at the foot of it, where foxes have always
bred. There have been a few mishaps among the chickens
periodically, and at one time we reared a cub until it got
what shepherds call "gid" (a disease of sheep) and it had
to be destroyed. I've seen foxes at close quarters more than
I have seen any wild animal, and I don't think that, hunted
or unhunted (using the word hunted in its usual sense), there
is much danger of the fox dying out. And, in spite of his
faults, which are after all only faults from our point of view,
I should be sorry to think there was. But the more he is pur-
sued the wilier he will become. Not for nothing does the
countryman say "crafty as an old fox."

I used to get a number of wild animals brought to me at
one time, both live and dead ones.

"Thought you'd like to have'n stuffed," I would be told.

I still have not a single stuffed animal in a glass case to show anybody, and I think my friends have grown suspicious. It is a long time since anyone brought me a fox cub, but I can thoroughly recommend them as endearing pets. "You stink like a fox," is only one degree less insulting than "You stink like a badger," but the domesticated fox does not stink. In friendly company it seems to have the scent glands, which are situated under the tail, under control and does not feel any need to use them.

There are otters in the Wye, and though I have not come across them as far down as Herefordshire they are probably more plentiful in the lower reaches than they are higher up the river. Observation of these animals generally is restricted to hearing the sound of a dive splashless enough to command the envy of an Olympic champion. That, and a shrill whistle from the side of the brook in the night. It is the furthest knowledge I can boast myself, though the whistle of an otter at play, perhaps teaching her cubs to swim, is familiar enough to me. I knew the otters were there, just as my neighbour knew they were there, for he kept ducks and, sooner or later, the ducks found the stream (and refused to come home to bed) and the otters found the ducks.

Few people realize how slow a process it is to learn, first-hand, about animals. If it were a conscious process it would be too tedious to relate. One notices something now, something again, and in time, perhaps after many years, the realization suddenly comes that all the bits of knowledge add up into something resembling a whole.

And very often the only things a person learns are what he has been able to see for himself. The fact that the next person has seen something contradictory does not signify. One will say the rabbit is a miserable coward; another that the rabbit will fight hard in defence of its young. The truth is that animals vary as much as people do.

Imagine two Martians in cloaks of invisibility just arrived on earth to study the behaviour of *Homo sapiens*. One sees an author who has just received a cheque for a thousand pounds from his humble and grateful publisher. Number two sees a man who became irritated with his wife's habit of eating off her knife and hit her on the head with a chopper, and at the moment tears of repentance run down his cheeks the insurance company are handing *him* a large cheque.

To the learned societies of Mars, Observer Number One says, "*Homo sapiens,* when given a cheque, throws his hat in the air, hugs his children, laughs, dances, takes his wife to the local, and shows signs of the greatest joy."

"My learned friend," says Observer Number Two, "is talking the most arrant rubbish. When *Homo sapiens* is given a cheque he sobs, beats his breast, tears at his collar, and, in general, is evidently in the deepest dejection. . . ."

Then the wigs are on the green and their friends try to tear them apart. Henceforth naturalists on Mars will be split into two groups on the worst possible terms. . . .

I had a little experience of the same sort of thing. I stopped the car on a hill-top one morning to watch a heron fly past. I particularly noticed that its legs were *tucked up,* not extended. Very shortly afterwards I noticed a drawing of a heron in flight and the legs were extended full-length along the body. Naturally, I laughed. Then I found that many people entertained the same fallacy as the artist. I became very argumentative about it. I *knew*.

I kept on knowing—until I noticed herons flying with legs extended.

Perhaps my heron liked flying that way (oh yes, it *was* a heron!) or had rheumatism. Or perhaps they draw in their legs on long flights, or high flights.

The fact that somebody, no matter how learned a naturalist, has observed that a certain animal does a certain thing does not mean that that animal always does that certain thing or that all other animals of that kind do that certain thing.

Perhaps I'd better revise what I said about the fox just now. *Our* fox did not stink.

The red squirrel is perhaps the prettiest, most endearing of all our woodland creatures. I've never known anyone have a harsh word to say for the squirrel, unless it is the gamekeeper. I'm sorry to keep knocking at the gamekeeper's head like this. I've known some gamekeepers who were excellent fellows, and some who have been keen naturalists as well, but their failing always has been a tendency to make pheasants' eggs the orbit round which their pleasant lives swing. Red squirrels make the most delightful pets it is possible to have if you rear them from the right age. They do not hibernate as much as is generally supposed, and my own observation has been that the sight of a lively squirrel during the winter is a sign of mild weather for some time to come.

But likeable as the squirrel is, it is not nearly so interesting a creature as the hedgehog. The hedgehog, very occasionally called hedgepig, got its name from the pig-like shape of its snout. I'd not like to eat hedgehog any more than I'd like to eat, say, a puppy I was rather fond of, but I'm told it is distinctly good food. Gypsies cook it exactly as they cook chicken—in a ball of clay in the embers of a fire.

The hedgehog is rather unpopular with most country-people. They will insist that the hedgehog milks the cow, a legend that Pliny told and that may have been stale when he heard it. For one thing the hedgehog has not a large enough mouth to take hold of the teats; it certainly could not even tackle the job unless the cow were lying down; and it is extremely unlikely that most cows would lie quiet to be milked by a hedgehog. The story is as widely believed in Herefordshire as it is everywhere else. I met one man who said—in answer to a direct challenge—that he had *seen* the hedgehog performing its foul theft. I did not call him a liar. He was rather a big man.

There is another old country belief, common in Herefordshire, that hedgehogs climb the apple trees and shake down the apples. Then they tumble down themselves, roll on an apple so that a spine sticks in it, and in this way carry it home to the nest. Though plenty of people who believe the-hedgehog-milks-the-cows theory will scoff at this, it *is* possible that at some time a hedgehog did get an apple stuck on its back—perhaps a dog or a fox rolled it over—and somebody saw it going home afterwards, apple on back. . . . How I wish I could have seen it!

Anyhow, apples are the last thing Herefordshire folk are greedy with.

The hedgehog's spines are enlarged and stiffened hairs. There are about two hundred and fifty to the square inch of body and some fifteen to sixteen thousand on the whole body of a normal adult. The muscle that gives some clever people the power to wiggle their ears and move their scalps is the same muscle, the *panniculus carnosus,* that enables the hedgehog to raise and lower its spines, only where the *panniculus carnosus,* which all mammals have, is in man a feeble or practically useless agent, in the hedgehog it covers almost the entire upper surface of the body.

Very few animals will tackle the hedgehog. At the first sign of danger it rolls into a ball, quills erect, and can remain so almost indefinitely. It may be this instinct that has caused a high mortality among them on the roads in recent years. A hedgehog crossing the road, at the first beam of a headlight, would probably curl up instead of keeping on running (and considering its tiny legs, it can get along quite well) and so get run over. There are stories of foxes and badgers getting the better of its armour, but on the whole I think they would prefer to go for easier prey.

They are very fond of eggs—pheasants' eggs, of course! Did any wild animal ever eat any other kind? On country roads, in fields, copses and woods, they are plentiful in summer, but in the winter they hibernate. They possess what are called hibernating glands, the use of which are not properly understood, though since the glands are enlarged before hibernation and get smaller as it goes on it is thought that they perhaps store anti-toxins to combat bacteria that invade the body when the winter sleep begins.

We had a baby hedgehog once, a pinkish creature with soft spines, which the children fed on milk from an old-fashioned fountain pen filler. In spite of getting the milk without having to trouble a cow, the poor creature died. Adult ones we have had for longer periods without casualties. The method used to be to keep them in the house until they were apparently friendly and then take them to the greenhouse where they were expected to repay our hospitality by eating the woodlice. They invariably dug their way out and cleared off after a very short time and I can't say I noticed the woodlice had anything to worry about. It is rather shabby treatment bringing a solitary hedgehog home, anyhow. They mate for life, and an old man put the situation in a nutshell by writing this on a bit of paper, "man $\frac{B}{\text{meddling}}$ wife," and challenging me to read it. The interpretation is, "Be above meddling between man and wife." The advice seemed sane enough and apparently refers as much to hedgehogs as people. All the same, I'd welcome a couple in my garden, though they are touchy little beasts when they have young. But most parents are.

Herefordshire snakes are mostly the harmless grass-snakes, but there may be more vipers than one sees. Hardly anybody likes snakes, harmless or poisonous. The aversion is so deep-rooted as to be almost instinctive. The sight of one of them is a signal for an involuntary prickling of the scalp—and attack.

Thou art cursed above all cattle, and above every beast of the field; upon thy belly shalt thou go. . . .

And I will put enmity between thee and the woman, and between thy seed and her seed; it shall bruise thy head, and thou shalt bruise his heel.

True, every word of it.

I have killed many a grass-snake when I was a boy—simply because it was a snake. I remember chasing one over some rough open ground once and it went into a large pool and I had my one and only sight of a snake swimming. It swam so well I was too amazed to throw stones at it. They move amazingly fast on land. Though they appear legless they have, actually, vestigial forms of legs, similar to the legs of the lizards, just under the skin.

Their capacity for swallowing bulky foods—eggs, mice, even small rabbits—is explained by the fact that the lower jaw is joined to the head by very elastic muscles, enabling them to open their mouths wide enough to allow these dainties to enter and pass into the gullet. The oesophagus is similarly elastic.

In most poisonous snakes the poison comes from the poison glands to the base of the fangs and then runs down grooves in the fangs. This groove, in the viper, is closed and forms a duct in the centre of the tooth, and the poison runs through this and is ejected through a hole in it. The mechanism of the fangs themselves is simple, efficient, and wonderful. They are mounted under the upper jaw on a bone that is hinged so that it can swing freely. At the back of the skull is another bone that can swing in the same way. The two are connected by a thin bone known as the *pterygoid*. As the snake opens its mouth the rear bone is automatically swung forwards and, impelled by the *pterygoid*, the fangs are erected, ready to strike; when the mouth closes the bone at the back swings backwards and the fangs are lowered to lie along the roof of the mouth. Thus the viper has only to open its mouth to be ready for striking.

The viper's venom is seldom deadly. I have known of only one case of death occurring from snake-bite and it was not in Herefordshire. The victim was a child and fright and shock may have had a good deal to do with her death. Many more people have died in this country of gnat-bites than from "adder-stings." I'll admit there are more gnats than adders. An old man I knew intimately was bitten in the arm when he thrust his bare arms into a heap of trash he was going to carry to the bonfire. He belonged to the belly-God-send-thee-good-ale-enough school and, except that his arm swelled up to look something like a vegetable marrow, I don't think the bite did him much damage. Some of his friends said he was so thoroughly pickled that all the cobras in Asia couldn't have hurt him. A few said Tal (short for Talbot) hadn't been bitten by a snake at all. I remember arguing about it.

"Then what *did* bite him?" I demanded.

"One o' they li'l cuddy-evacks.[1]"

"Huh!" I scoffed. "Cuddy-evacks can't bite."

"They obscenely well can. Bite like an obscene shark, boy."

"They can't bite," I said emphatically.

"Hows't thee know?"

"My father said they can't."

"Thy father don't know everything."

"My father picks up cuddy-evacks. He'll let them run all over his hands."

They looked at me in horror. "If he do they'll bite'n one of these days, and his arm'll swell up like Tal's. That's if they don't kill'n."

[1] Pembrokeshire for lizard.

Not all I and my father knew would persuade them lizards didn't bite. They wouldn't have picked one up for anything. Neither would I have done. It was all very well to take one's father's word. But there's nothing like being on the safe side.

Lizards are common enough, though it is on the higher ground where there are rocks for them to sun themselves on that they are seen most. I have sat for a long time on a stone with a lizard on the next one, neither of us moving. So long as human beings are good enough not to fidget they don't seem to mind their company. Snakes are seldom seen on the hills, but plenty of lizards are. In fact, the best place I know for finding lizards (on a warm summer day) is an old ruined house in Bwlchysarnau, one of the highest, and in winter the coldest, places of Radnor.

A lizard, caught by the tail, will sometimes let the tail break off in order to escape. It does this without hurting itself, as the tail consists of muscles fitting into sheaths at the end of the body. When the tail breaks it does so between two vertebrae, the muscles come out of their sheaths, and the only actual breakage is in the skin. The animal can grow another tail, and more tails after that if necessary, but it seems rather shabby treatment to put it to the trouble of doing so.

The slow-worm is a lizard, but, poor creature, has to the unknowing eye all the appearances of being a snake, for which misfortune it is usually set upon and killed as soon as seen, and identified afterwards. Country people themselves are as often at fault as anyone else. Next to the hedgehog I don't think there is any animal I would welcome so readily to my garden as the slow-worm. It eats all kinds of insects, but its favourite food seems to be that small greyish-white slug that eats all the best seedlings. But perhaps people would prefer the slugs to this reminder of a hated tribe.

The Wye is as good a salmon river as there is in the country. The fact has been known, and recognized, for long enough, great quantities of cured Wye salmon being commandeered by Edward I for feeding his troops in the Scottish wars. Wye salmon going to Scotland! That is a compliment indeed. But then they had other things than fishing to keep them busy. In the higher reaches of the river it has become almost a national pastime to poach the salmon coming up to spawn in autumn. No doubt this has been done since Welshmen found salmon good to eat, but a lot of impetus was given to the habit some century ago when, at the dying-down of the Rebecca Riots, men banded together still, not to smash turnpike gates, but to catch fish. They had found that there are some things that can be done better in company. This went on for so long that many people living far up the Wye know nothing of Rebecca's original purpose and believe that catching salmon was what Rebecca organized "her" bands for.

This pastime never seems to have been the fashion to the same extent in Herefordshire. I don't say nobody living near the river has ever tasted salmon in late autumn, but circumstances were different from those in the hills, the river was easier to watch, the preserving better organized, and, perhaps, the fish not quite so easily caught.

There are plenty of good trout streams about also, but it is the grayling that give distinction to the fishing in the county. Good grayling streams are none too common and efforts to introduce the fish not uniformly successful. Artificial cultivation, where it has been tried, has been a failure. The Lugg is one of the best grayling streams that fishermen know.

This handsome relation of the salmon has a distinctively large striped dorsal fin. It is better to eat than the trout and, giving just as good sport, is very popular with anglers. It spawns in spring so is in season in the autumn, when trout are not.

Chapter XIV

THE SPARROW ALSO IS A BIRD

HEREFORDSHIRE provides an ideal home for birds. There is water, there are woods and hedges everywhere, the climate is mild. Sea-birds are not here, except as visitors, nor are the birds, relatively few in number, of high moorland and mountain, but I believe most of the others may be seen at one time or another, in one place or another, by those who know them when they come.

I confess to being the most inexpert of bird-watchers. The birds most easily recognized are those obliging enough to stand still to be recognized, and hardly any seem to have acquired the habit; or those so big that it is impossible to make a mistake. To see and know a really uncommon species is one of the high-lights of the bird-lover's life. Yet the others are good, and who would be without them?

"How do you get rid of your sparrows?" a friend asked me. He had a pair of nuthatches visiting his bird-table and apparently they took offence at the bad table-manners of the sparrows, and this was driving the poor man crazy.

"I don't," I said.

"You don't?"

"I don't even try."

He looked at me as if I'd just come out in pimples. I added maliciously: "I encourage them."

He looked as if they were big pimples.

The truth is, I'm getting tired of people being nasty about the house-sparrows. One person says something unpleasant about them and it is repeated. Slanders get around that way. Don't believe it. The sparrows aren't half bad. Their only real vice is that, like the poor, they are always with us. And very much pleasanter that way. The sparrow also is a bird.

I don't think it is a nice habit (it is only a thoughtless one) to provide bird-tables and good food to spread on them

212

and expect only the aristocrats to take a meal there. I admit it is most satisfying to see the best company arrive at one's door. But if we're feeding birds we must feed birds. During the winter when the snow was deep we had to keep piling scraps on the bird-table. And in the middle of the feast arrived—two crows! They alighted some distance away in the snow and came plodding through it, looking like awkward old gentlemen in black knickerbockers, very shy and uncertain of their welcome. I had only to bang on the window and they would have taken the hint. Tramps, that's what they were. And tramps of bad character. But hunger is a great leveller. We were out to feed hungry birds and, however unwelcome, that is all those two were. They plucked up courage at last, snatched the largest pieces and were gone. No manners at all. But that was not our business.

This all leads up to an apology for not having seen more rare birds in Herefordshire where they might so easily have been seen had I watched more carefully. I've been too easily satisfied with ordinary company. Nor have I wished it otherwise, being no rare bird myself. A man finds his own level. He gets the friends he deserves.

It is not a good thing to be satisfied with one's weaknesses. But who would grumble at the robins, the skylarks, hedgesparrows, finches, tits, a blackcap or two, whitethroats, chiff-chaffs, swallows and martins and swifts, wagtails, yellow-hammers, blackbirds and thrushes, woodpeckers . . . ?

Did I offer apologies for my friends? I take them all back. And I've hardly started the list. Those are only some of the little ones.

Luckily there are people more observant and more knowledgeable than the run of us. Members of the Woolhope Club, for instance, give records from time to time of uncommon birds seen. A recent list includes the red-backed shrike, willow tit, tree sparrow, corn bunting, reed bunting, landrail, whimbrel, great grey shrike, and golden plover. In the eighties of the last century an enthusiastic Hereford naturalist, Dr Bull, published his *Birds of Herefordshire,* which contained notes on every bird that had been seen in the county.

A golden eagle, for instance, was once caught at Berrington near Leominster. It had been observed in the district and a trap, baited with half a rabbit, was set for it. "It measured eight feet from point to point of the wings and stood nearly three feet high."

It was killed and stuffed.

It is a wonder that Herefordshire sees any rare birds at all. The custom of those days on seeing a rare bird was to run for the gun. A manx shearwater was killed at Peterstow, another at Woolhope. A red-throated diver was killed on the Wye at Sellack. A skua was caught at Foxley. It was frightened away from a young pheasant it was eating, so a trap was set with the rest of the pheasant as bait and the skua came back and was caught—and stuffed. A specimen of the little tern was shot by someone out shooting partridges. Rather a long list could be made of visitors who met their end in this way. I'm not sure Dr Bull was altogether easy about it. Of course, many of the people who gave him notes of birds were the ones who did the shooting, and a number of them must have been his friends, so he could not very comfortably reprove them. But he does repeat from time to time in his book, and with some satisfaction, that certain birds would have a better chance of survival now there was a ten-shilling licence required to carry a gun. On the face of it that was aimed at the poor man, but no doubt the cap would fit, and be worn, by others.

A pair of fire-crested wrens was seen in a garden at Sellack in 1864, records Dr Bull. "It was an effort of self-denial on the part of Mr —— not to shoot them."

That could be praise or reproof, or both, or just mild sarcasm.

Luckily, stuffed birds as an ornament are no longer popular. Hereford Museum has a collection, but I try to avoid looking at it. If we must have them we must, but I think, to be fair, that every collection of stuffed birds should contain also at least one stuffed ornithologist.

Quails are not, as they once were, common in Herefordshire. Near Ross there was once a field known as Quail Field because of the birds feeding there. It is a pity they could not be persuaded to return, as they are great weed-eaters, feeding on the seeds of such plants as docks, persicaria, and chickweed. There is a recorded instance of three thousand five hundred seeds of chickweed being found in the crop of one bird. Quails are great fighters and among the Romans they were kept, like gamecocks, for fighting. They are migrating birds, flying north in spring and south in autumn, and some of the Mediterranean islands turned this to good account, catching them in enormous quantities. Dr Bull records, but without special indignation, that as many as a hundred and sixty thousand had been taken on Capri in a single season. It was left for a later writer, Axel Munthe, to rouse the anger of the world against the cruelties practised in catching them.

The pheasant is surely the tamest bird to be seen in Herefordshire. I have had to stop the car in the road near Garnons to avoid running over a couple of fighting cock pheasants, and then they have taken no notice.

I was laughed at when I told that story.

"Keepers about? Hard luck!"

There weren't any keepers about. But you couldn't wring the necks of birds as confident in you as that.

The pheasant was introduced into this country hundreds of years ago. It comes from the south-west of Asia and according to mythology was discovered by Jason and his Argonauts on the banks of the Phasis (from which it gets its generic name, *Phasianus*) in Colchis some three thousand years ago. The first reference to its existence in England is in a twelfth-century manuscript referring to food served in the Canon's household at Waltham. The monks had geese, fowls, blackbirds, magpies, partridges, and each was allowed *unus Phasianus*. Thomas à Becket dined on pheasant the day he was murdered (December 29th, 1197) and "he dined more heartily and cheerfully that day than usual."

By the Middle Ages they were plentiful and no feast of any consequence was complete without them. They cost fourpence each in Edward I's reign, and at the enthronement of the Archbishop of York in Edward IV's reign two hundred were provided. The full list was "Fessauntes 200; Partridges 500; Heronshaws 400; Quailes 100 dozen; Plovers 400; of the fowles called Rees 200 dozen; Peacockes 104; Mallards and Teals 4,000; Cranes 204; Swannes 400;

Geese 2,000; Bittern 204; Curlews 100; Egrittes 1,000;
Pigeons 4,000; Capons 1,000."

These were only the birds! There was "large quantity of
other meats."

The list is given by Leland, and is interesting in containing both herons and cranes. The crane is not a native bird
and there is no record of its ever being seen in Herefordshire, but the country people often refer to the heron as the
crane.

Pheasants were sometimes the quarry in hawking. The
Household Book of d'Estranges of Hunstanton mentions
"vj fesands and ij Ptrychys kyllyed wt the Hawks," and,
"Item, a Fesant kylled with a Goshawke."

In the early sixteenth century pheasants were worth a
shilling, a good sum for those days. This is the price quoted
in the Household Book of the Earl of Northumberland. In
comparison "Hennys" were twopence, "Geysse iiid or iiiid
at the moste," and "Pertryges iid a pece."

The pheasant has become naturalized in this country, but,
apart from the Game Laws, it is doubtful if it could survive
without some help. It should be fed in any winter, and in
severe ones this feeding is essential. Personally, I have no
quarrel with so handsome a bird, but I wonder sometimes if
it would not have been better to have left it at home by the
Caspian Sea. Pheasant-rearing on some estates and in some
periods has been a matter of such importance as to over-
shadow everything else. All kinds of native animals and
birds have been destroyed lest they do the visitor some
harm; its high price and the ease with which the silly creature
may be caught have encouraged the hungry, the fanciful,
and the poacher equally, and have been the cause of much
bad feeling and an immense amount of actual suffering. The
unwisdom of bringing strangers into our midst has been
stressed with reference to the musk rat, the grey squirrel,
and the little owl. The pheasant, delightful creature though
it is, has caused more trouble than those three put together
many times over.

The partridge, on the other hand, is a native, and, giving
less trouble to rear, has not been regarded quite as jealously
by the keepers. Where they have been shot they are wary

birds, but in the wilder places on the hills they can be approached much more easily. They are plucky little things. Aubrey in his *Miscellanies* has a second-hand story of partridges attacking a hawk.

"When I was a Freshman at Oxford 1642, I was wont to go to Christ-Church to see King Charles I at Supper: Where I once heard him say, That as he was Hawking in Scotland, he rode into the Quarry, and found the Covey of Partridges falling upon the Hawk; and I do remember this expression further, viz. and I will swear upon the Book 'tis true. When I came to my Chamber, I told this Story to my Tutor; said he, That Covey was London."

The parent birds will go to a great deal of trouble to lead one away from their chicks, fluttering along the ground and feigning a broken wing. It seems mean not to play out the game and pretend to be taken in. They won't do this trick with a car so long as it keeps going, however slowly, and it is from a car one has the chance to see the old birds leading the chicks from one place to another.

The birds' habit of "jugging"—that is, settling down in the open, generally in the middle of the same field and in the same spot—has been of great advantage to the poachers who net them with comparative ease. The keepers' counter move has been to stick thorns in the place, which has the double advantage of sending the partridges elsewhere, and spoiling the poachers' nets.

In olden days many more kinds of birds seem to have been used for food than we eat to-day. No doubt the shortage of fresh meat during the winter had something to do with that. The curlew was once quite highly priced, varying from five-pence or sixpence to a shilling. The curlew are seen more commonly in the Black Mountains than in the lower parts of Herefordshire. They are shy birds and prefer the comparative quiet of the hills, where they are found in large numbers. They nest in company with the plovers and though both species lay their eggs in little more than a "scratch" in the open the nests are not easy to find. In fact, finding either a plover's or a curlew's nest was quite an event to me until some children showed me how it was done. Then it was easy. It consisted only of finding a place to lie in, keeping perfectly still, and watching. I may add that it often meant a long wait. Once the nest is seen, you wonder how you could miss it. If the bird is on the nest it is practically invisible. This is understandable in the case of the curlew, for its plumage merges into the background of the moors on which it nests (it nests sometimes in ploughed fields), and the golden plover has a sort of camouflaged colouring. But I have stood a dozen yards from a lapwing's nest and have known the position of the nest and even then had difficulty in seeing the bird's black-and-white head. Lapwing fledglings are lovely little creatures, but baby plovers are a pure delight, the most beautiful of all young birds, and, until their parents have taught them caution, they are tame and friendly as well.

Two bar-tailed godwits have been shot in Herefordshire and one black-tailed godwit has been recorded. This last was another of our early table delicacies according to Ben Jonson.

> Your eating
> Pheasant and Godwit here in London, haunting
> The "Globes and Mermaids," wedging in with lords
> Still at the table.

In those days they were fattened in Lincolnshire for the London market.

"A fat Godwit," says Thomas Muffett, an Elizabethan doctor, "is so fine and light meat that noblemen . . . stick not to buy them at four nobles a dozen."

The knot, two of which have been shot in the county, were also netted and fattened to be sold for the table. "Being fed with white bread and milk they grow very fat and are accounted excellent meat."

Snipe and woodcock are no new dainties. Snipe are not as common now as they were before the low marshy land was drained, but there are parts, mostly on the fringes of the Black Mountains, where they may still be found.

About woodcock there is an old Herefordshire belief that if the October full moon is between the 10th and 25th, and wind and weather are favourable, cocks will be plentiful, but if the full moon falls on any other date they will go elsewhere.

218

Dr Muffett had a good opinion of the corncrake, or land-rail as it was called.

"Rails of the land deserve to be placed next the Partridge, for their flesh is as good as their feeding is good."

"The Rayle that seldom comes but upon rich man's spits."

But first catch your corncrake. Frankly I have never seen one, and not for want of searching. I've listened to them, dozens of them, it seemed, monotonously complaining from scented hayfields, hour after hour through the night. But for all that I ever saw of them, they might have been ghosts.

Herefordshire, having no lakes or large pools, is not frequented much by the various ducks, though mallard used to breed in one or two places, and teal and widgeon have been winter visitors to the Wye, and sheldrake, garganey, and shovellers have been shot at infrequent intervals. These birds are more often seen outside the county boundaries in the pools of Radnor and Brecon. The same thing may be said of the geese. Some of them seldom come inland except in the severest weather, and those that come most frequently go to the little lakes in the hills. Odd specimens have been shot and stuffed—bean goose, pink-footed goose, white-fronted goose—while both the brent goose and the Canada goose have been seen a few times in flocks. The barnacle goose is a regular migrant to our north-western shores, but it has been seen only once (and shot and stuffed!) in Herefordshire. The barnacle goose is the least shy of the goose family and comes inland more than the brent. I have a particular affection for the barnacle goose because of old Gerard's story, which he really seemed to believe, of the barnacle tree, surely the most wonderful plant in his *Herball*. He told of a small island in Lancashire "wherein are found the broken pieces of old and bruised ships . . . whereon is found a certain spume or froth that in time breedeth unto certaine shells, in shape like those of the Muskle, but sharper pointed, and of a whitish colour; wherein is contained a thing in forme like a lace of silke finely woven as it were together, of a whitish colour, one end whereof is fastened unto the inside of the shell, even as the fish of Oisters and Muskles are: the other end is made fast unto the belly of a rude masse or lumpe, which in time commeth to the shape and forme of a bird: when it is perfectly formed the shell gapeth open, and the first thing that appeareth is the foresaid lace or string: next come the legs of the bird hanging out, and as it groweth greater it openeth the shell by degrees, til at length it is all come forth, and hangeth onely by the bill: in short space after it cometh to full maturitie, and falleth into the sea where it gathereth feathers and groweth to a fowle."

And that was how the barnacle goose was born.

". . . if any doubt, may it please them to repair unto me, and I shall satisfie them by the testimonie of good witnesses."

Cormorants are seen from time to time in the Wye valley. As a rule they are resident only on rocky and precipitous coasts, but occasionally they come inland to the mountain pools, and in Merionethshire there is a colony five miles inland. They are smelly, dirty birds, but they are marvellous divers and swimmers, as graceful in the water as they are clumsy on land.

A more common bird on the Wye is the heron. In fact, the heron may be seen in all parts of Herefordshire and there is a heronry at Berrington Park and one has recently been started at Aconbury and occasionably they may be found nesting alone. As a rule, they feed at the river's edge, standing mournfully as if pondering on weighty matters, but not long ago I saw at least half-a-dozen standing in a field that had been cleared of sugar beet. This was near Ledbury. I don't know what they had found that interested them. It may have been frogs. In Tudor times the heron was protected because it was highly thought of as a quarry in falconry. Killing herons, except with the longbow or by hawks, was forbidden and taking the eggs meant a penalty of twenty shillings. The theft of a young bird from the nest incurred a smaller fine, ten shillings, a distinction hard to understand unless the herons are more ferocious when the young are hatched, and so taking a young bird a more risky affair and less likely to be attempted. I have had a live heron brought to me, and the force with which it strikes with its long, heavy, pointed beak is amazing. Being tackled by a heron at the top of a tall tree would be no joke. They were once considered fine table birds. I think our ancestors had stronger stomachs than we have to-day. Perhaps the farmer in W. H. Hudson's essay, *The Heron as a Table Bird,* kept his hanging too long. At the first mouthful "a change came over his face, he turned pale and stopped chewing; then, with mouth still full, he suddenly rose and fled from the room."

His sisters, who had not tasted their share, buried the rest in the garden.

Fine feathers don't necessarily make fine birds. The kingfisher is the loveliest bird you will see in Herefordshire, with the exception perhaps of the green woodpecker, but it has a most regrettably dirty nest. It builds its nest in a hole it makes itself in the river bank, and the hole can be identified with some certainty because the bird always makes the height of the entrance a little greater than the width, and the passage inside has an upward slope.

The kingfisher was Halcyone, daughter of Œolus, the god of winds and storms, and her husband Ceyx was drowned on his way to Claros. She found his body on the shore and in her grief threw herself into the sea. They were changed into halcyons, or kingfishers.

They built their nest at sea and as it floated they hatched out their young and during this time Œolus kept the winds at peace so that they should not be disturbed. Thus fine days at sea are Halcyon days.

"Expect St Martin's Summer, Halcyon days."

There was an old superstition that if a dead kingfisher were hung up its beak would always point in the direction from which the wind came. Sometimes they were skinned and hung up for this purpose.

Marlowe was aware of this when he wrote *The Jew of Malta.*

> How now stands the wind,
> Into what corner peers my Halcyon's bill.

There are records of a number of hoopoes being shot in the county towards the end of the last century. Another lovely bird that can't keep its house clean.

Most of the hawk family are seen in Herefordshire as visitors from Wales. The buzzard is no longer uncommon there, nor is the kite, and the peregrine is seen occasionally.

In the county itself the kestrel and sparrow hawk cling rather precariously to existence, hated by both farmers and keepers. Indeed, the hill-farmers dislike the whole tribe just as thoroughly, but up there is more space and the birds stand a better chance of survival. A few years ago the buzzards had increased to such an extent that they were a menace to message-carrying pigeons and the Home Guard received orders to shoot them when possible (and cartridges to shoot them with).

These attacks on bird-life are not new, but sparrows and crows were once the chief victims.

There is an entry in Ledbury parish registers: "A.D. 1711 Jany 9th. An order that a rate of threepence per dozen for all sparrows yt shall be taken and killed between this and the first of August following in this parish be allowed by the churchwardens."

Another entry the same year:

"Pd for a hoop's head and a fitchett's head 2/3."

A hoop was a bullfinch. Evidently its persecution is no new idea. A fitchett was a polecat. There are hardly any polecats in Herefordshire now, unless they have migrated recently, but in Radnor they are much more numerous than they have been in recent years, and the Radnorshire name for polecat is still fitchett. They do not stand up to persecution well because of their habit of going through the lowest hole they can find—a drain-pipe laid down on purpose, for instance—and so they are easy to trap.

Leominster, also, has some records of bird-catching. A large net called the chafnet for the capture of crows and choughs used to be suspended from the western tower of the church, and windows had to be boarded over to keep out the pigeons. But the townsmen of Leominster don't seem to have taken their duty very seriously. At a Court leet in 1576 the jury "present the churchwardens of this Towne to have incurred the penalty of the Statute in that case made and provided for not keeping of such nets as whereby crowes and such other vermine might be destroyed which devoure and spoyle corne to the greate prejudice of many of the Inhabitants within the Borough."

In 1615 they had a go at the windows.

Paid to John Exley for boordes and nailes for the windows of the back side the church to keep out the pigeons.

iijs iiijd

Not having used Irish timber as they did at Goodrich Castle, they had to tackle the spiders, too, as this entry in the Churchwardens' Accounts for 1624 shows:

Item.   Paid to Tho. Houton for sweping off the spiders.

iijs iiijd.

In 1635 the constables and churchwardens were again in trouble with the jury of the court leet over the chafnet—the net to catch crows "and other vermine."

"Item.   They present the Constables and Churchwardens of this Borough to have incurred the payne of xs. for not having a sufficient Chafnet according to the Statute in that case provided."

It is doubtful if this bird-catching did the slightest good to anyone. Indeed, it must have done an untold amount of harm, for there is hardly a bird—even birds that are disliked, and there aren't many of those—that on balance does not do a great deal more good than harm to man. There is, as Professor J. Arthur Thompson has written, "a very short list indeed of those for whom there is not a good word to be said from the point of view of the farmer and gardener." He adds, "This last list includes the wood-pigeon and the sparrow."

But *why* the sparrow?

I have for years been an enthusiastic gardener. At the same time we always have a large colony of sparrows. And my garden has never suffered from them, excepting perhaps a few radishes thinned out in spring, and radishes are nasty indigestible things anyhow, and perhaps an odd crocus pulled to pieces. As for damage to fruit or fruit-beds, we always have more fruit than we can eat and sometimes more than we can give away as well. To cap this, I never bother to spray or dust to destroy insects. I leave greenfly and such undesirables as the raspberry fly to the birds. Up to the present they have never failed me.

The sad fact about that bird-catching is that it was not

223

only the commonest birds, which had a strong power of recovery, that suffered. Where crows were the quarry, choughs, hooded crows, rooks, and jackdaws were the victims as well, and probably ravens, too. Where sparrows were aimed at it is almost impossible to draw up a list of birds that may have been killed. For one thing, not many churchwardens, neither then nor now, would know a sparrow from a nightingale. Sparrows meant, widely, small birds. Then there was that threepence a dozen. Threepence was a useful sum two hundred years ago. A number of threepences was more useful still. All this in a county where there was mistletoe in every orchard for making quicklime, and there was no compulsory education to prevent a boy from earning an honest penny to help his parents.

I have compiled a list of birds which I think must have been destroyed in large numbers. Some obviously would suffer more than others, and there must have been many killed which I have not included. But these I feel are a safe guess: nightingales, whitethroats, blackcaps, all the warblers, hedge sparrows and tree sparrows, tits perhaps, wrens, tree creepers, wagtails, pipits and larks, flycatchers, finches, linnets, twites.

It all happened a long time ago, but, since it went on all over England, I really believe that the bird-catching of those days may explain why certain birds are not a lot more common than they are.

There is another point that I have not seen mentioned anywhere, but which is worth considering. From time to time our ancestors suffered from epidemics, like the Black Death and the Plague, which wiped out large numbers of them. With the ideas they seem to have had of sanitation I think they needed some help in cleaning up. Small birds—especially, in towns, the humble sparrow (I feel I'm scoring a point there!)—would be invaluable for this purpose. They would eat most of the scraps of food thrown away and much of the garbage, and they would make short work of the flies, which carry disease germs, that bred in the remainder.

But, of course, once cut down the bird population by half, or even three-quarters—at threepence a dozen . . .

It is an old tale, a sad tale, and better forgotten. We *never*

make the silly mistakes our great-grandfathers made. But
was there, some time ago, word from Whitehall that sparrows should be destroyed? Perhaps I dreamt it.

On the whole, birds, with one or two exceptions, have
never been better liked, or better protected, than they are
now. I don't think the wren, a shy little bird and a first-rate
singer, is in much danger in Herefordshire to-day. It always
was considered unlucky to kill a wren.

> Malisons, malisons, more than ten,
> Who kills the Queen of Heaven's Wren.

But in parts of Ireland it was anything but popular at one
time and the reason is given in a story by Aubrey.

"A party of the Protestants had been surpris'd sleeping
by the Popish Irish, were it not for several Wrens that just
wakened them by dancing and pecking on the Drums as the
Enemy were approaching. For this reason the wild Irish
mortally hate these Birds to this day, calling them the
Devil's Servants, and killing them where ever they catch
them. They teach their children to thrust them full of
Thorns: You'll see sometimes on Holidays a whole Parish
running like madmen from Hedg to Hedg a Wren-hunting."

All the tits may be seen in Herefordshire with the exception of the crested tit. The long-tailed tit is sometimes called
the bottle tit and older people will sometimes refer to it as
a mumruffin. I don't think I have actually seen the coal tit
in Herefordshire, but as there are a number in the next
county of Radnor they probably inhabit milder Herefordshire as well. The blue tit, or tom tit, as befits the commonest member of the family, once had a bad reputation and, as
with sparrows, some parishes set a price on their heads.

A number of birds had local names. Hedge sparrows were
known as aizacks and yellow hammers as writing larks.
Writing lark is as good a name as yellow hammer (barring
the fact that it is not a lark), for the markings on the eggs
are exactly like scribbles done with a pen. The green woodpecker is still often called the yaffle, probably on account of
its cry, so like derisive, not very polite, laughter. Starlings
were referred to as stares or sheep-stares, and the song
thrush was, and is, as in so many other places, the mavis or

throstle. Herons are called cranes as often as not; the old name hern seems to have gone out of use. Dippers, quite understandably, are water blackbirds, and chaffinches are pinks, or, more rarely, pinkins. Pipits (when not mistaken for larks) are known as titlarks.

The missel thrush, as might be expected in a county where mistletoe grows so widely, is very common. It has the local name of storm cock, and its song is said to foretell rain or wind in early spring. Herons also were regarded as sensitive to weather changes. Bacon noted this when he wrote, "the Heron when she soareth high, showeth wind."

Magpies, on the other hand, were birds of prophecy. There is a doggerel about them in many places. The Herefordshire version runs:

> One for sorrow,
> Two for mirth,
> Three for a wedding,
> Four for a birth.
> Five for a fiddle,
> Six for a dance,
> Seven for England,
> Eight for France.

Most counties have, as well as other differences, "Seven for a secret," and Mary Webb took this line out of the Shropshire version for the title of a novel.

Crossbills are seen occasionally. There is a record in an old *History of Birds* that crossbills used to visit Herefordshire and Worcestershire orchards in great numbers and destroyed the apples in order to get at the pips, from which habit they got the name of shell-pie. The crossbill is one of those birds having a legendary connection with the Crucifixion. It is supposed to have got its crossed bill through trying to pull out the nails that pierced our Lord's hands and feet, and the colour of its feathers came from the blood. Longfellow wrote a version of the legend:

> And that bird is called the cross-bill:
> Covered all with blood so clear.
> In the groves of pine it singeth
> Songs, like legends, strange to hear.

Baby crossbills have their bills uncrossed until they begin to feed themselves.

The four different doves are found in Herefordshire, the turtle dove being fairly common and the ring dove or wood pigeon, as everywhere else, very common. The rock dove, said to be the origin of all varieties of domestic pigeons, agreeing with them in habits, flight, manner of feeding, and, particularly, avoidance of trees, breeds in the Black Mountains and at Stanner Rocks. The stock dove, which gets its name from its habit of nesting in the stocks or boles of hollow trees, is uncommon in the county.

No bird is as unpopular in agricultural districts as the wood pigeon. Its crop will hold sixty acorns. This, translated into a capacity for corn, is formidable, more formidable when multiplied by the number of pigeons in any area. They are among the few birds who will eat slugs, but as a rule they don't seem to. Since they are the most wary of birds they are difficult to shoot and it is unlikely that we shall be without them for a very long time. A pity they are a pest, for, their feeding habits apart, they are handsome birds and a joy to watch. The pigeon is one of the few birds that hardly ever soars. My own very unscientific bird-watching has been very much concerned with the flight of different birds, and the thing that has struck me about a great many of them is how often they soar on spread wings and how seldom they beat their wings. The woodpecker's flight, for instance, provided its flight is, so to speak, taking it on the least downward gradient, is a series of swooping arcs. Like the daring young man on the flying trapeze—or a lot of trapezes, one after the other. I don't think I have ever seen wood pigeons swoop or soar. Their flight is swift and direct, impelled all the time by fast-beating wings. The power of their wing muscles in relation to their size must be enormous.

In Herefordshire villages the wood pigeon is called a quist. It would be interesting to know how long it has borne that name, for its cry is acknowledged to be plaintive, even lamenting, and the Latin word for lamentation is *questus*. That is not so far from queest or quist, and there were once nearly as many Romans as wood pigeons in the county

The wood pigeon's note is easily written as "Coo-roo-coo-oo-oo." The story of the Welshman stretches this rather near to improbability. He was down-country here stealing a cow when he heard what he thought was somebody calling to him from a tree, "Take-two-co-ows, Ta-affy." So, naturally, he did.

The wood pigeon's lament was used in an old piece of Herefordshire doggerel to poke fun at people with small families. If the verse is chanted, the "Coos" being sung quickly, the impression is remarkably like the pigeon's song.

> Coo, Coo, Coo, Coo!
> Too much ado
> To maintain two
> Coo, Coo, Coo, Coo!
> The little Wren
> Can feed her ten,
> And bring them up
> Like gentlemen.

A strange thing is that if those first four "Coos" are sung as they should be on one low note, in semi-quavers, one gets the beginning of a movement of a Beethoven Symphony. (The first *three* lines, on the same note, make it even more real.)

Many birds have tune in their song. Last year one of our blackbirds whistled many times the first few notes of a Verdi theme. I don't mean repeated as the thrush repeats his song, but sung on many different evenings. He also had an opening bar that someone should use, but, so far as I know, has not.

I wish some of our more difficult composers would try listening to the birdsong at daybreak on a morning in late April or early May. There, as I see it, you have a "no-harmony" (in the musical sense) and yet without discord.

I have sometimes wondered, while watching pigeons fly swiftly towards orchard or wood, whether any of them are descendants of the pigeons of long ago that were treasured so jealously for food. It was the Romans who first used domestic pigeons as an article of diet in our country. Pigeon-rearing was, with them, an art. Historians have written on the matter, giving details of the best breeds, housing ar-

228

rangements, how the birds were fed, how fattened. It was the squabs, the young pigeons, that were valued. Roman epicures had them crammed with white bread that had already been half-chewed by men paid for this work. To prevent the young pigeons from taking the least exercise, which might spoil the flavour of the delicate meat, the pigeon farmers used to break the birds' legs, a piece of barbarity that makes one think the Roman Empire fell none too soon.

The Romans in Herefordshire probably had their Columbariums (or Columbaria), though there is no record of them. The French certainly picked up the habit of pigeon-breeding, and, only the rich being allowed to keep them, the depredations of the kept pigeons must certainly have been one of the causes of the tyranny that led to the French Revolution.

If the Mercians forgot the Roman way of squab-raising the coming of the Normans brought it back. Throughout the Middle Ages fresh meat was always scarce in England during the winter. Winter feeding was neither understood nor practised until swedes and turnips were introduced as crops in the early eighteenth century. Farmers killed off most of their stock except those they kept for breeding and the meat was salted—not always properly salted—for winter use. In these circumstances young pigeons on the table were a delicacy. All over the country dovecotes were built to house the birds. Only the richer classes were allowed to have them, the right being jealously guarded by a law that was not repealed until as late as 1825—when it no longer mattered. The numbers of pairs of birds kept in a dovecote often ran into thousands, and it is reckoned that one bird needs something like two bushels of corn a year. It does not need much imagination to guess what the farmers said about the lord of the manor's pigeons. And in 1650 there were twenty-six thousand dovecotes in the country.

English farmers never suffered their hardships in silence. There must, at one time and another, have been a lot of bad blood over the doves. The introduction of winter-feeding with root-crops meant the end of the dovecotes. They were, for a while, still there, but any reason there had been for them was gone and presently the pigeons as reared birds were gone, too.

Mill Farm, Fownhope

Wild pigeons are bad enough. Think of thousands of privately owned ones that must not be interfered with!

Fourteen of the Herefordshire dovecotes have survived. At Sarnesfield the dovecote, dating from the thirteenth century, was in the tower of the little church.

The Garway dovecote (loft seems to have been the more usual name in the county) was built by the Knights Hospitallers, and contains an inscription: "In the year 1326 this dovecot was built by brother Richard." The walls of this one are 3 feet 9 inches thick, and there are six hundred and sixty-six holes.

Mansell Lacy, Dilwyn, Hampton Court, and Old Sutton all have good examples. The one at Richard's Castle is unique in having dormer windows. It is circular, built of stone, and has a flag roof. There are six hundred and thirty holes.

The dovecote at Yazor is hexagonal, while one at Weston, near Ross, has iron angle plates as a protection against rats, which were always a pest to the pigeon owners. Eardisland dovecote is made of brick and is very large.

The most beautiful dovecote in the county is the one at Kings Pyon, the Butt House, or Buttas. It was built in the Gothic half-timbered style in 1632 by George and Elizabeth Karner, whose initials, G. E. K., may still be seen on it.

The Herefordshire dovecotes are no more than survivals and ornaments now. Farmers no longer look at them with hatred.

Instead they stare across their fields to the wood where the ring dove is flying to roost. They still say, "Drat those pigeons!" though.

Or stronger words to that effect.

I went to the Hereford Library where a fine and extensive collection of papers relating to the county is kept. I thought I'd see if I could find out how those old gentlemen of Hereford cooked their squabs. But the only manuscript cookery book Mr Morgan could find for me had nothing to say about them. It was dated rather late for the subject to have been of great interest. Perhaps it was a subject better forgotten.

I don't really enjoy cookery books. But I did notice one interesting recipe.

"To make soup for the poor.

"Take a beef's cheek, cut it into small pieces and bruise the bones, put it into 15 Quarts of water. . . ."

There wasn't a great deal besides. I know very little about cooking, but my wife assures me the fifteen quarts of water to one beef's cheek would not make a very exciting soup.

I stayed that night at the Red Lion at Weobley.

"Take a look at that," smiled Mr Wainwright, the landlord, pointing to a framed bill on the wall.

It was a bill for a show the Weobley Society was having in 1862. One of the prizes offered was a pound "to the Agricultural LABOURER who by his daily labour has reared the greatest number of children, who has not at any time been in receipt of Parish Relief, who has not at any time occupied more than a acre of ground, and who can produce a good character."

All that for a pound! It doesn't seem worth it.

CHAPTER XV

"A FAIRE FIELD FULL OF FOLKE"

COUNTRY people, for long periods of time, have very
little company. They are self-dependent, separated often from
their neighbours, thrown in on a small circle, perhaps the
family, or at most the village inn, for relaxation. They look
forward to a merrymaking, a fair (it used to be a wake), a
flower show, a village concert, a Sunday School outing. And
with a day's work ahead they will toil like slaves if there is
the prospect of a bit of fun at the end of it.

I remember the old communal hay-makings and corn-
harvets when everybody seemed to go to give his neighbour
a hand and every farm seemed to have more help than it
needed. The hot sunny days were glorious, but it was the evening that was best. Work stopped—generally was finished—
about dusk, and then there was supper in a big, low-ceilinged
farm kitchen, and after supper men lit their pipes and pushed
their mugs forward for more beer, and the talk grew intimate and a little coarse—but a clean, Chaucerian sort of
coarseness—and presently an old man would say, "I remembers my granny telling me—you mind my old granny,
Jim?"

At which Jim would nod gravely and take a drink of beer
and for five minutes they would discuss where she lived and
her characteristics and how many children she reared on how
little money.

"Well, I remembers my granny telling me——"

At which point somebody (almost certainly a woman)
would tap me on the shoulder and exclaim, "You still here!
I promised your mother I'd send you home an hour ago.
There's a naughty boy! Run you home now, quick."

I'd pass the yellow lighted window sadly and the old fellow could still be heard.

"It was the time I finished schooling. Only a year's schooling did I have in my life, didn't I, Jim?"

Oh, the hard-heartedness of grown-ups!

Herefordshire men are like countrymen anywhere else. They dearly love a merrymaking now and then. It may be a football or cricket match, a music festival, an agricultural show, or a day's trip to the seaside. Their grandfathers had their own ways of enjoying themselves. They saw to it that no occasion went by uncelebrated: mumming, burning the bush, a wake—it might have been a crab wake—a harvest home. . . .

But the grandest, most rollicking, happiest jollification ever seen and enjoyed was surely the Morris dancing at Bacton in the early summer of 1609. Morris dancing (originally the word was *Morys,* a corruption of Moorish, for the dance was of Moorish origin, was Herefordshire's own specialty. At other forms of merriment you might equal a Herefordshire man; might even—he would generously admit as much—do better. But not at the Morris dance.

"The courts of kings for stately measures: the Citie for light heeles, and nimble footing: the country for shuffling dances: Western-men for gambouls: Middlesex men for tricks above ground: Essex-men for the Hey: Lancashire for Horne-pipes: Worcestershire for Bag-pypes: but Herefordshire for a Morris-daunce puts downe, not onely all Kent, but verie near (if one had line enough to measure it) three quarters of Christendome."

And the occasion for this honest claim? A day in May, when twelve dancers whose total ages amounted to twelve hundred and twenty years were to perform for the pleasure and enjoyment of His Majesty King James I on the occasion of a visit he was paying to the county.

"Never had Saint Sepulchre's a truer ring of Bels: never did any Silke-weaver keepe braver time with the knocke of the heele: never had the dancing horse a better tread of the toe: never could Beverley Fair give money to a more sound Tabourer, nor ever had Robin Hood a more deft Mayd-Marian."

There were four "Marshals in the fielde"

Thomas Price of Clodacke,	105 yeares
Thomas Andres of Beggan Weston,	108 yeares
William Edwards of Bodenham,	108 yeares
John Sanders of Walford,	102 yeares.

Can we blame them that "they had no great stomacke to daunce in the Morris but tooke upon them the Office of Whifflers"?

The dancers were twelve in number, eleven of them being men.

James Tomkins of Lengerren.	106 yeares old.
John Willis of Dormington.	97 yeares old.
Dick Phillips of Middleton.	102 yeares old.
William Waiton of Marden.	102 yeares old.
William Mosse (who had no mosse at his heels).	106 yeares old.
Thomas Winney of Homer.	100 yeares old.
John Lace of Madley.	97 yeares old.
John Carlesse of Homlacie.	96 yeares old.
William Maio of Egelton.	97 yeares old.
John Hunt the Hobby Horse.	97 yeares old.
John Mando of Cradley.	100 yeares old.

John Mando, I think, must have been the Robin Hood. His Maid Marian put them all in the shade. She was "old Meg Goodwin the famous wench of Erdisland," and her age was one hundred and twenty.

"This old Meg was at Prince Arthur's death at Ludlow and had her part in the dole; she was threescore yeares (she saith) a Maide and twenty yeares otherwise."

The only mishap of the day was that one of dancers fell down and could not get up again. Quite likely one of the youngsters of ninety-six or ninety-seven. But it should have been no trouble to fill his place.

"For a good wager, it were easie to finde in that county foure hundred persons more, within three years over or under an hundred yeares."

Four hundred of them! Did Herefordshire men never grow old?

234

"Here is a doozen of yonkers that have hearts of Oak at fourscore yeares: Backes of steele at fourscore and ten, ribbes of yron at a hundred, bodies sound as Belles and healthful (according to the Russian proverbe) as an Oxe when they are travelling down the hill, to make that one hundred and twenty."

"Herefordshire for a morris-dance puts downe . . . three quarters of Christendom." Why not all of it?

Some people say King James never came to Herefordshire, and if he did not come he did not see the Morris, and if he didn't, he, for all his wisdom, was the loser.

Surely the sun shone that day. It was a real countryman's holiday, a proper randy, with coloured ribbons and laughter and good-natured chaff; people from near and far, the fiddlers tuning up, the dancers ready. A field full of folk. . . .

That's the Herefordshire I know.

"A faire field full of folke."

HEREFORDSHIRE

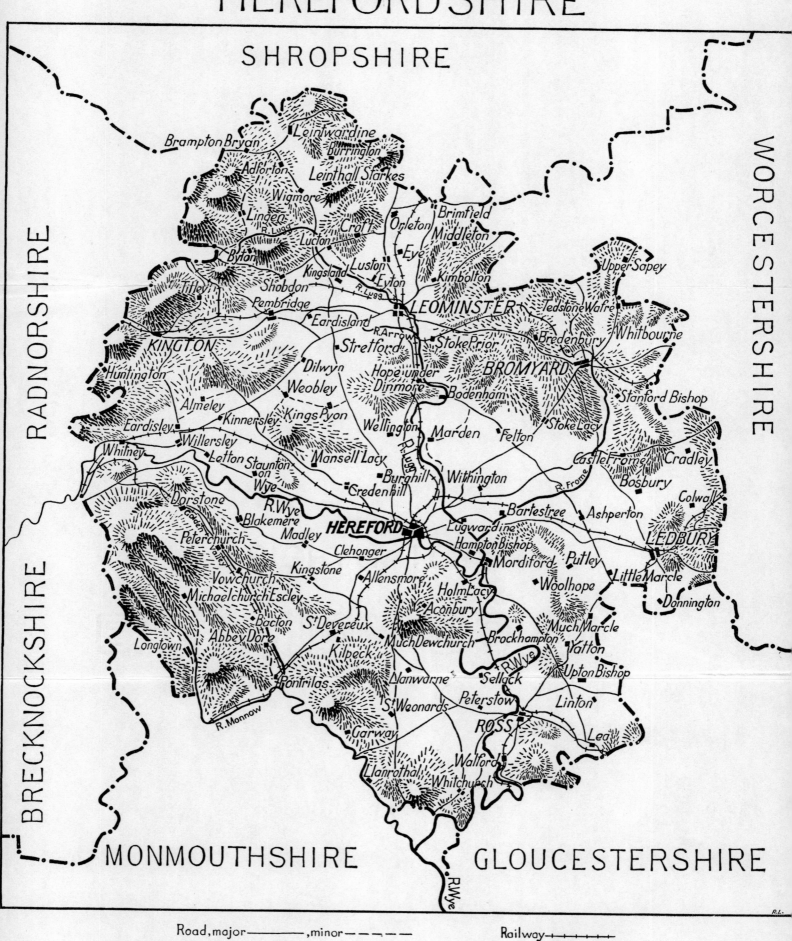

SHROPSHIRE

WORCESTERSHIRE

RADNORSHIRE

Brampton Bryan
Leintwardine
Burrington
Adforton
Leinthall Starkes
Wigmore
Croft
Orleton
Brimfield
Middleton
Lingen
R. Lugg
Eye
Byton
Lucton
Kimbolton
Upper Sapey
Titley
Kingsland
Luston
Eyton
Shobdon
Eyton
LEOMINSTER
Pembridge
Eardisland
TedstoneWafre
Whitbourne
R. Arrow
Stoke Prior
Bredenbury
KINGTON
Stretford
BROMYARD
Huntington
Dilwyn
Hope under
Dinmore
Bodenham
Stanford Bishop
Weobley
Almeley
Kinnersley
Kings Pyon
Wellington
Marden
Felton
Stoke Lacy
Eardisley
Willersley
Mansell Lacy
Castle Frome
Cradley
Whitney
Letton
Staunton on Wye
Burghill
Withington
R. Frome
Bosbury
Dorstone
R. Wye
Credenhill
Bartestree
Ashperton
Colwall
Blakemere
Madley
HEREFORD
Lugwardine
LEDBURY
Peterchurch
Clehonger
Hampton Bishop
Putley
Vowchurch
Kingstone
Allensmore
Mordiford
Little Marcle
MichaelchurchEscley
St Devereux
HolmLacy
Woolhope
Donnington
Bacton
MuchDewchurch
Aconbury
MuchMarcle
Abbey Dore
Kilpeck
Brockhampton
Yatton
Longtown
Pontrilas
Nanwarne
Sellack
Upton Bishop
R. Monnow
St Weonards
Peterstow
Linton
Garway
ROSS
Lea
Llanrothal
Walford
Whitchurch

R. Lugg
R. Wye

BRECKNOCKSHIRE

MONMOUTHSHIRE

GLOUCESTERSHIRE

R. Wye

R.L.

Road, major ——— , minor ———— Railway ++++

Scale 0 ——— 5 ——— 10 ——— 15 ——— 20 Miles

BIBLIOGRAPHY

Herefordshire, A. C. Bradley (Camb. Univ. Press).
Notes on the Birds of Herefordshire, Henry Graves Bull (Jakeman and Carver, Hereford).
Cathedrals, Abbeys and Famous Churches. Hereford and Tintern, Edward Foord (Dent.).
Ross, Thos. Dudley Fosbrooke, (pub. locally, 1821).
Folklore of Herefordshire, E. M. Leather.
Herefordshire, edited by Arthur Mee (Hodder and Stoughton).
History of Kington, Richard Parry (pub. locally, 1845).
Diocesan Histories. Hereford, H. W. Philpott (S.P.C.K.).
Mansions and Manors of Herefordshire, H. Robinson.
Castles of Herefordshire, H. Robinson.
The Town and Borough of Leominster, G. Tyler Townsend (pub. locally, 1862).
Transactions of the Woolhope Naturalists Field Club. 1851–1941.
Hereford Cattle, Year Book of the Hereford Herd Book Society.
Aubrey's Miscellanies.
Camden's Britannia.
Leland's Itinerary.

The Hereford Public Library has an extensive collection of matter of local interest: pamphlets, letters, family papers, deeds and wills, scrap-books, etc.

INDEX

239

INDEX

Hereford Museum, 214
Hereford, Nicholas de, 24, 113, 159, 162
Hereford Riding, 22
Herefordshire, Area of, 105
Herefordshire Crops, 105
Herefordshire Orchards, a Pattern for All England, 114
Hergest Court, 33
Hergest, Red Book of, 33
Heriots, 159 *et seq.*
Hill, Miles, 28
History of Selbourne, 142
Hoarstone, 158
Hoarwithy, 8
Holm Lacy, 1, 8, 172, 173
Homer, 159
Honey, 116
Hope, 166
Hops, 45, 68, 105, 108, 109, 197
Hopton, Major, 72, 73
Hoskyns, John, 176
Hudson, W.H., 201, 221

Ithon, R., 1

Jews driven out of Hereford, 21
John, King, 56, 58

Kemble, Charles, 65
Kemble Family, 182 *et seq.*
Kemble, John, 30, 65
Kenchester, 3, 15, 149
Kentchurch, 29
Kent, John o', 153–155
Kidderminster, Thomas, 176
Kilpeck, 98
Kings Caple, 1
Kingsland, 103, 160
Kings Pyon, 106, 230
Kingswood Common, 131
Kington, 13, 32 *et seq.*, 96, 132, 146, 152, 155, 158, 160, 182
Kington, Commutation Survey of 1845, 45
Kington, Curfew at, 48
Kington, History of, Parry's, 5, 35
Kington, Murders at, 49
Kington, Old customs at, 45 *et seq.*
Kington Railway, 37
Kington, Tolls at, 50–52
Knight, Richard Payne, 178
Knight, Thomas Andrew, 178
Kyrle, John, The Man of Ross, 80–82, 87

Laci, William de, 96, 172
Iaud, Archbishop, 173

Leadon, R., 68
Lecke, Sarah, 64
Ledbury, 3, 13, 68 *et seq.*, 98, 108, 112, 119, 159, 220, 222
Ledbury Church, Constitution of, 70
Ledbury, Civil War at, 71, 72
Ledbury, Parish Registers, 71
Leinthall, Rowland, 165
Leintwardine, 168
Leland, 149, 216
Lemster, Comet at, 67
Lemster Ore, 53
Lemster, Strange News From, 63
Leofric, Earl of Mercia, 17, 55
Leominster, 3, 13, 22, 25, 26, 52 *et seq.*, 93, 96, 101, 103, 116, 160, 165, 166, 173, 180, 214, 222
Leominster, Curfew at, 48
Leominster, Danes at, 55
Leominster, Murder at, 66
Leominster, Trades in, 64
Letton, 132, 142
Leys, 158
Ley, The (Weobley), 93
Libraries, Chained, 23
Little Birch, 146, 173
Llandinabo, 78
Llanlieni, 55
Llanrothal, 78
Llanveyno, 146
Llewellyn, Prince of Wales, 18
Lollards, 23
Longtown, 153
Lugg, R., 16, 152, 211
Lupulin, 110
Lyall, Edna, 98
Lyonshall, 37

Madley, 7, 8, 102
Magna Castra, 83, 149
Mandeville, Sir John, 21
Mansel Lacy, 230
Mappa Mundi, 21
Marchers, Lords, 5
Marches, 5
Marden, 16, 152, 160
Mary, Queen, 24
Massey, Colonel, 72, 84
Matilda, Queen, 167
Mercia, 5
Merewald, King of Mercia, 55
Metheglyn, 112
Milfrith, 17
Milton, John, 174
Miracles at Shrine of St. Thomas, 19
Mistletoe, 7, 8, 98, 177
Monasteries, Dissolution of, 24
Monkland, 167

241

INDEX